UA 718 .P9 W5513 1986
Willems, Em ilio.
A way of life and death

D1242033

A Way of Life and Death

Other Books by Emilio Willems

Assimilação e Populações Marginais no Brasil. São Paulo: Companhia Nacional, 1940.

A Aculturação dos Alemães no Brasil. São Paulo: Companhia Nacional, 1946, 1980.

Aspectos da Aculturação dos Japoneses no Estado de São Paulo. São Paulo: Universidade de São Paulo, Boletim LXXXII, 1948.

Buzios Island: A Caiçara Community in Southern Brazil. Monographs of the American Ethnological Society XX. New York: J. J. Augustin, 1952.

Uma Vila Brasileira: Tradição e Transição. São Paulo: Difusão Européia do Livro, 1948, 1961.

Antropologia Social. São Paulo: Difusão Européia do Livro, 1966.

Followers of the New Faith: Culture Change and the Rise of Protestantism in Brazil and Chile. Nashville: Vanderbilt University Press, 1967.

Latin American Culture. An Anthropological Synthesis. New York: Harper & Row, 1975.

Der preussisch-deutsche Militarismus: Ein Kulturkomplex im sozialen Wandel. Cologne: Verlag Wissenschaft und Politik, 1984.

A WAY OF
LIFE AND DEATH

Three Centuries of Prussian-German Militarism
An Anthropological Approach

by

Emilio Willems

Vanderbilt University Press
Nashville, Tennessee
1986

D. HIDEN RAMSEY LIBRARY
U.N.C. AT ASHEVILLE
ASHEVILLE. N. C. 28814

Copyright © 1986 by Emilio Willems
Printed in the United States of America

This book, in slightly different form, was
first published in Germany in 1984.

*Der preussisch-deutsche Militarismus: Ein
Kulturkomplex im sozialen Wandel*

© 1984 bei Verlag Wissenschaft und Politik
Berend von Nottbeck, Köln
Umschlaggestaltung Rolf Bünermann
Gesamtherstellung Werbedruck Zünkler, Bielefeld 11

ISBN 3-8046-8630-3

ISBN 0-8265-1214-3
Library of Congress Cataloging-in-Publication Data
Willems, Emilio.
  A way of life and death.

  Translation of: Der preussisch-deutsche Militarismus.
  1. Militarism—Germany—Prussia.   2. Sociology,
Military—Germany—Prussia.   3. Prussia (Germany)—History, Military.   I. Title.
UA718.P9W5513 1986   355'.0213'0943   85-22488
ISBN 0-8265-1214-3

Contents

Foreword

Emilio Willems approaches the theme of Prussian-German militarism from the intentionally unilateral standpoint of cultural anthropology. In contrast to the usual presentations, this means, somewhat paradoxically, a considerable gain in depth rather than a limitation—as the reader will discover almost immediately. There is, in addition, a highly personal involvement in the problem of German militarism, which, in its final phase, shook the world so violently that it has not yet recovered. One may assume that this problem, among others, prompted Professor Willems to emigrate from Germany in 1931, first to Brazil and, in 1949, to the United States following an invitation from Vanderbilt University. Now a professor emeritus, he has been living ever since in Nashville, Tennessee.

Professor Willems's professional activities have been recognized in the Federal Republic, where he was elected first a corresponding member and later an honorary member of the German Society for Sociology. He has published regularly and has repeatedly lectured as a visiting professor in West German universities. He is at home in three cultures and has written in three languages. His numerous earlier publications in Brazil are being reprinted as valuable contributions to basic social research. In the United States, he has acquired a solid reputation as a Latin Americanist (see his comprehensive work *Latin American Culture: An Anthropological Synthesis*. New York, Harper & Row, 1975.) Recently, he has begun to bring the results of his research to the attention of the German public. The present book represents a highly stimulating and thought-provoking sample of his work.

This becomes particularly obvious in his definition of militarism. If one considers military confrontations generally as "the organized use of violence between belligerent parties," to quote a conventional definition, one sees immediately how different Willems's approach is. He sees militarism as a culture complex, *i.e.*, as "a cluster of interrelated traits or elements deriving their meaning and function from a dominant or focal element," which has to be dealt with as a unit. The culture complex *militarism* has systemic character, and "it would be quite unrealistic to assume that such a complex with all its components and ramifications throughout the fabric of a given culture could possibly arise on the spur of the moment, as the result of a sudden political decision. Even the most cursory survey can hardly fail to recognize that numerous changes are necessary to generate a militaristic system, and very few of those changes are amenable to improvisation." Decisionism in the friend-enemy relationship has little explanatory value, as the introduction of highly intricate systems of interest, such as the military-industrial complex, shows. Even a superficial examination reveals that the armament industry represents no more than one sector of the industrial system, "the major part of which is unrelated to the production of armaments."

The main thesis of the book Willems summarizes in a single sentence: "The powerholders of the Prussian state succeeded in building a society in which *all* sectorial structures and institutions were gradually shaped to support the exigencies of war and preparation for war." This interpretation closely resembles what Anouar Abdel-Malek, an Egyptian living in France, called "société militaire" (1962), or Franz C. Endres's earlier, somewhat paradoxical definition of militarism as "the mental attitude of the non-military," or Friedrich Wilhelm Foerster's statement that militarism was "simply *the* form of Prussian society," an interpretation proposed much earlier by Alfred Vagts (1938, 1959). In a more recent book on military sociology, militarism is defined as "a state of mind in which generally soldier and war are glorified and military ways of thinking and acting transferred as models of behavior to other sectors of society" (Roghmann and Ziegler 1977, 208). In this process, the following factors play a decisive role: a centralized political structure; the existence of a more or less exclusive, self-recruiting military elite; special privileges and strong relationships with the political powerholders; and socially mobile classes that, without the use of revolutionary means, strive to gain political influence through association with the ruling classes. A clear distinction between *military* and *militaristic* is established. As Vagts says: "Militarism presents a vast array of customs, interests, prestige actions and thoughts associated with armies and wars and yet transcending true military purposes. Indeed, militarism is so constituted that it may hamper and defeat the purposes of the military way" (Vagts 1959, 11).

Emilio Willems's distinctive accomplishment lies in the fact that, with Prussian-German militarism as an example, he investigated the origin and evolution of the culture complex, revealing the structural conditions it shared with other cultures but noting that from the time of the Teutonic Knights it moved along a line of increasing radicalism. Only in the spring of 1945 did it reach its logical end, and German militarism in its ultimate manifestation was destroyed by a tremendous effort of the nonmilitaristic powers. Willems abstains from developing a "critique" of militarism. He offers instead an analysis of its underlying cultural system, including the supportive infrastructures of historical origin that helped to mobilize all the adaptive forces capable of serving the complex. He notes that militarism is not necessarily synonymous with war, but primarily with the active preparation for war through the militarization of human, technological, and economic resources. "The structure of the armed forces was more than a reflection of the social structure; it actually *was* the stratification system of Prussian agrarian society transferred to the barracks." In a parallel development, the bureaucracy was militarized and there also was a continuous flow of retired military officers into civil professions (teachers, administrators, judges, etc.). "Towards the end of the formative period, the diffusion of military patterns throughout the social structure had reached a point at which it may well be questioned whether the division of Prussian society into 'civilian' and 'military' sectors was still meaningful."

The latter remark may be considered typically "anthropological." So too may the discussion of the careful control of the social and cultural background of the military, who at first were frequently aliens, even the officers. However, the total transformation of the society through the militaristic credo could be completed only after a radical conscription system had been so firmly implanted that among the younger generations an attitude of "anticipatory conformity" came to prevail, an attitude that ultimately led to ideological conformity and changed the whole value system.

Emigration was the only way of avoiding this process, and the exodus of political nonconformists resulted in an increasingly homogeneous German society, particularly after the catastrophic defeat of the democratic movement between 1820 and 1830, again in 1848, and especially in 1850, when the entire Prussian army was mobilized to prevent further "revolutionary eruptions." The intellectual elites, particularly the professoriat, disgracefully failed to measure up to the challenge (as in 1933 too). The theme "emigration" has, of course, a personal significance for Emilio Willems, who left Germany partly because the intellectual atmosphere of the twentieth century was no less pernicious than it had been in the nineteenth century, and militarism at the University of

Berlin, where Willems and I studied under the same teachers, was flour-
ishing as always, long before the dominance of National Socialism (see
Sombart's *German Socialism*, 1934). National Socialism certainly did not
create anything new; it merely took up what was already there. What we
social scientists found particularly nerve-racking was, above everything
else, the idea of a military organization to be imposed on business and
industry which even a man like Goetz Briefs found defensible. Incidentally, the idea survived World War II when numerous officers went into
industry, where they set a decidedly militaristic tone.

This foreword is not intended to present a content analysis of the
whole book. I merely wished to alert the reader to the perhaps unusual
analytical technique of cultural anthropology, which does not lose itself
in particular aspects of militarism but emphasizes the way it is rooted in
a complex cultural system.

René König
Professor Emeritus of Sociology
at the University of Cologne

A Way of Life and Death

1

Militarism as a Culture Complex in Evolution

There has never been complete agreement about the meaning of the term *militarism*, but very few, if any, students of European civilization would take exception to the statement that Germany was, at least until 1945, a militaristic state. Just what different analysts, mostly historians, mean by this term has been the object of rather thorough scrutiny, resulting in the identification of five categories of broad conceptualizations covering numerous specific formulations. The most common meaning attributed to the term refers to the tendency to use war in preference to other means of solving international conflicts. Another set of definitions points to the political power of the military as the essence of militarism. A third group focuses on the discretionary appropriation of a society's resources for the maintenance and development of an army. A fourth group of definitions centers on a kind of discipline conducive to unconditional compliance with orders issued by superior authority and, associated with this submissive attitude, a boundless respect or reverence for military status symbols. Finally, many analysts believe that the glorification of war and the warrior and the diffusion of military ways of thinking and acting among nonmilitary sectors of a society represent essential characteristics of militarism (Roghmann and Ziegler 1977, 200–201).

We mention these various conceptualizations here not to propose options, but rather to contend that *all of them* apply to Prussian-German militarism. Indeed, we assume that no full understanding of the phenomenon being examined could be achieved without giving careful attention to the five sets of traits we intend to consider here as constituent attributes of the militarism that emerged and developed in Prussia and later spread to the member states of the German Empire.

1

The association of so many diverse characteristics suggests that we are dealing here with a phenomenon of considerable complexity, which eventually affected all aspects of German culture. In view of the formidable obstacles holding back the development of Prussia as a great military power, the assumption that it could possibly have emerged all of a sudden, perhaps as a personal creation of a "great king," seems highly unrealistic. As we shall see, even the most warlike rulers had to build Prussian military power step by step, constantly hampered by the painful poverty of the country, the sparsity of its population, and the lack of contiguity of its territory.

The historical facts that we think had a definite bearing on the emergence and evolution of Prussian-German militarism have been known for some time, but their significance has not always been fully realized, nor have their structural interrelations been clearly perceived. The fairly common view that only certain phases or aspects of Prussian history can be identified as militaristic reflects a fragmentary understanding of the processes involved in laying the structured foundations of a political system whose rather inconspicuous beginnings can be traced back to the seventeenth century. Gerhard Ritter thought that Prussia's "problem of militarism" started only with the conquest of Silesia by Frederick the Great in 1740. Frederick's father, the "Soldier king," who created a powerful army and successfully initiated the militarization of Prussian society, was not a militarist in Ritter's opinion because he carefully abstained from warfare and even enjoined his successor to avoid "unjust" wars (Ritter 1954, 23). The idea that militarism necessarily implies frequent or continuous warfare, although quite common, is nevertheless questionable and, in the case of Prussia, seems outright fallacious. The history of Prussia and the German Empire is characterized by several long periods of peace, which were well utilized to build a fighting force equal or superior to most. Continuity and longevity are two of the most salient features of Prussian-German military evolution, and neither one would have been feasible without long intervals between armed conflicts. Furthermore, abstention from war does not mean that an army could not otherwise be used in international politics. Often a demonstration of available means of physical coercion, or "power capabilities," may be enough to decide the outcome of a power contest (Anderson 1964), and no demonstration appears to be more effective than a large, well-prepared fighting force, especially if, as happened in the nineteenth century, it is supplemented by warlike ideologies.

Obviously, Ritter, like some of his contemporaries, questioned the appropriateness of the term *militarism* for any phase of Prussian-German history not affected by its more radical or extreme manifestations, such as those usually identified with the Wilhelmian and National Socialist periods. Among the historians taking issue with Ritter, Dehio argued that a militaristic tradition had indeed been established in eighteenth-century Prussia and that adherence to the tradition transformed Germany into a redoubtable continental power (Dehio 1955, 43–64). Dehio referred to "200 years of militaristic politics," and following Dehio's lead, some younger historians inquired into the "socio-economic power structures of Prussia-Germany" (Berghahn 1982, 59). Although more attention has recently been paid to continuity and the sociocultural context of militarism, apparently no one has perceived the heuristic advantages of an evolutionary approach to the subject. Unilateral emphasis on tradition tends to obscure the evolutionary process, which may be defined as a sequential change of form moving in a discernible direction.

The main purpose of this essay is to identify the changes that had a recognizable bearing on the emergence and development of militarism in Prussia and, later, in the German Empire. It is not assumed here that change and tradition were necessarily at variance with each other. We propose to show that interaction between tradition and change lent support to both. Radical changes in Prussia's political structure initiated a tradition that in turn made further changes possible or indeed necessary; with each change, the military tradition gained in strength. If evolutionary criteria are used, it becomes clear that Prussian-German militarism lasted not two hundred but nearly three hundred years.

Any specific evolutionary process begins with a change that can be identified as a prime mover in a sequence of events, each of which is contingent upon previous ones. The creation of a standing army and the ruler's coercive appropriation of economic resources were the crucial changes acting as prime movers in Prussia's military evolution. Both were manifestations of an emerging absolutism, and both were results of a prolonged power struggle between monarch and the estates (Stände). None of the subsequent changes in territorial, political, and economic development of Brandenburg-Prussia would be explainable without taking into account the momentum provided by these events. As military development continued, additional prime movers emerged, acting in conjunction with existing ones. However, evolutionary changes should not exclusively be understood as deliberate creations of the monarch and his collaborators. Many intentional or institutional changes of evolutionary significance generated secondary effects, sometimes quite unexpectedly or at variance with the intentions of the innovators. To the extent that they advanced, distorted, or even undermined particular aspects of the evolutionary process their role must be included in our analysis.

The success of evolutionary changes, whether intentional or not, is determined by their relative superiority as adaptive devices in particular environmental conditions. These conditions can be defined here in terms of an ongoing international power contest and, to a lesser extent, internal confrontations designed to subvert the existing political order.

An increase in military strength may be considered an adaptive change to the extent that it prevents aggression from external and internal enemies. However, the more militaristic a society, the higher the probability that the adaptive value of such changes is measured in terms of an increase in offensive capabilities, resulting perhaps in territorial conquest and appropriation of other peoples' resources. In other words, the adaptive value of military changes of evolutionary significance is obviously relative. The concept is meaningful only insofar as the political perspective of a particular society and a particular class system is concerned.

Yet it happens that changes of this kind fail to live up to the expectations of their originators. As we shall see, this was the case of the German battle fleet, which was intended to challenge Great Britain's position as a world power. Not only did the German fleet fail to accomplish this objective, but its precipitate construction diverted scarce resources from other sectors of the German armed forces that were sorely needed during the ensuing war.

It seems difficult to determine the point at which the doctrine of militarism with its adaptive implications began to be contradicted and eventually invalidated by the ever-growing emphasis on the technological aspects of military development. Quite in contrast to other cultural phenomena, the militaristic approach to international relationships always contained a risk factor whose growth seemed directly proportional to the technological development of warcraft. At the time of World War I, the risk factor had already reached a level at which the adaptive value of war seemed highly questionable. Subsequent developments, particularly atomic warfare, multiplied the risk factor a thousandfold, totally belying the major tenets of militaristic doctrine. Thus, militarism as the comprehensive prime mover of military evolution foundered on its inherent inconsistencies. Attempts to revive it have been inextricably caught, as we shall see, in a tangle of insoluble ideological contradictions.

There may be a tendency to perceive the evolution of Prussian militarism as a purely endogenous process. Actually, during its formative phase the country lacked most of the human, scientific, and technological resources that would have been necessary to develop an effective military force from within. Almost all crucial changes concerning the formation of an internationally effective army were based on transfer or diffusion from militarily more advanced European countries. And often enough, the adaptation of borrowed elements to internal conditions proved difficult and time-consuming. One should keep in mind that Prussia's rise as a military power is understandable only in the context of European civilization as a whole. The evolution of Prussia-Germany from a recipient into a donor society, insofar as military development is concerned, was initially dependent on innovations that, with few exceptions, did not originate in Prussia or Germany. But once Germany had entered a phase of intensive industrialization, it became a focus of autochthonous invention and diffusion of weaponry and other military equipment. The reversal of Germany's role as a consumer into that of a producer and distributor of military hardware was reflected in an increasingly uncompromising militaristic posture.

Perhaps a clearer understanding of militarism may be obtained if it is perceived as a culture complex (i.e., a cluster of interrelated traits or elements deriving their meaning and function from a dominant or focal element). The focus of militarism is war, or the use of organized violence as the preferred or only admissible way of resolving major international and certain forms of domestic conflict in the pursuit of particular political objectives. Charged with the preparation for and conduct of war, the armed forces are to be considered a major component of the complex. A military establishment is, of course, a manifold thing, and if disassembled, it differentiates into distinct organizational patterns, ideological tenets, institutionalized rules of behavior, and technological resources encompassing specialized skills. Military evolution comprehends quantitative growth of the complex and increasing internal differentiation. No genuine militarism is thinkable without such growth, but expansion and increasing differentiation of the military complex do not by themselves generate militarism. If they did, most, if not all, modern nations would have developed forms of militarism quite similar to that of Germany. Almost everywhere in Europe the military complex evolved roughly in the same way, but militarism did not. A highly developed military establishment may or may not reflect militaristic values and attitudes. In Prussia and Germany it did, but in other societies it did so to a much lesser extent or not at all.

Whether or not a particular society may be considered militaristic lies in the nature of the linkages between the military complex and the society at large. Fundamental, of course, is the way political power is distributed. If it is concentrated in the person of an absolute king and if, as it happened in Prussia, he perceives his role primarily as that of supreme military commander, the power structure would seem to facilitate militaristic developments. Furthermore, if the king has, as the Prussian monarchs did, the undivided loyalty and support of the nobility, the most powerful of all social strata, the prerequisites for a militaristic state are fulfilled.

It is not surprising, then, that the rulers who promoted the most decisive changes in the evolution of Prussian-German militarism put their function of commanders in chief ahead of that of chief executives of a "civilian" government. This structural arrangement had at least two major consequences. The military complex and the government established a close linkage through the person of the ruler and his immediate collaborators. The military priorities implicit in this association proved conducive to the marshaling of human and economic resources necessary to military development. At the same time, the existing power structure paved the way for the gradual militarization of Prussian-German society. (Militarization, of course, is militarism viewed as a process.)

Under the aegis of the triple alliance, monarchy-army-nobility, the military complex and different sectors of Prussian, and later German, society established numerous linkages, which gradually increased the orbit of the militarization process. During the nineteenth century, three particular aspects of this process merit special attention.

The first aspect is the rise, perhaps proliferation, of support structures such as paramilitary organizations or patriotic leagues advocating expansion of the armed forces and the pursuit of political objectives that presumably cannot be attained without international conflict.

The second is the emergence of an ideological support system designed to maintain and, if deemed desirable, to elaborate the assumptions that war is historically necessary or inevitable, that its benefits exceed its costs, and that instant preparedness for violent conflict outweighs any other political pursuits. A special task of the supportive ideological media is to nurture suspicion and animosity against presumptive foes by imputing hostility, perfidy, duplicity, and secret political machinations to their leaders. Consequently, so it is argued, they must be dealt with from a position of great strength derived from military preparedness. Supportive ideology is expected to provide moral justification of war, and none seems more convincing than the right to defend the fatherland against imputed aggression. Militaristic ideology must build up a flexible conceptual arsenal that can be manipulated in such a way that *any* war can be presented as "defensive," or at least as morally defensible.

Since it is the task of the support system to build up consensus about the desirability of militarism, its ideological tentacles may go well beyond endeavors directly concerned with war. National cultures are extremely complex, and many of their components are unrelated to specific political pursuits, whatever their nature, scope, or relevance. Some may even deflect from, or be inconsistent with, the kind of concerted effort required by the politics of belligerency. To bring the entire culture into accord with the extreme forms of nationalism underlying the "heroic warrior spirit," discordant or "neutral" elements are subjected to reinterpretation, while irreconcilable traits may be suppressed or destroyed, possibly together with the persons or groups with which they are identified. Institutional devices designed for reinterpretation or elimination are to be considered components, albeit peripheral, of the military complex.

The third aspect is the diffusion of military patterns of behavior throughout the society. Processes performing this function may be spontaneous or organized. One may argue that spontaneous adoption of military modes of thinking, acting, and feeling is a more reliable indicator of genuine militarization than organized ways of attaining the same objective, but the two forms may coincide and thus reinforce each other. At any rate, whether spontaneous or organized, the channels and mechanisms of diffusion have to be identified and analyzed as significant traits of the military complex.

These three aspects of militarization are neither mutually exclusive nor independent of one another. Their cumulative occurrence in a given society would suggest that a radical form of militarism has been developing, but the conclusion that *all* three processes ought to be considered as thoroughly functional with regard to the conduct of and preparation for war may not be supported by all pertinent facts. One should refrain from assuming that militarism is necessarily a well-integrated culture complex. In fact, no complex is, and militarism constitutes no exception to the rule. The evolution of warcraft demands frequent changes in military organization, technology, and strategy, but certain sectors of the armed forces often resist such changes because they would imply modifications or perhaps elimination of status privileges, ranking principles, or power positions tied in with the stratification of the society as a whole. Although obsolete and a possible threat to the nation's capability of waging successful wars, these traits nevertheless are integral parts of the militaristic system and should be analyzed as such. They help in discovering the reasons why even the most militaristic societies are by no means immune to defeat on the battlefield.

The current expression "military-industrial complex" suggests a close relationship between military establishment and industrialism. The linkage does indeed exist, but it does not imply that the industrial system *in toto* was or is an integral part of the military complex. Neither its origin nor its development was or is contingent on demands for weaponry, but at certain times and in particular societies the expansion and modernization of the armed forces has strongly affected the industrialization process. On the other hand, the industrial revolution not only created the technological prerequisites for a diversification and specialization of the armies, but it also dramatically increased the capability of the militaristic state to wage war. An analysis of the mutual dependence of military establishment and armament industry should not overlook the fact that the latter represents only one sector of an industrial system, the major part of which is not concerned with the production of military equipment. It may be argued, therefore, that the military establishment and the industrial system constitute two different culture complexes. Even so, the possibility of coalescence should not be disregarded, especially in totalitarian societies where the state exercises absolute control over the industrial system.

If full-fledged militarism may be considered a way of life, it most certainly is also a way of death. Preference of war to other means of conflict resolution involves immense risks that call for institutionalized restraints. Instead of rushing headlong into open war, even the most militaristic nation seeks to attain disputed political objectives by mere demonstration of power capabilities, which simultaneously enhance military might and delay, perhaps indefinitely, the eruption of actual war. Certain patterns of restraint, such as military maneuvers, massing of troops in critical border regions, gunboat diplomacy, military alliances, and the like, tend to be perceived as manifestations of blatant militarism. Actually, they imply deferment of violent confrontation and therefore restraint. They may be defined either as steps toward war or as attempts to intimidate the enemy into submission without violent engagement. It is this ambiguity that allows deferment of war without loss of face.

Hardly less ambiguous are the strategies and conventions intended to regulate the actual conduct of war. Codes of honor punish cowardice and encourage bravery, but they also rule out "unfair" or "dishonorable" ways of dealing with the enemy, although what is regarded as honorable or dishonorable tends to change in time and space. Even the most militaristic societies have accepted, at least in the past, internationally established norms intended to reduce the risks of war. On the other hand, the availability of increasingly effective weaponry has caused a rather generalized move from conventional to total forms of warfare implying disregard for traditional restraints.

The occurrence of militarism is by no means limited to modern, complex societies, however. It is not an upshot of the industrial revolution, nor is it a product of capitalism and its attendant class structure. The present study will show that exploitation, a rigid class structure, and a vigorous capitalistic system played no minor role in the development of Prussian-German militarism, though these phenomena occurred elsewhere with similar intensity without generating militarism. Conversely, militarism existed in societies that had neither a class order nor an economic system lending itself to exploitation or to capitalistic entrepreneurship.

Perhaps no other case is more appropriate to demonstrate the essence of militarism than certain Indian societies of the Great Plains, such as the Cheyenne, the Kiowa, the Comanche, the Sioux, and others. There were no resources that could be monopolized by anyone. There were no social classes that could be exploited by any group or person, nor was there the remotest possibility that any such group could be involved in a competitive "armament race." Once they had obtained the horse and the buffalo hunt had become far more productive than ever before, they devoted themselves to warfare with a single-mindedness that no modern, complex society could possibly match. Among the Comanche, we are told, "war became the pattern of life; the military cult became the ideal of the aspiring young man" (Wallace and Hoebel 1952, 245). The most coveted rewards built into the cultural system went to the distinguished warrior, and "war honors provided the basis of the whole system of rank and social status in Comanche society" (Wallace and Hoebel 1952, 245). The famous military societies, fraternal associations of warriors, cut across band lines and made it possible to mobilize military manpower for major objectives. Like the sons of the Prussian nobility, the "boys and youths of the Cheyenne were trained to feel that the most important thing in life was to be brave; that death was not a thing to be avoided; that, in fact, it was better for a man to be killed while in full vigor rather than to wait until his prime was past, his powers failing, and he could no longer achieve those feats which to all seemed so desirable" (Grinnell 1956, 12). Only to a very limited extent did economic interest (in the form of plunder) account for the glorification of warfare in the Great Plains. "Love for fighting," a "desire for glory," the achievement of personal status, and "eagerness for revenge" ranked high among the motives of war (Wallace and Hoebel 1952, 245).

Neither among the Plains Indians nor in any other genuinely militaristic society can the apotheosis of warfare be fully explained in terms of economic interests or other purely rational motives. Neither a large army nor the availability of the most modern and destructive weaponry per se generates militarism, no matter whether the structure of the society is built upon capitalistic or socialistic models. The mass production of modern weapons, always in competition with potential enemy powers, may be little avail if the members of such a technologically advanced society are allowed or even encouraged to make up their individual minds about whether war—in general or in particular—is ethically justifiable and about whether they should accept or refuse military service in war or in peace. A society that cannot depend on the willingness of its soldiers to fight *under any circumstances* cannot be considered militaristic. Equally unmilitaristic is the attitude in most Western societies that military service is a chore and a burden rather than an honor.

There is no suggestion here that militarism is exclusive to Germany and a few other nations. Virtually *all* nations have standing armies, which may or may not have developed certain characteristics of militarism. If total immunity to militarism is difficult to detect, full-fledged militaristic systems displaying the whole gamut of traits previously outlined are rare. But between the extremes is a broad spectrum of societies that, at certain points in history, may be regarded as militaristic to a degree. However, the military governments mushrooming in the so-called Third World bear little, if any, resemblance to a thoroughly developed militaristic system, German or otherwise. In the contemporary world, seizure of government by a general or junta of generals is usually tantamount to dictatorship imposed upon a recalcitrant society deeply divided by irreconcilable political ideologies and economic interests.

The military's usurpation of political power seems to be the only criterion to justify the classification of such societies as "militaristic" (Lieuwen 1960, 7; Johnson 1964, 3). The differences between these military dictatorships and Prussian-German (and other versions of) militarism are quite obvious. Military dictatorships have little support among the people, and as a rule the existing military-civilian dichotomy shows signs of exacerbation. In German society this dichotomy faded almost to the vanishing point, which suggests consensus rather than opposition. Furthermore, there has never been the slightest indication that military patterns of behavior tended to spread to other segments of the society as they did in Prussia and, even more so, in imperial Germany. Analysts of Third World "militarism" have emphasized the way the military have arrogated political power by subversion, rebellion, or revolution. In three centuries of militarism no Prussian or German general ever overthrew the established government by violence or threat of violence. There is no doubt at all that the German military wielded enormous political power, but its basis was firmly imbedded in the political structure of the society itself. In fact, the dominant position of the military complex was so secure that the generals were vitally interested in supporting the government rather than in subverting it.

Three events in Prussian history are sometimes referred to as cases of actual or potential insubordination, "oppositional defiance," or rebellion of military commanders. The first was the Convention of Taurogen (1812). The Prussian general, York von Wartenburg, agreed with the Russian commander to separate the Prussian troops from the fleeing French army and to put them under the command of the czar. Acting without authorization of the king or anybody else, von Wartenburg attempted to precipitate a war of liberation against Napoleon.

The second case is connected with the revolution of 1848. The ambiguous attitude of King Frederick William IV, who for a time seemed to sympathize with the liberal ideology of the revolution, provoked the reaction of some of the most conservative military leaders. Those closest to the king apparently discussed the restoration of the pre-March regime by means of a coup d'etat. No attempt was made, however, and if action had been taken, it would have served to restore the dignity and authority of the monarchy as the military perceived it.

The third case was the Kapp *Putsch*, a 1920 military uprising of the radical right under the leadership of Wolfgang Kapp, former governor of East Prussia. The intent was to overthrow the republican government. Involved in the *Putsch* were remnants of the German army in the process of disbandment. Disagreements between Kapp and the commanding general, but particularly the firm stand taken by the *Reichswehr*, led to the collapse of the movement.

Of these three cases only the third bore characteristics of political subversion, and none could possibly be attributed to the military as a group or an institution. In fact, the Kapp *Putsch* failed because it was opposed by the military establishment.

Militarism seeks to maximize the nation's preparedness for war, but there is always the possibility that the rewards built into the system do not agree with the pursuit of its main objective. Certain organizational patterns, services performed by particular groups, and whole branches of the armed forces may become obsolete but be allowed to survive because abolishing them would threaten the status privileges of high-ranking military leaders. Inversely, changes introducing new weaponry or strategies may fail to live up to the expectations of their originators and thus constitute a potential or actual threat to the survival of the system. Cases of such internal inconsistencies will be presented later.

Since militarism, as defined here, cannot be regarded as an inevitable ingredient of specific evolution, the possibility of its disappearance has to be admitted. Militarism itself may become a casualty of evolutionary changes, although repeated military defeats may be required to reveal its obsolescence.

Our inquiry proposes to single out the historical determinants that played a role in the evolution of Prussian-German militarism. The propositions we wish to examine may be formulated as follows:

1. Certain political, economic, and demographic developments antedating the emergence of the Prussian state may be considered to be structural prerequisites to the implantation of militarism.

2. Based upon these earlier developments, Prussian militarism evolved gradually over a period of approximately three centuries. During that time it underwent major changes, some of which were caused by the transfer and adaptation of exogenous models of military organization invented and put into practice by neighboring states. As the armed forces expanded and their privileged position consolidated, the military pattern of behavior performed increasingly significant integrative functions. Integration in this sense was first achieved in the eastern provinces of Brandenburg. Much later it spread to other areas of the country.

3. The powerholders of the Prussian state succeeded in building a society in which *all* sectorial structures and institutions were gradually shaped to support the exigencies of the preparation for war. This tendency has been described as a "pervasion of civilian society by military imperatives which shape the self-image, the environment and the culture (including educational substance and style) of civilian society" (Senghaas 1975, 153) or as "transfer of military structures and modes of thinking to other areas of life" (Rohe 1975, 267). At least one analyst went as far as to perceive militarism as *the* form of Prussian society" (F. W. Forster as quoted in Endres 1975, 99).

4. Prussian-German militarism developed in interaction with other nation-states where similar forms of militarism were rampant, although those manifestations suggest less consistency and commitment than in Prussia. Comparison with Germany's major rivals will show that German militarism was unique among the European nations.

5. If one considers the longevity of Prussian militarism and the increasingly effective role it was allowed to play in Prussian society, it probably did perform adaptive functions, not only in the process of territorial expansion and integration (national unification) but also in the maintenance of a particular social system. The apparent worthiness of militarism became an article of faith of a substantial and ever-growing proportion of German society. Under no circumstances could it have been preserved and expanded by sheer force, although coercion served as a relevant ingredient in certain phases and aspects of militaristic developments.

Yet almost imperceptibly at first, German militarism began to veer from the functional to the dysfunctional and nonadaptive as war tended to become *total* war and, consequently, a lethal threat to national survival rather than a means of settling international conflict. Two world wars were necessary to uncover the obsolescence of militarism.

2

The Antecedents

Conquest and Colonization of Slavic Territories

Long before Prussia acquired its political identity as a militaristic state, war had been endemic in the lands east of the Elbe River. It was clearly directed against the Slavic tribes inhabiting Thuringia and what later became known as eastern Germany. The objectives of these extensive campaigns were conquest, conversion, and resettlement. Beginning in the twelfth century, the east developed into a vast frontier where military conquest was followed by a flow of settlers from various regions of Germany and adjacent areas. Great reserves of unexploited forests and marshland offered economic opportunities no longer available in the west. All social strata were represented among the migrants: clergy, knights, traders, craftsmen, and peasants. The indigenous Slavs, thinly spread over extensive areas, were neither exterminated nor driven out, but in the course of time they became Germanized and eventually merged with the conquerors (Aubin 1941, 366, 369).

Eastward expansion proper began in 1134 when Count Albrecht the Bear was enfeoffed with the North Mark by Emperor Lothair II. Over a period of two centuries, Albrecht's successors gained control over various Slavic territories including Brandenburg. Eventually, a large and relatively powerful principality emerged, the center of which was located between the Elbe and the Oder rivers. Westward it extended beyond the Elbe, and its eastern territories reached far beyond the Oder into the valley of the Vistula (Carsten 1954, 5). Named after Brandenburg, one of its component territories, the principality became the direct predecessor of the kingdom of Prussia.

Prussia Under the Rule of the Teutonic Knights

The martial traditions of the Ascanian dynasty were surpassed by those of the Knights of the Teutonic Order, who in 1211 assumed a leading role in expanding the eastern frontier. Thoroughly militarized, they embarked upon the conquest of Prussia and the conversion of its pagan tribes, located between the Vistula and the Niemen rivers (Lamprecht 1913, 3: 383ff.). To the Knights, war was a way of life, far beyond mere conquest and territorial expansion. At the peak of their power they controlled Prussia, Courland, Livonia, and Estonia. Eventually, Poland vanquished them.

The warlike traditions and rebellious attitudes of the indigenous Prussians compelled the Knights to maintain a constant state of military vigilance. Numerous uprisings had to be beaten down, and the eastern boundaries had to be defended against invaders. The suppression of the last great revolt, which lasted from 1261 to 1275, sealed the fate of the Prussians. The rebels who had not been killed or driven out were made serfs, while the natives who had remained loyal to the Order were allowed to retain their holdings and to become "Prussian freemen." To the extent that the loyal Prussians belonged to the nobility, their status was recognized as legally and economically equal to the German nobility. In fact, the Prussian freemen and nobles quickly became Germanized, and many Germanized Prussian aristocrats became the ancestors of Junker families (Carsten 1954, 66). Many other Junker families descended from Slavic peoples, such as the Wends, the Kashubians, and the Poles. Prior to 1806, one-fifth of all East Elbian counts and one-fourth of all noble families of lower rank were of Polish ancestry (Görlitz 1950, 12).

The cultural heritage of the Teutonic Knights did not vanish as the Order declined. During two hundred years of a highly effective rule, the aboriginal culture of the Prussians was thoroughly transformed, but the regime erected by the Order should not be interpreted in militaristic terms alone. Militarism as practiced by the Knights is to be understood within the context of superior statecraft, unmatched by the contemporary German and Polish principalities. Close association with the Norman Empire in Sicily and the political experiences gathered in the Near East enabled the Order to transfer Norman, Byzantine, and Italian influences to northeastern Europe. "To the present day the vast archives of the Teutonic Order bear witness to its uniform standards of administration, its division of labor among numerous professional officials, its highly centralized organization, its great wealth and financial power" (Carsten 1954, 7).

Before assigning to the Teutonic Knights the role of bearers of "German culture" in the east, one should use extreme caution. Prussian nationalism of the nineteenth century contributed to the idealization of the Teutonic state insofar as it projected political characteristics of Bismarck's time into the Middle Ages, uncritically emphasizing those achievements of the Order that could be used to glorify Prussia's past. Undoubtedly, the incessant wars the Order waged against the native Prussians transformed them into Christians and obedient subjects to such a degree that the aboriginal culture eventually disappeared almost without a trace. The Knights had the mentality of medieval crusaders prepared to eradicate paganism, and the state they implanted bore no resemblance whatever to the national state of the nineteenth century.

However, two aspects of the Teutonic Knights' rule should be pointed out here. The militaristic regime of the Knights was expressed not only in the subjugation of the native Prussians but also in violent confrontations with the Poles and the estates of the Order's own territory. Many of the burghers and nobles who had come from the western principalities considered the political rule of the Order to be tyrannical, and in 1454 the fateful thirteen years' war broke out, which pitted the Knights against the rural aristocracy and the burghers of Danzig, Thorn, and other towns. No longer was the Order able to maintain control over the western part of its domain, but the general decline had already begun earlier. In addition to prejudicial wars, mismanagement, economic crises, and moral decay had befallen the Knights (Wippermann 1981, 337; Rosenberg 1980, 107).

Internal warfare and the general decadence of the Order's rule are often glossed over in idealistic descriptions of this alleged model of Prussianism. The question to be posed here refers to the frequently discussed hypothesis of a cultural continuity between the state of the Teutonic Knights and that of the Prussian militarism of later years. The main difficulty lies not so much in the dissolution of the Order's rule as in the fact that the cultural heirs of the Knights, namely, the Prussian nobility, enjoyed a long period of peace extending throughout the entire sixteenth century until the time of the Thirty Years' War, offering little opportunity for warlike activities (Rosenberg 1980, 109).

At any rate, a comparison of essential culture traits of the sociopolitical system established by the Order with those of latter-day Prussia yields surprising similarities:

1. The Order had implanted the "profound doctrine of the supreme value of the State, and the civic subordination to the purposes of State, which the Teutonic Knights perhaps proclaimed more loudly and clearly than do any other voices speaking to us from the German past"

(Treitschke 1942, 21). Much later, unquestioning subordination to the State and its living symbol, the king, became the cornerstone of Prussia's political structure.

2. The Order, which recruited its members among the German aristocracy, was "endowed with the triple pride of Christians, Knights and Germans" (Treitschke 1942, 39). This ideological trinity was to play a significant role among the Junkers, the landed aristocracy of eastern Prussia, in subsequent centuries.

3. The terribly severe internal discipline of the Order was matched by the unrelenting harshness with which paganism and any vestige of political autonomy of the Prussians were suppressed, particularly after the rebellion of 1261. Absolute loyalty demanded by the Order included unconditional acceptance of the conquerors' culture. These were the beginnings of "Prussianism" in the sense of uncompromising discipline.

4. The Order strongly encouraged immigration from Germany. Along with German nobles, there was a broad stratum of German peasants and urban settlers from almost every major region of Germany (Treitschke 1942, 53ff.).

5. The Order laid the foundations of a social structure in which the landed aristocracy was clearly the ruling class and a free peasantry ranked above the serfs, who were mostly Prussian natives. Along with these strata there were the beginnings of an urban bourgeoisie. This feudal structure may be considered the prototype of the stratification system found in later Prussia. It proved particularly adaptable to military objectives. Indeed, the institution of the militia and the obligation of the peasantry to participate in the wars fought by the Knights anticipated certain aspects of eighteenth-century Prussian military organization.

Though the structural prerequisites for the militarization of the Prussian peasantry can be traced back to the stratification system instituted by the Order, the existence of a direct linkage between the two forms of militarism would be difficult to prove. A century of peace afforded the Prussian Junkers the opportunity to shift their interests from militaristic to economic pursuits. It hardly seems surprising therefore that, oblivious of their remote military tradition, they should initially refuse to accept the military role the Prussian rulers proceeded to impose upon them after the Thirty Years' War. Whether or to what extent the Prussian officer corps of the seventeenth and eighteenth centuries was actually prompted by the behavioral model of their warlike ancestors remains an open question.

In 1525 the Order of the Teutonic Knights was dissolved, and the Reformation took hold in Prussia. The last Grand Master of the Order, Albert von Hohenzollern, became the first duke of Prussia and a liege man of the king of Poland. Transformed into a local, land-holding nobility, the former Knights constituted a "homogeneous upper class with identical economic and political interests" (Carsten 1954, 150).

In 1618 Prussia fell to Brandenburg by succession, and under the "Great Elector" Frederick William (1640–88), Brandenburg-Prussia became a unified state. However, the rule of the Knights had left permanent marks on Prussia. Throughout the seventeenth century, Prussia continued far ahead of Brandenburg in population and in economic development (Carsten 1954, 203). In the present context, the political fusion of Brandenburg and Prussia seems relevant because it marks the convergence of two distinct military traditions looking back on two centuries of conquest and subjugation of peoples indigenous to the conquered territories.

The disintegration of the Teutonic Order's state encouraged violent confrontations, the outcome of which was related to the later political and economic power position of the Junker aristocracy. In Prussia as well as in Brandenburg, the Junkers descended from a "heterogeneous colonial aristocracy" composed of native nobles of Baltic and Slavic provenance, of immigrated German aristocrats and mercenary chieftains (Rosenberg 1980, 95). These pioneer settlers became robber knights who ruthlessly exploited the political weakness of the country by coercively appropriating land. While this anomic situation lasted, robbery and murder ceased to be considered crimes and became greatly admired patterns of behavior instead (Rosenberg 1980, 123). Many Junker families thus "acquired" extensive rural estates. As the agrarian economy became increasingly profitable, demanding the recruitment of a docile labor force, a system of servitude was forced upon them that spread rapidly, always in unison with the illegal usurpation of the local jurisdiction and administration by the state owner (Rosenberg 1980, 115, 131).

3

The Formative Period of Prussian Militarism

The Road to Absolutism and the Emergence of a Standing Army

The emergence of modern Prussian militarism was predicated upon the growing concentration of power in the person of the ruler. As long as he had to share the power to make high-level political decisions with the estates, he had little chance to obtain the resources necessary to build a permanent military establishment capable of playing a decisive role in international or domestic conflicts. Traditionally, the ruler had to approach the estates, particularly the nobility and the burghers of the corporate towns, for the allocation of funds to organize and equip an army in the case of war. The existing system did not make allowance for the establishment of a permanent army without which no truly militaristic state could possibly be erected. Thus, the main bone of contention between the ruler and the estates was the right to levy taxes. The issue became momentous in the seventeenth century when the Thirty Years' War engulfed Brandenburg-Prussia. Unable to offer effective resistance, the country was invaded, occupied, and ruthlessly exploited by imperial and Swedish armies. Completely overruling traditional privileges, the invaders imposed arbitrary taxes and collected them by force. Particularly galling to the political elite, the Junker nobility, was the contempt for their inherited privilege of exemption from taxation. After a century of relative peace in the eastern territories, the Junkers, hemmed in by parochial interests and perspectives, were unable to cope with or even understand the complexities of international politics (Carsten 1954, 179–80; Rosenberg 1958, 33).

Succeeding George William, the "Great Elector" Frederick William had to yield to the pressures of the Junker nobility, at least temporarily. He abolished the war council and reconstituted the privy council with a Junker majority, but the power contest between the ruler and the estates continued unabated. Temporary successes alternated with strategic retreats until eventually another international conflict, the war between Sweden and Poland (Northern War, 1655–60), shifted the power balance between elector and nobility definitely in favor of royal absolutism, which appeared to be the general trend of the era.

Participation in the Swedish-Polish war implied a significant change of Brandenburg's role in international politics. Instead of being victimized by international conflicts, Frederick William intended to use such conflicts to gain political advantages. In fact, at the end of the war Brandenburg's claim to the sovereign possession of Prussia, against the interests of Poland and Sweden, was recognized (Carsten 1954, 270). The elector had increased the army during the war, and when the estates refused to grant the necessary appropriations for the maintenance of a peacetime army, he raised the funds without their consent (Carsten 1954, 189). What played further into the ruler's hands was the invasion of Prussia by the Tartars (1656–57), who burned thirteen towns, killed 23,000 people, and enslaved another 34,000 (Carsten 1954, 208). Clearly, a standing army seemed necessary to protect the country, and the Prussian estates were forced to grant funds to maintain a small force in peacetime (Carsten 1954, 216). At any rate, once a standing army had been created, it could be used to break any resistance to the levying of taxes earmarked for its own maintenance. Toward the end of his reign, Frederick William had succeeded in monopolizing the powers (1) to make foreign policy without consent of the estates, (2) to introduce permanent taxation, and (3) to maintain a standing army that by the time of his demise numbered about 30,000 (Rosenberg 1958, 35). The first crucial step in a long series of evolutionary changes had been carried out.

The Nobility Becomes a Military Elite by Royal Fiat

The destruction of the *Ständestaat* and the ruler's assumption of absolute power did not, per se, generate militarism. They should be viewed as mere aspects of a more complex process affecting all sectors of the society. Above all, the way this process altered the position of the Junker nobility deserves careful scrutiny. The fact that Frederick William curtailed the traditional privileges of the nobility did not imply the wish to destroy it. On the contrary, he perceived the Junkers as potential military leaders and protagonists of a militaristic state, a role they were not prepared to assume without specific incentives and pressures the ruler brought to bear upon them. To understand how Frederick William actually succeeded in militarizing the Junkers, several facts have to be taken into account. The economic situation of the land-holding nobility had deteriorated considerably during the great depression, which lasted from 1618 to 1650. Profitable expansion of the agrarian economy had come to an end (Rosenberg 1958, 33). The depression was instrumental in directing the "new poor among the wellborn" toward military job opportunities "which gave a fresh lease on life to illiterate noble boys, landless noble bumpkins, unemployed nobles returned from service in foreign armies, and impoverished or bankrupt squires with little or no formal education" (Rosenberg 1958, 59).

In 1701 when Prussia became a kingdom, nearly one-fifth of its nobility were classified as "poor" (Carsten 1954, 272). Whatever the criteria of poverty may have been, there can be little doubt that the Junker squirearchy was highly differentiated, and that indigence, often associated with lack of salable skills, played into the hands of the ruler, who wished to transform the Junkers into a "service nobility" expected to identify its interests with those of the state in return for positions of honor and profit (Carsten 1954, 272). Such positions were to be had in the officer corps as well as in the burgeoning bureaucracy. The only obstacle preventing the Junkers from immediately taking advantage of military job opportunities was the general lack of prestige associated with soldiering. Only the dregs of society joined the army, and the moral and intellectual level of the officers was hardly above that of the rank and file from which they had been promoted. The first steps in making the officer corps more attractive were weeding out the "bad elements" and no longer promoting plain soldiers to officers (Lamprecht 1913, 3: 691; Craig 1955, 12–14).

Although successful, this change drove a wedge between officers and soldiers that, in the long run, would produce consequences damaging to army morale. At that time, the problem lay in overcoming the social difficulties of the transition period. This did not happen without coercive measures on the part of the monarch, who ordered all young noblemen aged twelve to eighteen to be registered. From these lists he arbitrarily selected the ones who had to enter the newly founded cadet academy in Berlin. The youngsters, in groups of eighteen or twenty, were then taken to the capital under military guard (Schmoller 1981, 763). However, in the course of several decades the status of the Prussian officer was raised to the level of a privileged group whose members took advantage of otherwise unavailable opportunities to achieve positions of professional competence, great authority, and social prestige. Furthermore, the social status of high-ranking officers was enhanced by close association with the ruler and, a little later (1701), with the king, their supreme commander, who did his utmost to indoctrinate the Junkers with the belief that military service was the "natural" vocation of the nobility (Craig 1955, 12–14). Actually, the officer corps, as well as the bureaucracy, became the new estates, offering prestigious and profitable career opportunities in a changing social structure.

One of the major aspects of this change is to be seen in the Great Compromise of 1653 between the ruler and the Junker nobility. A victorious absolutism excluded the nobility from participating in top-level decision making. In return, the elector respected the undisputed rule of the Junkers at the local level, particularly insofar as complete control of the peasantry was concerned. Nevertheless, the interests of the crown never completely coincided with those of the agrarian nobility. On the one hand, the feudal structure of the rural society fostered the development of militarism, as we shall see. On the other hand, the crown found it desirable to protect the peasantry from the estate owners' encroachment upon their customary rights (Baumgart 1981, 73). Apart from paying taxes, the peasants performed militarily important services and provided recruits for the army (Büsch 1981, 53). In spite of such relatively minor differences, the Great Compromise performed an invaluable function. Without losing the characteristics of semifeudal landholders, the Junkers became a "service aristocracy" bound to the ruler by the "unviolable law of obedience and unflinching loyalty." Inverting their historical role of opponents to monocratic rule, the militarized nobility became the main instrument of regal absolutism (Lamprecht 1913, 3: 661). The conventional image of the monarch that gained currency with Elector Frederick William was one of a military leader symbolized by the officer's uniform and sword. Pictorial representations of Prussian kings and German emperors most often depicted them with their military paraphernalia.

Subordination and loyalty to the king were linked to the officer's sense of honor internalized in the cadet corps. That sense of honor has been appropriately defined as "a moral compulsion which forced the officer to bear hardship, danger, and death without flinching and without expectations of reward" (Craig 1955, 16). *Todesverachtung* (contempt of death) became the supreme virtue of the officer. Frederick the Great (1740–86), who stressed the importance of honor perhaps more than his predecessors, apparently believed that the virtues of honor existed only among the nobility. Consequently, he refused to follow the policy of his father, who had appointed commoners to the officer corps.

The transformation of an agrarian nobility into a military elite represents the second major change in the evolution of Prussian militarism. It marks the inception of a professional officer corps and, at the same time, the genesis of a triple alliance between monarch, officer corps, and Junker nobility, the extraordinary stability of which ought to be considered the prime determinant of the longevity of Prussian militarism. To state this in more abstract terms, a major change gave birth to a new structural pattern that would soon become a firmly established tradition.

The Disfranchisement of the Peasantry

It would be difficult to explain the emergence of militaristic absolutism in Brandenburg without considering the structural changes affecting the peasantry and urban bourgeoisie. As long as the territories east of the Elbe River served as a frontier, access to land was free, although often to the detriment of the native population. Though never completely enfranchised, the peasantry enjoyed an economic situation that compared favorably with that of western Europe. However, even in the fifteenth century the legal status of the smallholders began to decline. The feudal lords imposed tributary services that became increasingly oppressive, inducing numerous peasants to desert the large estates. The lords reacted by tying the peasants to the soil, which in turn caused more people to escape serfdom by desertion. In fact, the successors of the Teutonic Knights in Prussia were confronted with a real peasant war in 1525 (Carsten 1954, 150). In spite of their sporadic resistance, neither peasants nor serfs had enough power to prevent the steady tightening of subordinative relationships to the land-holding nobility, in Prussia as well as in Brandenburg and Pomerania. In the seventeenth century the previous changes were legalized, and the peasant's legal status was fixed at a uniformly low level (Carsten 1954, 152–62). Military structures could easily be erected on this kind of social order if the powerholders deemed such a step desirable.

In contrast to the peasantry, the urban burghers formally participated in decisions concerning taxation and foreign affairs. Under the Elector Frederick William, the traditional rights of the "Third Estate," the burghers, were gradually curtailed, municipal self-government became a thing of the past, and increasing taxation dealt heavy blows to the urban economy. During the Swedish-Polish war, the tax burden imposed upon the towns was so heavy that they were "almost deserted." Peace brought some reprieve, but taxation continued to weigh heavy on the urban bourgeoisie. Eventually, a controversial excise tax became a permanent part of the urban tax structure (Carsten 1954, 190–91, 197).

Brandenburg's military action in the west against Louis XIV of France, in 1672, brought renewed pressure to bear on the towns. Opposition proved futile as in the case of Königsberg, which was occupied by the army, and people "had the tiles of their roofs seized" if they failed to pay (Carsten 1954, 209). It should be emphasized, however, that the Junker nobility remained exempt from taxation. "Servile land tenure and peasant bondage by legal status, an empoverished burgher class, crippled municipal liberties and Junker dominance were from the start fundamental characteristics of the modern Prussian system" (Rosenberg 1958, 28).

The Ruler's Monopolization of Fiscal Power

If the monarch's monopolization of fiscal power and the ruthless use of such power to build a militaristic state jeopardized the rural and urban economy (peasantry and burghers), one may ask how militarism thrived while the economic resources necessary to its development were systematically depleted by excessive taxation. It may be argued that in view of its economic implications, incipient Prussian militarism constituted a threat to the survival of the society and, as an institution, had little or no adaptive significance. The argument is undoubtedly correct as long as one has in mind the survival of the traditional *Ständestaat*. However, the point is that militarism was perceived, by its protagonists, within the context of the absolutist state and its power politics.

Morris Janowitz has charged Prussian militarism with "the modification and destruction of civilian institutions by military leaders acting directly and premeditatedly through the state and other institutions." This remark seems unobjectionable if it refers to the institutions of the *Ständestaat* or to those of the Weimar Republic. However, the so-called civilian institutions, developing during the formative and efflorescent periods of Prussian militarism, were built out of ideological and structural principles in which military modes of thinking, feeling, and acting loomed large *since their very inception*. This is particularly true of the Prussian judiciary and the bureaucracy in general. Whether administrator or judge, the Prussian jurist represented a unique breed in which professional expertise, military authoritarianism, and political conservatism (monarchism) were combined in a way that would have made interference by military leaders redundant (Janowitz 1975, 59).

The rulers of seventeenth-century Brandenburg-Prussia could choose between two political alternatives. They could simply remain, as most German principalities did, a mere satellite of the more powerful states, or they could attempt to marshal available human and economic resources to achieve the status of a European power to be reckoned with in international politics. The latter alternative carried additional weight in view of the fact that the elector ruled an aggregate of noncontiguous territories spread over northern Germany from the Dutch border in the west to the Russian border in the east. They had been acquired through dynastic succession or conquest. In other words, there was not *one* state but a number of separate principalities that "happened to have the same ruler, but no other bond between them" (Carsten 1954, 178). The inhabitants of those heterogeneous territories certainly had no awareness of belonging to the same political structure and were thus, geographically and culturally, extremely vulnerable to the vicissitudes of the international power struggle. Frederick William was probably the first monarch to pursue an active policy designed to weld this heterogeneous aggregate into a unified state, and he perceived the armed forces and increasing centralization of power as key elements of political integration (Lamprecht 1913, 3: 654). Thus the question of whether or not Prussian militarism had adaptive value should be related to the survival chances of the political structure about to emerge toward the end of the seventeenth century.

Of course, these considerations do not eliminate the fact that the fiscal burden must have been oppressive, judging from the effects it had on the peasantry and the urban economy. Available resources did not suffice to maintain the standing army, and the elector sought and received subsidies from such countries as the Netherlands, Spain, France, and Austria. If foreign financial assistance saw the military establishment through difficult times, it also compromised Brandenburg's position in international politics. The subsidy tractates created dependency relationships that explain Brandenburg's comparatively small political influence in spite of its military accomplishments (Hintze 1915, 221).

The Harnessing of Economic Resources

Development of economic resources was the only way to escape the satellite role imposed by financial dependency. During the second half of the seventeenth century, the elector increasingly concentrated his efforts on economic development. To raise the level of the national income, he introduced new industries, improved the existing ones, promoted trade, mining, and agriculture, and encouraged immigration capable of developing new economic activities. In fact, by the end of the century about twenty thousand French Calvinists (Huguenots) had settled in Prussian territories (Dorwart 1953, 129, 135). The elector conceived his development plans in terms of mercantilistic doctrine, and as such they were at variance with the economic interests of the estates.

Mercantilism was intended to generate a "total transformation of society and its organization, as well as of the state and its institutions, in the replacing of a local and territorial economic policy by that of the national state" (Schmoller 1931, 51). Particularly in Prussia, mercantilism meant the *Gesamtstaat* (united state) capable of establishing "one national army supported by a national economy" (Dorwart 1953, 129). The military were instrumental in imposing the new order upon the institutions representing economic particularism.

Finally, in an appraisal of the adaptiveness of militarism, it should be emphasized that militarism is not synonymous with warfare, as some authors seem to believe (Service 1967, 169; Webster 1976, 815). Militarism, as defined earlier, is active preparation for war through the mobilization of human, technological, and economic resources. In this sense, it means, above everything else, demonstration of power capabilities by holding in readiness a large, well-trained, and disciplined army, by submitting various sectors of the society to military discipline (implying instant readiness to support war), and by providing the ideological underpinnings conducive to strong military and civilian morale.

In retrospect, there can be little doubt that the demonstration of power capabilities throughout the formative period of Prussian militarism was more effective than actual war. If population increase, territorial growth, and economic development are acceptable criteria for measuring the effects of militarism, then it must be considered adaptive. Between 1740 and 1806 the territorial size of Prussia tripled and its revenues and population quadrupled (Rosenberg 1958, 175).

The Military Revolution

Prussian militarism originated during a period in which the art of war went through a series of changes radical enough to justify the term *revolution*. In the Middle Ages warfare was virtually a privilege of the feudal nobility; it was highly individualized and unresponsive to any attempt to impose a semblance of battle discipline. Only the king's authority was respected, but "often even the king was powerless to control his nobles" (Oman 1953, 58). Any petty nobleman capable of mustering a body of retainers could carry out forays or engage in feuds. Major engagements centered on the heavily armed cavalry composed of mailed horsemen who considered war an "honorable business" and fought according to a generally accepted code. To the extent that they played any role at all, foot soldiers "without discipline and with a miscellaneous assortment of dissimilar weapons" rarely stood their ground against cavalry charges

(Oman 1953, 64). There were no standing armies, and structured officer corps were virtually unknown.

Changes originating in various countries and at different times were intended to break the tactical superiority of the medieval cavalry. Partially based on the rediscovery of classic Roman models, most innovations were designed to rehabilitate the infantry, providing it with weapons and tactical skills effective enough to withstand the impact of the armored cavalry. This was accomplished before portable firearms became widely available. In fact, the massing of foot soldiers in the form of the Spanish *tercio* and the Swiss column proved highly effective against the mounted knights. The eighteen-feet-long pike of the Swiss infantry outreached the lance of the cavaliers, and the offensive shock of the cavalry failed to prevail against the dense, deep formations of the infantry (Roberts 1967, 56). The new tactic gave the Swiss column a military superiority temporarily unmatched in continental Europe. While the success of the Swiss pikeman rested on the "irresistible impact and steady pressure of his solid column with its serried edge of spear point," the longbow provided the English archers of the late Middle Ages with a weapon capable of defeating the feudal cavalry by rapid shooting of armor-piercing missiles (Oman 1953, 74).

Jan Zizka, the military leader of the Hussites, has been credited with another tactical innovation, the so-called *Wagenburg* (wagon fortress), which played a significant role in the military revolution of the fifteenth century. Equipped with a variety of weapons, four-wheeled wagons were variably used for defense and attack. Disposed in a vast circle and chained to one another, the wagons proved impregnable to cavalry charges and, at the same time, provided protection to the foot soldiers. The Hussite generals successfully used the wagons, advancing in cuneiform order, so that their two wings protected the marching infantry. Soon Bohemia's neighbors eagerly adopted this new tactical device, and Margrave Albrecht von Brandenburg effectively used the *Wagenburg* in the war against Pomerania (1478–79) (Jähns 1889, 1: 305–6).

Among these and many other initiatives designed to change medieval warfare, none had greater revolutionary significance than the Swiss column and the Spanish *tercio*. Of course, the increasing use of portable firearms accelerated the demise of the feudal cavalry. Yet the *tercio* and the Swiss column merely represent first steps on the way to more significant changes that came about between 1560 and 1660, primarily in Holland and Sweden. Maurice of Orange, the Dutch statesman and military reformer, substituted the "unwieldy squares" of the Spanish *tercio* and the even larger but asymmetrical blocks of the Swiss column for "a multiplicity of small units ranged in two or three lines and so disposed and armed as to permit the full exploitation of all types of weapons" (Roberts 1967, 196). As innocuous as this change may seem at first glance, it had far-reaching implications. The new tactic could be effective only if the many small units acted in strict coordination and in accordance with commands given by officers who has been trained to take full advantage of the newly gained maneuverability. A previously unheard-of training system became mandatory, implying adherence to the equally unknown principle of mass subordination. To provide the necessary drill and to master the intricacies of the new tactics, a much larger and better educated officer corps had to be created.

Maurice of Orange's innovation was intended for defense rather than attack, but Gustaf Adolf, king of Sweden, went much further in transforming the Dutch type of deployment into a battle array designed for offensive action and annihilation of the enemy. Yet far from freezing into a rigid mold, Swedish tactics allowed for "adaptation and variation" (Roberts 1967, 73, 203). Under Gustaf Adolf's rule, Sweden developed into one of the top military powers of the seventeenth century. Although widely recognized as a model and emulated by many countries, Sweden proved quite inimitable, at least temporarily, in two aspects of its military organization. Mercenary armies were believed to be superior to citizen militias because the drilling and professional skills required by the new tactics could not possibly be exacted from militias. Indeed, these failed disastrously in the seventeenth century, except in Sweden where conscription dated from 1544. By 1630 Gustaf Adolf commanded the first standing national army of conscripts in Europe (Roberts 1967, 64, 200). In contrast with its counterparts elsewhere, the Swedish army proved equal to the demands of a vastly improved fire discipline and the combined use of firearms and pikes. The scope of Swedish warfare, during the seventeenth century, remained unsurpassed until the age of Napoleon. Gustaf Adolf developed a "gradualist strategy" designed to conquer Germany by occupation and "methodical consolidation of successive base-areas." At one time, seven Swedish armies acting in coordination extended from the Vistula to the Brenner Pass, and from Glogau in the east to Lake Constance in the west (Roberts 1967, 73, 203).

Gustaf Adolf also thoroughly remade the cavalry. Lance and heavy armor disappeared, and instead of the caracole—the firing of heavy pistols by horsemen executing rapid turns while avoiding close contact with the enemy—the charge with the sword was introduced. To the extent that the light cavalry eliminated differences in mount, arms, and equipment between noble and esquire, it symbolized social subversion, but as we shall see later on, the nobility was compensated for the loss of its own distinct military organization by being called to fill the most prestigious, if not all, positions in the newly created officer corps (Roberts 1967, 196, 217).

The tremendous expansion of the scale and scope of warfare implied the harnessing of human, technical, financial, and administrative resources only the state could successfully manage. Unlike his southern neighbors, Gustaf Adolf was spared power contests with the estates, for Sweden had never known feudalism. In the Articles of War Gustaf Adolf set a new standard of royal control over things military. Private and irregular armies were no longer tolerated, and the monarch assumed the functions of recruiting and paying his soldiers. The previously existing system of mercenary armies acquiring their own equipment was considered incompatible with discipline and efficiency. By 1630 the War Office *(krigsrät)* had become a true center of military administration, and after 1630 a domestic armament industry proved capable of supplying most of Sweden's military needs at a "relatively inconsiderable cost" (Roberts 1967, 65).

Sweden's national army turned out to be not only more efficient but also less expensive than most mercenary armies of that time. The king no longer had to contend with the customary peculations by captains, and payment was made in "land-grants, revenue assignments, tax-remissions, or in kind" (Roberts 1967, 200).

One essential aspect of the military revolution was the harnessing of science to war. No longer could warcraft be learned "on the job." Gustaf Adolf insisted that commanders be able to use the tools provided by scientists, and no tool ranked higher in his opinion than mathematics. Reflecting the general trend toward providing some measure of formal education for officers, Johan of Nassau founded the first military academy in 1617, and others followed in Scandinavia, France, and Austria (Roberts 1967, 212).

Some innovations had a definite impact on warcraft. The invention of corned powder increased the effectiveness of firearms. A portable telescope was used by both Maurice of Orange and Gustaf Adolf, and a whole century of progress stood behind the Swedish light field artillery, which set standards until King Frederick the Great of Prussia succeeded in adding further improvements (Roberts 1967, 74, 211).

The concept of military rank developed only in the first half of the seventeenth century. Of course, some men had been officers before that time, but in the mercenary armies of the Thirty Years' War their position had been rather vague. Now, a genuine hierarchization of command positions was introduced, and by the end of the century the structuring of the officer corps was complete in its basic aspects. Although its organization differed vastly from that of the medieval knights, it became like the chivalry of bygone times a "European supranational entity, with its own ethos, its own international code of honor, its own corporate spirit" (Roberts 1967, 213). It ought to be mentioned at this juncture that the supranational code of honor imposed a moral restraint on modern warfare, which in spite of occasional setbacks preserved its cross-cultural validity, at least within the orbit of Western civilization, up to the time of World War I.

The military revolution was contingent upon the marshaling of economic resources far greater than anything that had been possible in previous times. The new system of mercantilism made available commodities without which no war could be waged. The state's centralized control of manufactures and international commerce was designed to avoid situations in which a country would be at the mercy of a foreign power for the production of strategic goods. Because of the international competition for such commodities, economic warfare tended to become wider in range and more effective (Roberts 1967, 214).

Annihilation rather than mere defeat of the enemy had been practiced often enough before the military revolution, but Gustaf Adolf raised it to the level of a strategic principle, thus foreshadowing Clausewitz' *Vernichtungskrieg* (war of annihilation). From time to time, extreme militarists have advocated total destruction of the enemy, but within the confines of Western civilization only the bombing strategy of World War II came close to the *Vernichtungskrieg*.

The origin and development of Prussian militarism ought to be understood in the context of the military revolution. No mistake could be more serious than the assumption that the Prussian military establishment, particularly in its early phases, ever was a self-contained entity and that it was capable of choosing an evolutionary course contrasting with what had been happening in the rest of Europe. From the very beginning, Prussia was wide open to the changes brought about by the military revolution. Its gradual transformation into a great military power would have been completely inconceivable without the continuous borrowing of organizational and technical elements invented, discovered, and rediscovered primarily in Holland and Sweden. From Sweden, Prussia received military discipline, the organization of firepower, the light regimental and mobile field artillery, among other traits. Prussian rulers emulated Gustaf Adolf's role of supreme drill master and commander, a pattern that remained dominant in Prussian military organization long after Swedish militarism had subsided.

Prussia was not the only recipient of imported military skills and technology. A vast, dense network of channels crisscrossed Europe, and cultural diffusion continuously influenced the development of warcraft everywhere. International connections worked at all levels of military establishments. Officers and soldiers

learned all manner of things from allies and enemies. In their professional business the quicker they could imitate the best foreign models, the better for them, and there was a remarkable uniformity all over Europe in drill, in naval architecture, and no doubt in the manners and outlook of the military and even of naval officers. . . . Warfare itself thus did something to draw the community together, and so did the diplomatic organization behind it (Clark 1958, 97–98).

The composition of the mercenary armies contributed significantly to the ease with which military innovations spread over Europe. Soldiers were recruited with little regard to national origin, and every officer corps had foreigners in its ranks. It may suffice here to mention that toward the end of the seventeenth century almost one-third of all Prussian army officers were French Huguenots (Rosenberg 1958, 59).

Changes in Prussian Military Organization

The changes to which the Great Elector subjected the armed forces could not possibly have been accomplished in one single act. The military heritage of the Thirty Years' War was not easily amenable to the reforms the Elector and his immediate successors had in mind. Military commanders often refused to obey orders given by the elector, and descriptions of "Brandenburg's officers of those times seem to obliterate the differences between bandit chieftains and colonels . . . . Officers and generals fight duels and treacherously assault or stab each other to death, while the Elector does not dare to interfere much" (Schmoller 1981, 750). The relative impotence of the elector was closely related to the appalling poverty of the country, which had turned the appropriation of necessary funds into a chronic problem. Frederick William was indebted to the colonels who threatened mutiny of the troops whenever payment of wages was delayed.

Traditionally, the formation of an army or a single regiment, as the case might be, was a private enterprise of military leaders who hoped to reap large profits by renting out their troops to a ruler engaged in war. The elector's task was to transform the private army, recruited for a particular purpose, into a permanent institution at the exclusive service of the monarchy. Following the models established by Holland and Sweden, the elector himself proceeded to form regiments, and he appointed their commanders, the colonels, but this is as far as he went during the first phase of the reform. For a long time the regimental commanders, appointed by the elector, continued to select the officers under their authority and to recruit the soldiers to keep the regiments up to the prescribed strength. Although they had ceased to be private entrepreneurs, the colonels still drew substantial perquisites, both legal and illegal, from the "regimental economy" *(Regimentswirtschaft)*. The fact that between 1655 and 1688 seventy-five regiments were established and dissolved indicates that permanency should not be confused with stability of the military institution *(Militärgeschichtliches Forschungsamt* 1964, 25).

Responsibility, discipline, loyalty to the monarch, and professional esprit de corps were slow in developing among the officer corps. Insubordinations of the colonels were rather frequent, and only gradually could they be induced to act as components of larger army corps and to accept the authority of commanding generals (Hintze 1915, 220).

Among the rulers of Prussia, none was a more "passionate soldier" and "fanatic militarist" than King Frederick William I (1713–40), but he was also "the most peaceable of the Hohenzollerns of the seventeenth and eighteenth centuries" (Rosenberg 1958, 41). Surnamed the Soldiers' King, he valued the army as "the basis of his temporal bliss," his "true interest as well as security, but equally his glory and prestige" (Rosenberg 1958, 38). Under his reign and that of his successor, "Prussia was not a country with an army, but an army with a country which served as headquarters and food magazine," as a Prussian minister remarked in 1800 (quoted in Rosenberg 1958, 40). Frederick William I was primarily responsible for the establishment of military modes of behavior as models for the bureaucracy but, more generally, for all sectors of the society not directly involved in military affairs (Rosenberg 1958, 41). Berlin became a replica of Sparta "such as the world had never seen before." The capital resembled a military camp; the soldier was honored, but the civilian was degraded (von Archenholz n.d., 15). Frederick William enlarged on the changes initiated by his predecessors. Troops once billeted in private homes were increasingly concentrated in barracks. Uniforms and weapons were standardized, and a drill manual, strictly enforced in the smallest details, brought unheard-of rapidity, uniformity, and precision to the execution of military maneuvers. The king established a cadet school for the sons of the aristocracy, and one of his pet projects was the recruitment of unusually tall men for his elite guard (Ergang 1941, 66, 81).

A rigid disciplinary system was enforced by inflicting draconic penalties on violators. Harsh treatment and forcible enlistment produced a high rate of desertions among the rank and file and so much emigration of younger men that at times agricultural production suffered from the scarcity of able-bodied laborers. Sometimes entire villages emigrated (Büsch 1962, 16).

Contrary to the practices elsewhere, the promotion of Prussian officers depended on competence or merit, "at least in principle" (Ergang 1941, 73, 76, 80). The king considerably tightened the demands made on the officer corps. The officer's duties and services were spelled out in great detail; he had to be present at all times to train, correct, and supervise, no matter how minor the duty or drill. The regime thus established required total subordination of the officer's personality in service to the king, who kept in the closest possible contact with the higher echelons. Since the king's wish was that no personal involvement should divert an officer from his duties, he preferred unmarried men. Before a member of the lower ranks could marry, he had to obtain the consent of the regimental commander, and from 1717 on, approval of the king was necessary. Different versions of this sort of control haunted the officer corps up to World War I (*Militärgeschichtliches Forschungsamt* 1964, 37, 38, 43–44).

Frederick William succeeded in creating a highly homogeneous and honor-conscious corps—one characterized by the same social origin, the same values and attitudes, and the same rights and responsibilities. He gave the final touches to the dependency relationship between monarch and officer corps. The nobility accepted such an exacting and relatively unprofitable position because hardly any alternative, except the civil service, was available to the sons of the East Elbian nobility. However, admission to the higher levels of the bureaucracy required a longer and costlier training period, and not enough openings were available to employ all those seeking a professional career. Of course, the nobility was hemmed in by its unenviable economic situation on the one hand and its prejudice against a "bourgeois" occupation on the other (*Militärgeschichtliches Forschungsamt* 1964, 42–45).

The Coming of the Huguenots

The efforts of the Great Elector to create a professional officer corps were greatly enhanced by the arrival of some twenty thousand French Huguenot refugees, many of whom had been officers in the armies of Louis XIV. They were almost immediately incorporated into the Prussian armies, and toward the last decade of the seventeenth century approximately 29 percent of all officers were French Huguenots (Rosenberg 1958, 59; Holborn 1964, 66).

What the Prussian ruler had in mind was to supplement his own cadres with military specialists whose professional qualifications were undoubtedly superior to those of his incipient officer corps. In other words, it was a deliberate attempt to accelerate the evolution of the Prussian military establishment by implanting new attitudes, new organizational patterns, and new technical devices.

The elector's assumption that he was dealing with representatives of the most advanced forms of warcraft was based on the fact that under Louis XIV France had become one of the foremost military powers of Europe. A good figure to characterize the French military of that time is the incomparable Marquis de Vauban, known as a resourceful innovator of military architecture and an even more outstanding pioneer of new siege techniques. Vauban inspired a number of disciples, among them several Huguenots who built fortresses for Prussia (Jähns 1885, 2: 1439; Erbe 1937, 67).

That the refugee officers were French *and* Huguenots (or Calvinists) was of extraordinary significance. The cultural history of the Huguenots indicates an unusually high level of achievement in almost any endeavor they undertook. To some extent their accomplishments may be due to the social origin of most members of the sect. A large proportion, perhaps the majority, came from the more privileged strata of French society. In the rural areas, up to 80 percent of the Huguenots were members of the nobility, and in the towns a disproportionately large number of professionals, scholars, wealthy merchants, and artisans had joined the reform creed (Erbe 1937, 15). On the other hand, the Huguenots professed Calvin's doctrine, which, as Max Weber long ago found out, strongly stimulated all sorts of worldly endeavors. Thus, warcraft was only one of the many fields in which the French Calvinists attained extraordinary distinction. A century before their descendants sought asylum in Prussia and elsewhere, the Huguenots produced outstanding military specialists who joined the court of Henry IV as collaborators and experts. The most brilliant of these men was the Duke de Sully, who modernized the French army, creating a "formidable" artillery and building fortresses, highways, and canals of strategic significance (Viénot 1934, 78, 99–101).

Still another factor contributed to the military achievements of the Huguenots. As a persecuted religious minority, they literally had to fight for survival. During the so-called crusades against the French Calvinists (1621–27), they defended themselves with great valor. In 1625 they rose against their oppressors and distinguished themselves in 1627 during the siege of La Rochelle, one of the strongholds of French Calvinism (Viénot 1934, 254, 274). Although in the long run their resistance turned out to be hopeless, it probably reinforced their military tradition. Many of their officers went to fight under Maurice de Nassau to liberate the Netherlands from Spanish rule (Viénot 1934, 100). When the Edict of

Nantes granting political equality to the Huguenots was revoked in 1685, many thousands of them left France to seek asylum elsewhere.

This is the cultural background against which the arrival of the Huguenot officers should be appraised. The fact that virtually all of them were French noblemen added to their professional qualifications by the standards of that time and further justified the leading role they were expected to assume in the Prussian army.

It could be argued that a random distribution of the French officers throughout the ranks of the elector's army might have diluted their influence and diminished the chances to effect major changes. Shrewd enough to anticipate such a possibility, the Prussian ruler created a cavalry unit and an infantry regiment to be commanded exclusively by French officers. Following the French model, both units were divided into numerous small companies. In 1687 two companies of *Mousquetaires du Roi* were established, and they soon became famous as seminal schools for young cavalry and dragoon officers. The elector also took over the French institution of the *compagnies de cadets*, founded by Louvois. Composed of young French noblemen, these cadet companies established the pattern for officer training in the future (Jany 1967, 1: 297–98; Erbe 1937, 66); the cadets produced seventeen lieutenant generals and twenty-four major generals. The creation of these separate army units commanded by French officers also reduced the possibilities of personal friction with Prussian officers, who could not fail to perceive the newcomers as competitors and rivals.

Refugee officers assumed positions in all ranks and sectors of the Prussian military structure. The distinguished Huguenot Frédéric Armand Count von Schonberg, who bore the title of *Maréchal de France*, was appointed general in chief of all Prussian armed forces. Cayard and others built fortresses, and Charpentier became chief military physician (Erbe 1937, 67).

The Huguenot officers were not mercenaries in the usual sense of the word. Historical evidence reveals not only unquestionable loyalty to Prussia but also a commitment to the military profession that encompassed several generations of the same families. In the wars Frederick the Great waged during the eighteenth century, a great many Huguenot officers achieved unusual distinction commanding army corps and defending fortresses or fortified cities. At least seventeen Huguenot lineages were still represented in the ranks of the German army prior to or during World War I (Erbe 1937, 180–90).

The Militarization of Rural Society

More than any other sector of Prussian society, the rural social structure lent itself to thorough militarization. The Junker nobility controlled rural society, and members of the nobility constituted the officer corps. The rank-and-file soldiers were recruited from the serfs attached to the estates, while most of the noncommissioned officers came from the peasantry (Büsch 1962, 30).

The structure of the armed forces was more than a reflection of the social structure; it actually *was* the stratification system of Prussian agrarian society transformed to the barracks. The subordination of serf and peasant to the landlord became the subjection of the soldier to his officers. *They were the same people* (Simon 1955, 147). The landowner was almost always an officer or ex-officer; his authority as a landowner was as absolute as his military authority, for part of the reciprocal compromise between king and nobility had been the understanding that the monarch was not to interfere with the nobility's traditional control over the peasantry (Büsch 1962, 79). Since the authority of the officer was patterned after that of the landlord, the subordination of the soldier was conditioned by that of the peasant. The setting and the paraphernalia changed, but the basic human relationship remained. The two structures reinforced each other.

These structural similarities are revelant because by the early eighteenth century the Prussian kings began to recruit native Prussians instead of alien mercenaries. But the recruitment system was vitiated by so much abuse and violence that it defeated the objectives of the state. Young men were often recruited against their will and forced to serve even after a war. The rigor of the daily drill caused many to desert. In 1714 alone the infantry lost 3,471 men through desertion (Jany 1981, 771). Not only the deserters thwarted the objectives of the monarch; countless younger men took refuge in neighboring countries to escape the king's recruiters. The flight of an estimated 17,000 laborers in a single year (1714), including 7,000 craftsmen, jeopardized incipient industrialization attempts, which were being carried out for military reasons (Jany 1981, 184).

Repeated royal edicts failed to stem the abuses of the recruitment system. Often several regiments competed with one another to enlist future soldiers in the same district. In 1733 the king proceeded to limit each regiment to a particular territory where it was given the exclusive right to enlist recruits. Thus the canton system was established, which forced virtually all able-bodied men to have their names recorded in a special register. Since many of these "enrolled" men were actually called up to serve in the army, the canton system may be considered a transitory phase leading eventually to compulsory universal military service. After one or two years of active service, the cantonists were granted furlough, but over a period of twenty years they had to take part in the yearly exercises of their regiments. During his leave back in his native village, the cantonist was compelled to wear a piece of his uniform, even when working in the fields (Büsch 1981, 51). On Sundays he had to wear full uniform and attend religious service under the threat of being considered a deserter (Büsch 1981, 51).

Rather important was the fact that the cantonist belonged to a regiment stationed in his home district (Shanahan 1945, 17). Needless to say, the officers of cantonal regiments were members of the local landholding nobility. In other words, the cantonal soldier was simultaneously under military and manorial authority, a condition that significantly contributed to the stability of the system. Membership in a cantonal regiment, with its annual display of military discipline, reaffirmed the validity of the way the regional society was stratified, and the regional social structure provided the manpower and the pattern of subordination that reinforced military discipline.

One can hardly overemphasize the pervasiveness of military principles in the organization of rural society in eighteenth-century Prussia. The landowner's authority on the estate was absolute. He treated his serfs as harshly as his soldiers, and severe physical punishments of various kinds were as common on the estate as they were in the army (Büsch 1962, 42–43). Village, church, and school were under the landowner's control, as well as the local judiciary. The office of the *Landrat*, the representative of the king at the rural county level, was closely integrated with the military structure. Always a nobleman, an ex-officer, and an estate owner, the *Landrat* was also a military subcommissar exercising undivided control over troops, taxes, and police (Lamprecht 1913, 3: 686; Büsch 1962, 89). As such, he had the power to levy tributes, to enlist peasant labor, and to requisition peasant equipment (horses and wagons) for military transport and the construction of fortifications (Ludovici 1749, 213; Büsch 1962, 72). The military authority of the *Landrat* was kept as flexible as circumstances seemed to warrant and the king wished to make it.

The concept of desertion applied to peasants and soldiers alike. The villages were kept under strict surveillance to prevent the flight of peasants. Heavy fines were collectively imposed on villages that failed to carry out effective control of their people. Desertion was punished with death and confiscation of property (Büsch 1962, 28). The edict of 1713 decreed that any man leaving the country without permission was to be punished as a military deserter (Jähns 1885, 339).

Once Richelieu's idea of imposing military discipline on the nobility had been carried out (Lamprecht 1913, 3: 793–94), the policy of the Prussian crown became an all-out effort to preserve the status quo. The king perceived an enfranchised peasantry to be a threat to the system, and since he believed that without land-holdings the nobility would lose its aristocratic character and thus its military qualities, he did not allow the Junkers to sell their land (Büsch 1962, 103–4). Nor did he permit them to despoil dependent peasants of their holdings *(Bauernlegen)*, because out of their ranks came the noncommissioned officers. To preserve the economic viability of the landed estate, the crown provided funds to finance manorial credit associations *(Ritterschaftliche Kreditvereine)* whose facilities were restricted to the land-holding nobility (Lamprecht 1913, 3: 793–94).

The Urbanization of the Military

Relocation of the Prussian troops from the countryside into cities and towns was completed by 1721. Since the general urbanization process was very slow and most cities counted hardly more than a few thousand inhabitants, the permanent presence of an army unit with its numerous hangers-on entailed certain social and economic changes whose importance grew in proportion to the growing size of the army. For example, in 1740 Berlin had a population of 90,270, 21,309 of whom belonged to the army. By 1786, out of 147,388 inhabitants, 33,625 were garrisoned troops. During the entire eighteenth century, 20 to 24 percent of Prussia's urban population consisted of military personnel and their dependents.

Attempts to analyze the relationships between civilian and military should emphasize that the troops were not isolated in barracks but assigned to private quarters. In other words, many civilians shared their dwellings with soldiers and officers, a kind of involuntary contact that did not always generate desirable forms of association, according to reliable source material. In spite of obvious economic disadvantages, some cities refused to accept military garrisons within their walls (Schwieger 1980, 188). With few exceptions, however, the dovetailing of military and economic interests, which later played such an important role in the evolution of militarism, originated in the garrison towns of the eighteenth century.

The economic role of the troops was not limited to the consumption of local products. The soldiers took an active part in the production process, particularly the "soldier-workers" or those who happened to be on annual leave. The cantonists spent their furloughs in their native villages while the alien mercenaries had to remain in town as helpers of local craftsmen, spinners, and weavers (Jany 1981, 801; Büsch 1981, 57). Since wages were extremely low, the soldiers and their wretched dependents were forced to look for supplementary income however modest. The furlough system was a way of reconciling the political ambitions of the monarch with economic realities.

More relevant for the future of militarism was the presence of an officer corps in each garrison town. Although the officers were requested not to interfere with the city administrations, frictions and conflicts between civil and military authorities were rather common. In some cities, military governors and commanding officers found it possible to impose an autocratic regime on the population, mainly because the burghers were afraid of approaching the courts, which were not expected to redress abuses and transgressions (Schwieger 1980, 188–89). In this way, a pattern of impunity was established. By ordering his officers to refrain from social intercourse with the urban bourgeoisie, the king sanctioned the social and political ascendancy of the military (Schwieger 1980, 192). Later, when troops and officers had been assigned to barracks (or caserns), all mercenaries had been replaced by the conscripted Prussian natives, and the officer corps itself had been purged of its most undesirable elements after the unsuccessful war of 1806, relationships between the military and the urban population improved.

Although it may not seem to be the case, the urbanization of the military is one of the major changes in the evolution of Prussian militarism. Historians have often suggested that the association of absolutism and militarism resulted in a kind of atrophy of the self-esteem of the bourgeoisie. The continuing presence of an overbearing and high-handed officer corps generated an attitude of submissiveness in the Prussian bourgeoisie, which was still insubstantial and unassuming.

The "heroic" role the Prussian army played in the Napoleonic Wars, as well as the military reform following those wars, raised the status of the army, including the rank and file thereafter composed exclusively of Prussian subjects. The significance of a thoroughly urbanized army grew, of course, as urbanization of Prussian society accelerated at an unprecedented pace and the armed forces doubled and finally tripled. In the cities, the military faced the "enemy": first the liberal bourgeoisie, which was "defeated" in the suppression of the revolution of 1848, and a little later the far more "dangerous" Socialists, who eventually won (or so they thought) the revolution of 1918. In the cities the bourgeoisie, now wealthy and economically powerful, was won over to the militaristic model of the Wilhelmian era. Especially significant was the army's role in militarizing the member states of the German Empire, which had been independent monarchies prior to 1871. Again, this process took place primarily in the cities of those states, particularly in the ones that were residential seats of ruling monarchs. Furthermore, the urban environment offered previously unavailable opportunities for the military complex to develop linkages with an increasing number of support structures that were able to consolidate political consensus about German military policies.

Nobility of Descent and Nobility of Ascent

Attempts to freeze the social structure of eighteenth-century Prussia did not convert the Junkers into a caste. The term *caste* has so often been associated with the nobility, in Prussia and elsewhere, that an explication of the preceding statement seems to be in order. A *caste* is, by definition, "a *closed* stratum in which membership can be acquired only by birth." The Prussian aristocracy, however, was far from being a closed system. Not only were qualified commoners admitted into the aristocracy, but it preserved its power position, particularly in the army, only by replenishing its own ranks with men who had distinguished themselves in the service of the king. There was a nobility of descent and a nobility of ascent, the latter being composed of those who had been ennobled by the monarch. As the generations went by, the nobility of ascent merged with the nobility of descent. In the course of the present essay ample proof will be presented to support this contention.

Since the nobility had been chosen to play such a crucial role in the political design of Prussian absolutism, it would not have been expedient to lock out wealth and skills from a group that did not possess an abundance of either one. A wealthy man who made generous contributions to the recruiting funds could acquire the title of nobility (Demeter 1965, 5). Since the aristocratic officers did not seem inclined to learn the more complex forms of military technology, artillery officers, for example, had to be recruited from the ranks of the Prussian bourgeoisie. If such an artillery officer came from a rural estate and if he had served at least ten years, his status could be raised to that of a nobleman. Petty officers who had fought with distinction could eventually become officers and noblemen (Büsch 1962, 93–94).

The absolute power of the Prussian king was grounded in the standing army rather than in the cantonal reserves. The Great Elector left a highly centralized and disciplined army of 30,000, which his successors steadily increased throughout the eighteenth century. Frederick the Great commanded an army of 180,000. By 1740 Prussia was the thirteenth European state in population and the tenth in size, but its military power ranked fourth. At the same time, the total revenues of Prussia amounted to seven million talers, five million of which were spent for the armed forces (Lamprecht 1913, 3: 692). In the seventeenth and early eighteenth centuries the Prussian army was composed almost entirely of mercenaries, two-thirds of whom were aliens. Frequent desertions and the complaints of neighboring states about Prussian recruitment practices induced the monarch to decree in 1733 that, with the exception of Jews, "all men were born to bear arms" (Lamprecht 1913, 3: 690). He wanted to rely more on Prussian subjects, but universal conscription proved to be unattainable. At any rate, after the Seven Years' War, 67.8 percent of the Prussian army was composed of Prussian subjects (Jany 1967, 2: 645), but they were drafted almost entirely from the lowest level of the society. Men who were not "mendicants and tramps were exempted from military service by the cantonal regulations of 1792" *(Militärgeschichtliches Forschungsamt* 1964, 59).

Frederick II succeeded in tightening even further the rules restricting the behavior of the officer corps. Social interaction with persons of bourgeois extraction was not tolerated, and conflict about honor was not allowed to fester in times of war. Pressure to forgo marriage was intense among subaltern officers, and rarely were exceptions granted. The king also emphasized the need for scientific training of army personnel *(Militärgeschichtliches Forschungsamt* 1964, 49, 51, 54, 56).

Of course, the military ambitions of Prussia were incommensurate with the revenues of a relatively underdeveloped agrarian state. No matter how thrifty the financial management of the state, the standing army was poorly paid, and the soldiers ventured into crafts and trade to secure additional income. This was done to such an extent that the "barracks resembled factories" (Shanahan 1945, 31). The soldier-craftsman and the soldier-merchant competed with the guilds, whose grievances remained unheeded. Retired soldiers were often given jobs or land in newly acquired eastern territories (Shanahan 1945, 32).

Among the lower ranks of the officer corps, the family estate was expected to subsidize a life-style that required much more money than the officer received from his modest remuneration. However, a sharp contrast between the lower and higher ranks began with the rank of captain in command of a company. Higher officers enjoyed a number of financial perquisites, both legal and illegal. In times of war, plunder of conquered territories constituted a major source of income, and the almost unlimited power commanding officers held in their own garrison districts created opportunities for extortion and bribery among the local population. Needless to say, the civil courts had no jurisdiction in matters concerning crimes committed by officers. Büsch cites the case of a higher officer who was found guilty of accepting money to protect certain persons from civil justice. He was sentenced to four years of "fortress," but his misconduct was not considered dishonorable. Later he was allowed to resume his military career, and eventually he was promoted to the rank of field marshal (Büsch 1962, 128). Numerous sinecures were open to retiring officers, particularly in the higher levels of the civil service (Büsch 1962, 131).

The Militarization of the Bureaucracy

Political centralization, particularly concentration of power in a monocratic ruler, could succeed only to the extent that a subservient and reasonably efficient bureaucracy could be entrusted with the execution of the principles of absolute governance on all levels of public administration. Under Frederick William I, the army became the "backbone of the whole state administration which was geared to military needs and permeated with military spirit" (Hintze 1915, 287). The fiscal administration handled all matters concerning the maintenance of the armed forces, and out of the fiscal administration developed the entire internal administration. Given the militaristic framework within which the state was conceived, it is not surprising that the fairly rapidly expanding bureaucracy should be adapted to the already established patterns of military behavior. Since we are dealing here with a professional estate *(Stand)* that never ceased to ascend in the social rank order and eventually became the most prestigious of all professions, second only to the officer corps, the militarization of that group merits more than casual attention.

The militarization of the Prussian civil service was carried out in several ways. It should be emphasized that this process was concomitant with, or part of, its creation and subsequent development. First of all, the bureaucratic hierarchy was molded on the model of the army. Unconditional loyalty to the ruler, obedience, and strictest discipline reigned supreme. Under patrimonial absolutism all civil servants, even those of the highest ranks, were no more than "royal servants." The rigors of the disciplinary system were reflected in the sanctions inflicted, for example, on ministers and royal councillors. If such a dignitary was one hour late for a meeting, without written permission from the king, one hundred ducats were deducted from his salary. If he missed a meeting entirely, he would lose half of his annual salary, and if he missed another one, he would be dismissed from office *cum infamia* (Dorwart 1953,

173–74). Almost to the present time, Prussian students learned in their history courses that the Soldiers' King himself would not hesitate to cane a civil servant found to be remiss in the performance of his duties. The lesson was supposed to cause admiration for a king so palpably concerned with enforcing the pattern of rectitude and sense of duty that were to become the hallmarks of the Prussian civil service.

The military model was manifest in the organization of the state bureaucracy. A chain of command extended from top to bottom. No feedback from lower to higher levels was expected or tolerated. Obedience was taken for granted, as was obeisance to one's superiors. "Ministers of state, like generals and colonels, obeyed unquestioningly and carried out orders with military precision and punctuality. . . . Every minister was compelled in his own interest to maintain in his own department the same rigid spirit of order, punctuality and speed which the king imposed on his ministers" (Isaacssohn as quoted in Craig 1955, 18).

A second, equally significant aspect of the militarization of the civil service is evident in the recruitment of military manpower for nonmilitary functions. The "military bureaucrat" became a permanent fixture in public administration from the time of Frederick William I. Senior members of the officer corps were appointed to such high-ranking positions as *Regimentsquartiermeister* and *auditeur*. Whatever their rank, they were *definitely not* "civilians in uniform" but intransigent enforcers of military authoritarianism. The deployment of military personnel throughout the bureaucratic structure moved in four directions, to bring military principles and controls to bear not only on the bureaucracy but also on all conceivable sectors of the society in general.

1. In addition to its dominance in the officer corps, the nobility became increasingly involved in the Prussian bureaucracy. Noble officers were transferred to higher positions in public administration because they were expected to "set a model for blind obedience and quick action" (Rosenberg 1958, 64–65).

2. Military staff officers and generals, believed to be particularly reliable, were frequently appointed "members or chairmen of official royal committees and boards." As such, they were expected to report their findings, even to make decisions and to take action. These committees often investigated the conduct of civilian members of the civil service (Rosenberg 1958, 64–65).

3. In view of the cities' strong opposition to royal absolutism, the presence of the military in urban administration appears to be significant. Officers of the regular army were appointed to municipal committees, "usually as chairmen." In the numerous garrison towns, the military commander regulated local retail trade and the prices of basic

foodstuffs (Rosenberg 1958, 65). The military commissars had power to inspect the troops and to provide food and clothing for the garrison. They had their own specialized hierarchy and gradually expanded their orbit of influence to the point of becoming the main fiscal and police authority directly responsible to the king. Eventually, they gained control over all aspects of city administration (Lamprecht 1913, 3: 684–86).

4. It became an established practice to appoint military personnel unfit for active service to posts in the civilian bureaucracy. Many subordinate positions were reserved for "uneducated noble soldiers" and for "non-noble non-commissioned officers" who had no private income. Such appointments were made in lieu of a pension (Rosenberg 1958, 64–65). Collectors of town dues, mill inspectors, police inspectors, and police officers were exclusively military invalids, retired noncommissioned officers, and soldiers (Dorwart 1953, 171). The impact of this practice, which was to gain extraordinary importance in imperial Germany, will be discussed later. To the extent that the *Landräte* were recruited among retired noble officers, they ought to be included in the present category, and so should the generals who presided over the provincial governments (Büsch 1962, 138). Among the many positions available to retiring military personnel, teaching jobs in the Prussian public school system are notable because they were instrumental in transferring military discipline from the barracks to the educational sector. The schools were thus militarized long before education was entrusted exclusively to a body of trained professional specialists.

The Prussian judiciary was linked to the military in several ways. In many instances, military officers directly controlled the courts. For example, committees headed by officers investigated crimes committed by members of the civil service, and a military officer always presided over mixed civil-military courts (Büsch 1962, 138).

In all these cases military control meant transfer of barracks discipline to the institutions military officers happened to oversee. Their attitudes toward their subordinates and the public in general resembled those of commanding officers toward the rank and file.

The structural and ideological identification of the bureaucracy with the military establishment reached its most eloquent expression in 1723 when civil and military administration merged in a single *General Ober-Finanz-Kriegs und Domänen Direktorium* (General Superior Directory of Finances, War, and Demesnes) (Dorwart 1953, 164). Militarization of the civil service was made palatable by formally equating the ranks of the hierarchy with those of the officer corps. Thus, each officeholder had a military title, which put him on the same social level as a military man of equal rank.

From the very beginning, the Prussian bureaucracy was a relatively open system. Not only was it possible for a commoner with the right education to work his way up to the highest ranks of the civil service, but he often was ennobled in the process. Before long, a nobility of ascent competed with the nobility of descent for the highest positions in the administration and for equal status in society. By intermarrying with members of the old aristocracy and by acquiring noble estates *(Rittergüter)*, the nobles of ascent tended to consolidate their position and to become indistinguishable from the nobility of descent. "Assimilation by emulation" implied, among other things, the adoption of the whole military complex that had become identified with the Junker life-style (Rosenberg 1958, 148). In fact, the desire to share the traditional values and attitudes of the Junker nobility was strong enough to intensify and diffuse military modes of thinking, feeling, and acting throughout an urban sector of Prussian society barely touched by militarism.

Toward the end of the formative period, the diffusion of military patterns throughout the social structure had reached such a point that the division of Prussian society into "civilian" and "military" sectors had little meaning. "While in all other countries," wrote a major of the German army in 1885, "a 'civilian state' and a 'military state' confront each other like hostile brothers, Frederick William firmly welded them together through common endeavor" (Jähns 1885, 343).

The "militarization" of eighteenth-century Prussia was accomplished through the fusion of monarchy, land-holding nobility, and army. Together, and reinforcing one another, they held enough power, authority, and prestige to implant military patterns of behavior in those segments of the society within their orbit, mostly the bureaucracy and the peasantry. However, the growing urban bourgeoisie and the non-Junker nobility were hardly touched at all, either by militaristic ideology or by military conscription. Anyone owning property worth at least ten thousand talers was exempt from military service, and so were skilled workers and farmers (Shanahan 1945, 43). "Even whole cities and entire regions appeared to be exempt," particularly in the western territories where the social structure could not be converted readily into the agrarian-military complex characteristic of eastern Prussia (Lamprecht 1913, 3: 325). But in the western territories, exemptions were contingent on high levies (Büsch 1962, 49). Thus the integrative role of militarism appeared to be limited by a combination of class privileges and economic priorities. The state needed more soldiers and military equipment, but those resources depended on revenues and no significant increase of revenues could be expected without economic development. Bearers of scarce technical skills and entrepreneurial abilities had to be exempted from conscription because they were indispensable to expand manufactures and trade and, of course, to supply the armed forces. Again for fiscal and military reasons, Prussia developed a long-range policy of immigration, which proved to be successful. A continuous flow of immigrants came from other parts of Europe, and in its effort to attract settlers endowed with skills and capital, Prussia became an asylum for persecuted religious groups (Lamprecht 1913, 3: 694–95). Between 1756 and 1775 the population of Prussia increased from 4.3 million to 4.5 million, and in 1786 close to one-fifth of the population consisted of immigrants or descendants of immigrants (Lamprecht 1913, 3: 792).

Modernizing Warfare

If the gradual militarization of Prussian society was thought to increase the state's capability of waging war, one may ask whether warfare itself underwent changes of evolutionary significance during the eighteenth century. Changes in the political ideology certainly had considerable bearing on the evolution of warfare itself. Under Frederick the Great the so-called enlightened absolutism became the prevailing political dogma. By proclaiming himself the "first servant of the state," he raised the state itself to the level of supreme political authority. Political decisions, including those about war, came to be functions of the state on which were thus bestowed a will and a political intelligence. The assumption that the state possessed a rationality of its own turned service to the state into a moral duty and the most perfect form of human activity (Willoweit 1981, 267–68; Ranke 1981, 34). Since militarism comprehends service to the state, it moves out of the sphere of personal discretion into a suprapersonal, objective dimension that shields it from all human criticism. The idea of a "reason of state" (Staatsraison) contributed to the stabilization of Prussian militarism as a system.

Yet Frederick II was innovative in other areas too. The three Silesian wars, especially the last one, the Seven Years' War (1756–63), afforded vast opportunities for experimentation that under the king's imaginative generalship resulted in a series of strategic and tactical changes. Previously on the receiving end of military skills and techniques invented elsewhere, Prussia became a focus of diffusion. Some of the changes, which a half century later conferred immense superiority on Napoleon's armies, were clearly discernible in Prussian warfare as it developed under Frederick II. Like some of his contemporaries, the Prussian king was well aware of the shortcomings of the mercenary armies of his time. He did everything possible to replace foreign hirelings with Prussian subjects; he relied on the canton system to form regionally homogeneous army units that were obviously superior to mercenaries uncommitted to any ideological cause and prone to desert at the first opportunity. The troops from Pomerania and the Mark were bound together by local and regimental comradeship, by "patriarchal loyalty that the peasant owed to his squire whose sons and brothers led them in the field, and by confidence in the great and victorious king." Also, the Lutheranism of that time constituted a live cause for which the soldiers felt committed to fight: "Again and again we are told that on the march Frederick's soldiers sang the chorales that they had learned in their village church" (Ritter 1968, 133).

When Frederick acceded to the throne in 1740, 26,000 out of 76,000 soldiers were foreigners. In the Seven Years' War (1756–1763), the Prussian elite regiments were almost totally composed of Prussian natives. Yet in 1763, despite the king's continuing efforts to reduce the mercenary contingent, almost one-third of the Prussian armed forces of 103,000 consisted of foreign hirelings (Ritter 1968, 133–34).

Disregarding the predominant strategy of his contemporaries, who used their armies to outmaneuver rather than fight the enemy, Frederick trained his troops for attack. Whenever possible, he pressed for rapid decisions on the battlefield. Yet far from rigidly adhering to an established principle, the king remained flexible enough to turn unexpected situations to his advantage.

Frederick's "methodical cultivation of the offensive battle" did not mean that his armies, unlike those of Napoleon, were prepared for far-reaching strategic thrusts designed to destroy the enemy's power center (Ritter 1968, 138–47). The Prussian king intended to conquer Silesia rather than annihilate the Austrian armies. Without underestimating the inventiveness of Frederick, one should keep in mind that, unlike Napoleon, he did not have the manpower to garrison conquered territories and to build the logistic infrastructure necessary for effective control of occupied areas. Furthermore, in contrast to the rather frugal ways of the postrevolutionary French forces, the Prussian armies with their enormous baggage trains were incapable of swift movements. Nevertheless, in his time, Frederick the Great, "universally admired, studied and emulated," came to be regarded as the most "eminent preceptor of modern war" (Ritter 1968, 134–43, 148).

Victory in the three Silesian wars raised Prussia's international status almost, but not quite, to the level of the great European powers. Frederick II was convinced that the survival chances of the state lay in territorial expansion. The acquisition of West Prussia, for example, constituted in his opinion a "master stroke" of "enlightened" power politics (Baumgart 1981, 77–80). The fact that the population of West Prussia was Polish played no part in the political reasoning of the king and his contemporaries.

Initially, it was suggested that Prussian militarism was characterized by a combination of all the attributes ever associated with militarism. At this point it may be appropriate to ask to what extent the constituent attributes of militarism had taken shape during the formative period.

In view of the perennial conflict between Prussia's political ambitions and its relative poverty, it is not at all surprising that discretionary appropriation of economic resources for the maintenance and expansion of the army should have been one of the first fully developed characteristics of militarism.

With the consolidation of the triple alliance of monarchy-nobility-officer corps early in the eighteenth century, the military officers moved up to the highest level of the sociopolitical structure. The strength of their position stemmed from the power derived from the absolute power of the monarch and the status privileges of the Junker aristocracy to which they belonged.

The preferential use of organized violence as a means of resolving international conflict became a definite pattern only with the conquest of Silesia in 1740 and the successive campaigns to defend the conquered province against Austria. However, very little could be interpreted as glorification of war and warrior.

The implantation of military discipline met with serious difficulties insofar as it appeared to be inconsistent with mercenary armies and the way of recruiting and managing mercenary troops. And the transfer of military discipline to other sectors of Prussian society was successful only to the extent that the canton system took root and a militarized bureaucracy developed at the initiative of the king. The full development of the other attributes of militarism was contingent upon the emergence of Prussian nationalism in the early nineteenth century. At any rate, the system had been launched in a way that promised continuity, but its further evolution seems understandable only in the context of violent confrontations that upset the power structure of the whole continent.

4

The Transition: The Impact of the Napoleonic Wars

Defeat and National Awakening

The victorious wars of the eighteenth century, notably the Seven Years' War, had established Prussia's position as one of the great military powers of Europe. A sudden and radical reversal occurred when Prussia suffered crushing defeats at the hands of Napoleon's armies. The reaction to the military catastrophe of 1806 culminated in what may be termed a "national awakening," a concerted effort "to lift the nation's moral, religious and patriotic spirits, to restore its valor, self-confidence and willingness to make any sacrifice for national honor and independence from foreign rule" (F. vom Stein as quoted in Ritter 1969, 1:82).

The ideological outcome was something new: a militant nationalism committed to war as the only emotionally acceptable reaction to "foreign rule" *(Fremdherrschaft)*, even if it meant total defeat. To perish gloriously was felt to be preferable to dishonorable servitude. Whether it brought victory or not, war was praised as honorable, glorious, and ineluctable. "Most astonishing and momentous for the subsequent growth of ideas was the manner in which religious and political motivations were joined into a new morality of political militancy. The struggle for national liberation became virtually a holy war, a crusade against Satan in the name of God, or at least in the name of justice and virtue against evil" (Ritter 1969, 1: 81). The close association of highly inflammatory instigations to war with a sense of unshakable righteousness and intense religious feelings verging on mysticism provided the ideological foundations on which Prussian militarism was to feed for generations to come.

Although Prussia assumed the leadership of the nationalistic movement, the other German states did not remain untouched. Much of the literary and philosophical output, centered on the Wars of Liberation, was based on the assumption that reactions to French imperialism had somehow generated a common bond among *all* Germans.

Militarily, the "unified national mass army," the great innovation of the French Revolution, served as a model for Prussian ideas about army reform. Actually, Prussia had no viable alternatives if it was to stand a chance against the formidable fighting capability of the French army. Equally important was the adoption of "a corresponding new style of diplomacy," which "owed its greatest triumph to the aggressive use of bluff and intimidation, terrorizing the enemy to the point of paralysis; but it also wielded the weapons of deception and blandishment with sovereign mastery, ignoring laws and treaties with little compunction" (Ritter 1969, 1: 48).

Clausewitz' Version of Militarism

Carl von Clausewitz, a Prussian officer, "cast the essence of Prussian military spirit into a literary form none had found before him." His writings on warfare became the major treatise of German military science, but his main merit lies in his perception of the interrelations between politics and war. In fact, his peculiar standpoint was predicated on the political ecology of Germany, wedged as it was between powerful neighbors and, consequently, compelled "to adopt a policy of extraordinary militancy" (Ritter 1969, 1: 52–53).

Militancy is one of the central ideas on which Clausewitz developed his postulates, drawn to a large extent from the experiences of the French Revolution and French conquest of continental Europe. But to weld the disparate elements of a people into a single unit capable of sacrificing itself to maintain "independence," "honor," and "freedom," a deep emotional involvement of the individual participant is *conditio sine qua non*. Apart from "fatherland" and "national honor," Clausewitz wrote, the individual is but an "empty shell."

In accord with his general doctrine of militancy, he conceptualized the state as the "deliberate and forceful mobilization of the common national will that stakes its survival on freedom and independence" (Ritter 1969, 1: 49). These terms seem to imply an essential unity of war and statesmanship: "War is only part of the political intercourse, therefore by no means an independent thing in itself" (Clausewitz 1963, 596). Clausewitz insisted that "war is not merely a political act but a real political instrument, a continuation of political intercourse, a carrying out of the same by other means" (Clausewitz 1963, 16). As a political instrument, war is clearly subordinated to political exigencies (Clausewitz 1963, 596–601). The conduct of war, particularly the effort involved in carrying it to the desired end, should be proportional to the "political object" that determined its outbreak. "There can be wars of all degrees of importance and energy, from a war of extermination down to a mere state of observation" (Clausewitz 1963, 10).

Nowhere in his writings did Clausewitz advocate war for war's sake, which, according to Toynbee, would characterize militarism (Toynbee 1950, 15). What played into the hands of nineteenth-century military elites, in Germany as elsewhere in Europe, was Clausewitz' interpretation of war as an integral phase of the political process. Moving from the assumption that war is inherent in the political process to the belief in the inevitability of war was only a small step. And if war appeared unavoidable, was it not the most urgent responsibility of the militant state to prepare for war, overriding any competing demands for its limited resources?

Changes Tempered by Tradition

The immediate reaction to the military defeat of 1806 was a reform movement that might have produced radical change in the social structure had it been completely successful. The liberal forces' failure to change Prussia's authoritarian tradition decisively contributed to the preservation and future development of militarism. Significant changes were made, but they failed to affect the continuity of the military establishment. Though the aristocracy's privileged access to the officer corps was abolished on paper, the nobility's monopoly of leadership in the armed forces continued almost unabated. In 1806, 7,000 officers were on active duty in the Prussian army, but only 695 of them were commoners (Craig 1955, 17). In 1859, 65 percent of all generals belonged to the aristocracy (Ritter 1969, 1: 281). In 1906, 60 percent of the general staff were members of the nobility, a figure that in 1913 was reduced to 50 percent. However, in the cavalry, the most prestigious sector of the army, the aristocratic component of the officer corps represented 87 percent of the total in 1906, compared to 48 percent in the infantry, 41 percent in the field artillery, 31 percent in the supply services, and 6 percent in the foot artillery and technical troops (Ritter 1970, 2: 287). Out of the 2,516 officer cadets who passed examinations in 1862, 1863, and 1866, 49 percent belonged to the nobility while 51 percent were of bourgeois extraction. If one considers the occupations of the fathers of those cadets, it becomes obvious that a large majority (79 percent) came from three narrowly defined sectors of Prussian society: the military officer corps (33 percent), the higher echelons of the civil services (26 percent), and the owners of landed estates (20 percent). The remaining 21 percent were thus distributed: 7 percent teachers, 6 percent minor officials, 5 percent merchants and manufacturers, and 3 percent rentiers (Demeter 1965, 21–22).

The gradual increase of "commoners" among the officer corps was a question of supply and demand. The nobility of old Prussian stock was too small to provide, as it once did, enough officers to satisfy the demand of the expanding army. Among the higher ranks (colonels and generals), the proportion of aristocrats sank from 86 percent in 1860 to 61 percent in 1900, and to 52 percent in 1913. The nobility responded to this inevitable trend by monopolizing all officer positions in the elite regiments, especially those that were stationed in provincial capitals (Demeter 1965, 24, 28, 30).

The changes generated by the defeat of 1806 in some respects constituted breaks with tradition; in others, they reinforced the power of the officer corps to control its own composition. Reversing his previous stand concerning investigations of officers, the king agreed to a proposed self-purge of the officer corps. Investigating peers found that eight hundred officers had been remiss in discharging their duties during the disastrous war. Many were expelled, and others were condemned to "confinement in a fortress" *(Festungshaft)*. However, attempts to democratize the officer corps failed, mainly because it was formally allowed to screen all aspirants by regimental elections (Görlitz 1950, 46, 69). The candidates had to be acceptable to the regimental commander, and the vote of the regimental officers had to be unanimous to grant commission. However qualified a man might be, he was rejected if his social and political credentials were deemed objectionable. As a boundary-controlling device, this election performed the obvious function of preserving the homogeneity of the officer corps. It worked closely with the revised version of the military courts of honor, which enforced established ways of behavior (Demeter 1965, 126ff.). Violators of the officers' moral code could be reprimanded or expelled by the rulings of the court, which was also entitled to arbitrate cases involving officers and civilians. Together the two institutions were influential enough to impose what may be called "anticipatory conformity" of young men who planned military careers but had to compensate for the lack of social pedigree by adopting an ultraconservative posture, thus reinforcing the importance of newly acquired wealth and perhaps recent ennoblement. The admission of a steadily growing proportion of officers from the ranks of the expanding bourgeoisie did not destroy the attitudinal homogeneity of the officer corps. Of course, the monarch made all final decisions concerning the discharge and promotion of officers, who remained servants of the king rather than servants of the state.

The most relevant characteristic of the army reform was universal and compulsory military service, but the result was not the kind of people's army generated by the French Revolution. True enough, gone were the times when the soldiers feared their own officers more than the enemy. Corporal punishment was abolished, military service humanized and changed "from hated and humiliating servitude to an honorable privilege of free citizens" (Ritter 1969, 1: 101). The new army was a far cry from the mercenary forces of the preceding centuries, but class privilege crept into its structure nevertheless, primarily in the form of the *einjährige freiwillige Dienst* (one-year voluntary service) open to young men "of good family" who were to volunteer for one year. Such service "carried many advantages, including preferment in promotion and discharge with an officer's qualifying certificate, which was normally followed by election to Landwehr command" (Ritter 1969, 1: 102). Eventually, the successful conclusion of six years of study at a secondary school *(Gymnasium)* was required of candidates for the one-year voluntary service, an institution that was intact until the First World War.

More relevant to the present inquiry appears to be the fact that no class or group was exempt from military service. Furthermore, the tripartition of the Prussian military structure (line, reserve, and *Landwehr*) was clearly outlined in the Prussian Defense Act of 1814–15 (Lamprecht 1913, 3: 325). Yet no system of legal sanctions, elaborate and encompassing as it might be, could possibly capture the ideological orientation that the Prussian military elite, particularly Prince William (later King William I), wished to impress on the development of military organization. Ritter called it the "decivilianization" of the army, a process endeavoring to complete what the Great Elector and Frederick the Great had successfully initiated.

"What mattered most to the prince and king was to remove the recruit as far as possible from his wonted civilian life, to make him a soldier body and soul, so to speak. He was not merely to be well-drilled and thoroughly trained—a few months were enough for that. He was to absorb the spirit of professional soldiering for life. The business of being a soldier was not to be regarded as merely a passing thing, to be finished as soon as possible. No, the peculiar "soldier's estate" was to be looked on as something that endured throughout life. The soldier was to become so deeply immersed in active service that he would be reluctant to tear himself from it and prefer to re-enlist (Ritter 1969,1: 10).

Such an undertaking, taken literally, was doomed to failure. Not even three years of the most intensive military training and indoctrination could shape the recruit's personality so decisively that he would choose to be a professional soldier for the rest of his life. However, if one takes into account the extent to which most nonmilitary institutions were gradually infused with military modes of behavior demanding or at least encouraging lifelong adjustments, the pattern urged by Prince William was not inconsistent with the realities of the sociocultural process.

The General Staff: The Brain Center of German Militarism

The General Staff (GS), a form of corporate military leadership, has been regarded not only as a Prussian invention but sometimes as the very quintessence of German militarism. Whether one accepts the latter assessment or not, there is little doubt that the GS developed in Prussia and that it shaped the strategy of modern warfare in the most decisive way. Its function embodied the basic tenet of militarism, namely, to keep the nation in constant readiness for war.

Yet the structure of a fully developed GS was clearly at variance with the military leadership that had come into existence under the aegis of absolutism. Decisions concerning the strategy of war were prerogatives of the supreme commander, the king in the case of Prussia, or, if he lacked military skills as some Prussian kings did, his immediate delegate. Frederick II and Napoleon personally planned and directed the battles they fought. Of course, until the end of the eighteenth century, armies were relatively small and battles could be directed visually from an elevated position. Avoiding a battle rather than actually engaging in one was a major objective of military strategy. By artful maneuvering, one attempted to gain tactical advantages, which eventually might force the enemy to withdraw and desist from further engagements. One fought sparingly because mercenary armies were expensive, ready to desert under combat pressure, and difficult to replace. The limited size of the armies combined with the systematic avoidance of battles could not be considered as stimuli for the development of an internally differentiated and specialized institution such as the GS. But the military commanders of the eighteenth century were not without needed technical assistance. In the Prussian army a small group of officers known as the *Generalquartiermeisterstab* (General Quartermaster Staff) was entirely subordinated to the royal commander and was expected to execute orders concerned primarily with the logistics of military campaigns. Yet the General Quartermaster Staff constituted the nucleus that eventually evolved into the GS (Görlitz 1950, 17). This development, however, remains incomprehensible if considered in isolation. The evolution of the GS depended on other changes, and only in the continuing interaction of certain quantitative and qualitative transformations of warfare during the nineteenth century can one understand how and why the Prussian GS attained the influential position it has been credited with.

Modest as the beginnings were, by 1796 some staff officers had acquired the skill to sketch maps of battlefields. Even so, in the war against Napoleon, the Prussian generals failed to make proper use of the skills of this embryonic group of specialists (Görlitz 1950, 20, 42).

The French Revolution generated a new type of army and a new concept of warfare. Mass armies raised through compulsory conscription were "cheap" in comparison with mercenary troops, but the sheer size of the armies required extensive restructuring and coordination in which specialized staff officers were in charge of conveying and carrying out orders (Görlitz 1950, 29). A general staff with planning and commanding functions was hardly conceivable in Napoleon's armies.

Actual combat tended to dominate the conduct of wars in the nineteenth century. The new mass armies began to be used on an ever-growing scale to rout and, if possible, annihilate the enemy (Görlitz 1950, 58–59). Thus the risks of war multiplied as its objectives changed, and the growing size and complexity of the armies encouraged innovations to improve the chances of success. Prussia's defeat in 1806 and the ensuing reorganization of its armed forces contributed to the development of the General Staff, which first appeared under the name *Generalstab* in 1817. The man who had a leading hand in developing its cadre was Gerhard Johann David Scharnhorst. His appointment as director of the Prussian military academy indicated, among other things, that the army was becoming a channel of upward social mobility. Although rather well-known for his military expertise, Scharnhorst was neither a Prussian nor a nobleman. Before accepting the position for which he had applied, he requested ennoblement, a high command, and a military reform. Under his influence a new generation of officers developed; most of them were newly ennobled and later assumed positions on the GS (Görlitz 1950, 35).

Scharnhorst anticipated a major problem that, during the latter part of the century, would worry generations of staff officers. "Prussia cannot conduct a defensive war," wrote Scharnhorst. "Its geographic location and the scarcity of artificial and natural means of defense do not admit it" (Görlitz 1950, 40). It was implied, then and later, that national salvation lay in preventive war, or at least in the choice of the time and locale of confrontations. The wide-open plains of northern and eastern Germany seemed to invite invasion, and only an extraordinary degree of military preparedness could compensate for such geographical disadvantages.

By 1809 the GS had become a section of the Prussian War Ministry, and the minister himself was the highest ranking officer of the GS (Görlitz 1950, 51). The reforms following the Wars of Liberation emancipated the GS from the tutelage of the War Ministry. By 1824 there was a triangle of competing powers: the Military Cabinet, the War Ministry, and the GS (which was in charge of military training). Sciences and technical skills relevant to warfare were stressed, and war history was promoted with the objective of distilling as much knowledge as possible about the conduct of war. The concerted effort of the staff officers resulted in the systematization of available knowledge, much of which came to be published, but by the middle of the century the GS had not yet gained control over the organization and equipment of the army (Görlitz 1950, 85).

The period of efflorescence of the GS began with the appointment of Helmuth von Moltke to the position of chief of staff in 1858. Moltke, to whom war was an "integral part of God's world order," succeeded in establishing the primacy of the GS in relationship to the Military Cabinet (Görlitz 1950, 91). The military reform of the 1860s, in which Moltke played a leading role, introduced the coordinated deployment of separate army corps requiring a high level of training of the corps commanders. Moltke proposed to make ample use of the rapidly expanding railway network for the deployment (Aufmarsch) of troops. His position became even more powerful when Bismarck assumed the chancellorship of the Prussian state. The alliance between the two men—a great statesman and a great strategist—has been called unique in German history (Görlitz 1950, 107). It certainly did much to enhance the role of the GS.

The war against Austria in 1866 afforded an opportunity to test the skills of the burgeoning GS on the battlefield. The battle of Königgrätz (or Sadowa) has been regarded as the first major confrontation won not by a single general but by the GS under Moltke's leadership. The international prestige accruing to the Prussian GS gained immensely with Prussia's victory over France in 1870–71. When Moltke assumed office in 1858, the GS had 64 members; when he was replaced in 1888, it had grown to a total of 239 officers. By 1872, one-third of all staff officers had come from middle-class families (Görlitz 1950, 123). Generally regarded as a model, the organization of the German GS was emulated by a number of other nations, particularly by France whose GS achieved "legendary fame" (Görlitz 1950, 126).

The GS increasingly focused attention on the scientific preparation of real war and actively supported technical developments, such as long-range artillery, rapid-fire weapons, and steady expansion of the railway system, because they contributed to the nation's instant readiness to ward off sudden attacks from east or west. Under Moltke's successor, Count Alfred von Waldersee, the GS not only evolved into a great military bureau of war planning, but it also attained an unprecedented level of international influence, mainly through military attachés connected with German legacies abroad (Kitchen 1968, 2). Beginning in 1891 with the appointment of Count Alfred von Schlieffen to the position of chief of staff, the GS entered a phase of specialization and standardization that imposed severe limitations on certain areas of competence and consequently made internal interdependence and cooperation even more important (Görlitz 1950, 167).

Schlieffen divided the GS into four major sections: (1) strategic planning and details of military mobilization, fortifications, armaments, and the use of railways for troop deployment; (2) training and maneuvers of the armed forces and gathering information about other countries; (3) collection of information about Russia and France to assess their war potential; and (4) trigonometry, topography, and cartography relevant to the conduct of war. A few smaller sections were directly subordinated to the chief of staff. In 1914, the major sections had grown to six, and the total number of staff officers had risen to 625 (Kitchen 1968, 2, 5, 6).

The concentration of power in the GS passed its crucial phase under Moltke, who established the practice of not informing the War Ministry in advance of meetings with the emperor. In 1883, direct access of the chief of staff to the monarch was formally recognized (Kitchen 1968, 2). Since the War Ministry could not possibly shun dealings with the Reichstag, it was suspected of "dangerous compromise with parliamentarism," an attitude considered anathema in leading military circles. Such alleged compromising with parliament reputedly contributed to a considerable loss of authority of the War Ministry (Kitchen 1968, 9).

However, the growing preeminence of the GS cannot fully be understood apart from the industrial revolution that generated increasingly diversified and complex technology requiring an unprecedented degree of division of labor and specialization. The army reforms, particularly those adopted since the middle of the nineteenth century, reflected the evolutionary trend of industrialism. No single military commander could possibly hope to assimilate the growing body of knowledge related to warfare. It was definitely a task that could be performed only by a group of individuals divided into highly specialized, interdependent, and cooperating sections. In this sense the GS may be interpreted as a technocratic elite, whose power rested primarily on the implicit recognition of its indispensability. The members of this elite also happened to be members of a society in which the officer corps constituted a privileged social stratum. Shielded from parliamentary scrutiny and strongly supported by the monarch, the GS attained a position of power that technical expertise alone would not possibly have achieved. In fact, the traditional prejudice of the military elite against officers who specialized in technical matters vital to the conduct of war was by no means extinct. It survived all military reforms practically up to World War I, and some of its effects were clearly at variance with the militaristic principle of keeping fighting capabilities at the highest possible level.

However, this prejudice was associated less with technology itself than with the unimpressive social pedigrees characterizing those officers in charge of operating machinery and complex weaponry. Since the very beginning of the formative period of militarism, the Junker nobility had shown a strong aversion to serving as artillery officers so that commoners had to be recruited for this branch of the Prussian army. Once established, the identification of the more technically oriented sectors of the army with the "low" social origin of their officers came to be a self-perpetuating mechanism, which around the turn of the nineteenth century posed serious problems in the rapidly expanding German navy (Herwig 1973, 102ff.).

There was, of course, a vast difference between the technical skills required for the operation and maintenance of navigation equipment, for example, and the scientific expertise essential to the planning of the complexities of a military campaign. Although Admiral von Tirpitz attempted to justify status differences between engineer-officers and executive officers by proclaiming that the former "could only aspire to take charge of machinery" and the latter "commanded men," no such rationalization was possible with regard to the GS, which obviously did both at the highest and most comprehensive level.

The combined effect of the following conditions perhaps explains the incomparable position of the GS: (1) direct and close association with the monarch, the ultimate source of authority and prestige in German society (the GS was accountable to no authority except the emperor himself); (2) the virtual monopoly of increasingly complex knowledge absolutely necessary to the conduct of war; and (3) the demonstration effect of several wars won by the GS, and growing demand for GS assistance to other nations that wished to reorganize their armed forces in accordance with the German model.

In spite of having been abolished by the Treaty of Versailles, the GS survived the debacle of 1918 and became an integral part of the *Reichswehr* and Hitler's new army. But when World War II broke out,

Hitler proved increasingly intolerant and suspicious of the GS, and the conduct of war by the GS ended with the dismissal of General Franz Halder in 1942 (Görlitz 1950, 594–95).

If one attempts to assess the functional adaptiveness of the changes introduced by the GS, the following aspects should be considered:

1. The GS codified available information about the conduct of war, thus creating a systematic body of knowledge designed to train officers. Previously, the acquisition of such knowledge depended largely on the personal initiative and capabilities of individual commanders.

2. The GS produced *new knowledge* and *new tools* intended to provide a scientific basis for the conduct of war. Previously, the military sciences, if they existed at all, depended on the occasional initiatives of innovative individuals.

3. The increasing effectiveness of the GS derived, to a great extent, from its *permanency*. It allowed not only systematic selection and accumulation of knowledge but also, more specifically, long-range planning of military campaigns.

4. The activities of the GS presented a *corporate* effort performed on a *suprapersonal* level and therefore were relatively independent of individual officers whose shortcomings could be compensated for by corrective interactional devices.

5. Shielded from outside criticism and interference, the GS was able to establish and carry out policies deemed appropriate to maximize military preparedness. It was the realization of Moltke's demand that the "war machine must maintain complete independence of action in regard to the political leadership" (Ritter 1969, 1: 195).

6. The activities of the GS were *anonymous*. No military accomplishment or failure could be traced to individual officers, although in a general way the chief of staff was accountable to the supreme political authority, the king and emperor.

7. In view of these functional characteristics of the GS, there can be no doubt that it acted as an integrator of an increasingly complex military establishment. Permitting the new German navy to remain outside its control proved to be a major mistake.

In assessing the functional adaptiveness of these changes, we are considering them "from within" German society, in which war was widely regarded as inevitable as a natural force. Under given circumstances, there was supposedly no choice between war and peace, but only among the different means of winning the war. Thus the word *adaptive* refers to the conduct of a war ending in victory, not to war in general.

The German GS has often been accused of having been the driving force behind the "saber-rattling" groups that demanded preventive war against Germany's enemies. It has been suggested that continuous planning of military campaigns could not fail to generate among the staff officer corps the desire to put their elaborate war plans into practice. Such allegations are difficult to substantiate, although there is no reason to assume that the attitudes of the staff officers were different from those of the officer corps in general. Moltke, more than anybody else, shaped the GS, and Moltke has rightly been regarded as one of the most influential protagonists of Prussian militarism. He was certainly one of the first to advocate total war, carried to the point of rendering the enemy "utterly defenseless," and it was he who wanted the war against France (1870–71) to proceed to the complete annihilation of all French resources (Ritter 1969, 1: 196). Given Moltke's extraordinary influence, it seems reasonable to assume that many or most of his staff officers identified themselves with his point of view. Whatever the ideological position of the GS may have been, there is no doubt that it became the brain center of German militarism.

5

The Flowering of Prussian-German Militarism

Military Reform, Military Victories, and the
Emergence of the Empire

The Prussian military establishment received its definite shape in the reform law of 1860, a blend of traditional and new elements. Following the age-old concept of society as an organic whole composed of distinct estates *(Stände)*, the army was defined as such an estate but was set apart from other estates by an oath of loyalty and the surrender of the civil rights "of political criticism and free expression of opinion" (Ritter 1969, 1: 114). In other words, subordination was unconditional, and no civil commitment was allowed to interfere with loyalty and obedience to the king. Moreover, the lower echelons were forbidden to judge the morality, efficiency, and legality of orders given to them. Soldiers were sworn to serve the king and the fatherland, but it was primarily the king, as the living symbol of the nation, who demanded the undivided loyalty of the military without distinction of rank.

The military reform dovetailed nicely with the Prussian constitution of 1850, which had been drawn up by the king as a concession to the liberal forces' demands for constitutional limitations of the ruler's power. If Prussia became a constitutional monarchy, it did so in name rather than in fact. Legislative powers were shared by the king and the two chambers, but no decision could become law without the assent of the ruler. The king could do no wrong, nor was he legally responsible for his conduct (Constitution of the Kingdom of Prussia, 1894, Article 35). He was commander in chief of the armed forces, and he had the power to fill all posts in the army and to declare war and peace (Articles 46–47). Com-

61

pulsory military service lasted twelve years, of which three years were spent in active service, four years in the reserves, and five years in the *Landwehr*. In a national emergency, the *Landsturm* could be called, which was composed of all men up to the age of forty-two who did not belong to any of the other branches of the armed forces.

The demonstration effect of three victorious wars, against Denmark (1864), Austria (1866), and France (1870–71), played a decisive role in the further development of militarism, as did the establishment of the German Empire under the indisputable hegemony of Prussia. Although the federative character of the imperial constitution seemed to limit the power of the emperor, the processes of political unification and centralization, once set into motion, continued to strengthen and exalt the institution of emperorship (Huber 1963, 3: 812, 815). Nothing in the constitution exempted the emperor from being responsible to parliament, but actually he was inviolable and exempt from legal responsibility. Supernatural sanction of the ruler's untouchable position may be seen in the preamble "By the Grace of God," which preceded all imperial decrees. Such reaffirmation of monarchical autocracy fit the personality of William II, who pushed militarism toward its peak. Although he was not noted for his military expertise, he played the role of the supreme commander to the hilt, moving almost exclusively with a military entourage of the most conservative persuasion, signifying adherence to tradition and social preeminence of the military. William II treated ministers of state like military subordinates, and the attempted resignation of a minister was regarded as "a hair-raising instance of insubordination" (Ritter 1969, 1: 134).

The hegemony of Prussia should be viewed in the light of the rather widespread political underdevelopment of Germany. In the eighteenth century and before, there were literally hundreds of tiny principalities of questionable viability as sovereign states. Most of them had neither the resources nor the will to resist Prussia's pressure for incorporation. Gradually, Prussia was able to achieve territorial contiguity. The gap was finally closed in 1866, when the kingdom of Hannover was forced to surrender to the invading Prussian army. Hannover, Hesse, Nassau, and the city of Frankfurt were annexed to Prussia, whose territory at that time extended from the French border to the Polish provinces incorporated in the 1790s. The few remaining enclaves became federated units of the German Empire.

One should not take it for granted that military modes of behavior, expected in Prussia, would be acceptable to other member states of the federation, whose cultural traditions differed significantly from those of Prussia. The status of the military in southern Germany, prior to 1870, was hardly comparable to that of the Prussian army. Prussia itself had annexed territories that could not be expected to adopt the norms of eastern militarism. In fact, within six years after annexation, 170,000 men who did not wish to serve in the Prussian army emigrated from those territories (Obermann 1958, 185). There is a strong possibility that the substantial flow of emigrants from Germany to various American countries was, at least in part, determined by the rigors of military conscription. One may assume that the continuing exodus of nonconformists, beginning with thousands who had been implicated in the liberal revolution of 1848, was related to the astonishing degree of national consensus supporting the militaristic trend of the empire.

On the whole, the assimilation of Prussian military patterns by the different states was to some extent mediated by the German Confederacy, the precursor of the German Empire. After the revolution of 1848, a number of German principalities sought access to Prussian armament and institutions of military training. Not a few concluded treaties with Prussia, resulting in a more or less close association with, or incorporation into, the Prussian armed forces. This happened, for example, in the duchy of Baden, one of the larger units of the confederacy, where Prussian troops had to be called in to put down widespread rebellion (Jany 1967, 4: 177).

In the east, cultural differences from Prussia were less pronounced anyway, and in the south, Bavaria, the most powerful of the German states, began to adopt Prussian military models under Ludwig I (1825–48). In the course of time, Prussian weapons and equipment, regulations, and organizational devices were transferred to the Bavarian army, although not without critical scrutiny. Bavarian officers attended Prussian field maneuvers to familiarize themselves with more advanced military techniques of the age (Gruner 1972, 340).

After the incorporation of Bavaria into the German Empire, the social ascent of the officer corps occurred along the same lines it had followed earlier in Prussia, and as in Prussia, the reserve officer performed a key role in diffusing military ways of behavior throughout society (Rumschöttel 1973, 214–15).

Less conspicuous than in Prussia was the role played by the nobility in the development of the military establishment. At least since the turn of the eighteenth century, the proportion of bourgeois officers had surpassed that of their aristocratic peers. By the 1870s, only 25 percent of the officers were of noble birth, and at the outbreak of World War I, that figure had sunk to 15 percent. Yet it comes as no surprise that the Bavarian aristocracy held a virtual monopoly on all important command positions, and chances for early promotion were much better for members of the nobility (Rumschöttel 1973, 70).

Before 1872, when the prestige level of the Bavarian army was relatively low in comparison with the Prussian officer corps, educational requirements rather than social origin constituted the dominant criteria of access to the officer corps. During the decades following the army reform of 1872, social pedigree was increasingly substituted for educational qualifications; eventually, officer candidates of upper-class origin predominated. Actually, the social composition of the Bavarian officer corps came to resemble that of the Prussian corps, except for the insignificant contingent of sons of landed estate owners, a difference rooted in the diverse agrarian structure of southern Germany. Out of 1,230 cadets registered in the Bavarian War Academy between 1882 and 1894, 71.0 percent were sons of military officers and high-ranking civil servants, while only 3.4 percent were sons of owners of large rural estates. A total of 91.9 percent of all cadets was of upper-class extraction, while the remaining 8.1 percent belonged to the lower middle class (Rumschöttel 1973, 85).

As far as the adaptability of Prussian militarism is concerned, the case of Bavaria seems particularly relevant, because it is culturally farther removed from eastern and northern Germany than any other unit of the German Federation. These differences did not disappear with the constitution of the empire. In fact, Bavarian society took a great deal of pride in preserving its cultural identity, often in open antagonism to what it perceived as Prussian arrogance. Yet as different as its cultural traditions might be, it proved as receptive to the militarization process as any other regional culture of imperial Germany.

The Defeat of the Democratic Movement and its Implications

It may be argued that the adoption of a democratic regime by Prussia might have put a stop to further development of militarism or that some form of effective control exercised by a democratically elected legislature might have prevented the most radical manifestations of militarism. Although the assumption that a representative democracy (or any other political regime) is inherently inconsistent with militarism seems unwarranted, certain demands put forward by German political reformers of the 1830s clearly indicate an antimilitaristic posture. To create counterweights against the authoritarianism of the military, it was proposed that local militias or national guards be created and that the armed forces take an oath of allegiance to the constitution rather than to the king (Snell 1976, 64).

The Prussian Constituent Assembly of 1848 called for political changes, the "radicalism" of which sent shock waves through the more conservative sectors of the society. Democratic members of the Assembly, supported by certain newspapers and a profusion of handbills, proposed that the armed forces of all German states, including Prussia, be put under the command of a *Reichsgewalt* (federal authority), implying significant restrictions to be imposed upon the military authority of the king. The army would be required to take an oath on the constitution, officers would be elected by their subordinates, and all military personnel would be given the right to vote in general elections. Furthermore, voices were heard demanding, among other things, the disbandment of the royal guards and the abolition of all military academies, courts of honor, separate officers' messes, and marriage consent for officers. To neutralize the power of the army, antimilitaristic extremists even proposed that the people at large be armed (Jany 1967, 4: 173).

Such demands put an end to the king's vacillations. The troops, which had evacuated Berlin after a bloody fight in the streets of the capital, were ordered back. The commanding officer gave the Constituent Assembly fifteen minutes to evacuate the theater where the sessions were being held (Snell 1976, 117). This was a predictable, thoroughly Prussian response to a bold attempt to bring the military under the control of a democratic government.

The defeat of the democratic movement in Prussia was no isolated event attributable to unique political circumstances. Prussia's intransigent opposition to the liberal and democratic ideologies of the French Revolution ought to be understood within the context of European politics of that time. Democracy, as we perceive it today, was far more an ideal than a reality in a continent determined to follow the resolutions of the Vienna Congress (1814–15) and to restore the political order the French Revolution had overthrown. Yet the dissemination of egalitarian and liberal ideas had reached a point of no return. The French revolution of 1830, which unseated the last Bourbon king, was followed by uprisings in Brunswick, Saxony, and Hannover. Some constitutions and parliaments were adopted, but the actual political structure changed very little. The German Confederacy, an alliance of monarchical rulers formed by the Vienna Congress and determined to preserve "dynastic legitimacy," became an instrument of repression. Since most members of the confederacy could not afford a military organization capable of suppressing political violence, Prussian and Austrian troops were used to put down the many uprisings that flared up in 1848 and shortly thereafter. In November of 1850, the whole Prussian army was mobilized, ready to subdue further revolutionary attempts (Jany 1967, 4: 185).

Yet to ascribe the defeat of the democratic movement exclusively to military repression would not accord with the political reality. Actually, the success of the repression appears to be inseparable from the fact that democratic ideas attracted no more than a relatively small minority of supporters. Of course, monarchy, nobility, and bureaucracy were united in their uncompromising opposition to democracy as well as to liberalism. The Protestant and Catholic clergy equally anathematized the egalitarian and libertarian ideas of 1789. The Catholic clergy sometimes outdid the Protestants in pledging assistance against political "radicalism" and in assuring support to the throne to prove that Catholics were "first-class patriots" (Snell 1976, 26, 239). The schools were required to teach "patriotic history," emphasizing the perniciousness of social democracy and presenting the revolution of 1848 as a foolish aberration that reflected alien ideas. Although there was no censorship as such, the press law was strict enough to rule out anything that could possibly be construed as subversive. Profoundly elitist, the Prussian university professoriat had little sympathy with democracy, and many endorsed the famous jurist Friederich Julius Stahl, who publicly condemned it (Snell 1976, 137, 237–38).

"Democracy thereafter was widely associated with the threat of social revolution. Furthermore, from then on, middle-class Germans tended to see in democratic government a demagogic threat to the very rationalism, freedom, and orderly progress for which German liberalism was striving" (Snell 1976, 126). At the core of the problem lay, as the preceding statement suggests, the dissociation of liberalism from the democratic movement proper. Prior to 1848, liberalism advocated freedom for Germany through unification, and freedom for the individual in economic, political, and religious matters, but liberalism also opposed social equality and equal voting rights. The revolution of 1848 further accentuated the difference between liberals and democrats: The democrats were forced into the role of political villains "only soldiers could deal with effectively" (Jany 1967, 4: 178), while the liberals were allowed to gain some respectability as they became increasingly nationalistic and fought for a united but monarchical Germany. This was also the stated objective of most delegates to the German National Assembly, elected in 1848 by universal suffrage and empowered to write a constitution for a united Germany. Divided into moderate and radical-revolutionary wings, the democratic delegates had little chance against the liberal majority. In fact, the composition of the membership was anything but democratic: 81.6 percent of the delegates had a university education, and this at a time when it was still a privilege of a very few. Thus the bulk of the population, consisting of peasants, workers, and artisans, was not represented at all (Snell 1976, 96). Political unification rather than democratization of Germany was the main topic of discussion, but the delegates reached no agreement about the admission of Austria to the new political entity or about the degree of centralization that should characterize the new political structure. Finally, in March of 1849, the assembly proceeded to create a new empire, electing King Frederick William IV of Prussia as emperor of Germany. The king declined the offer, and Prussia, Austria, and most smaller states recalled their delegations. Rebellions broke out in Saxony and Baden when they attempted to impose the constitution written by the assembly, but the uprisings were put down by Prussian troops. A group of delegates who refused to give up moved the sessions from Frankfurt to Stuttgart, but the government of Württemberg finally used the army to disperse the first elected National Assembly.

The role the armed forces were allowed to play during the revolution of 1848–49 strongly encouraged the rebirth of Prussian militarism. First of all, from the standpoint of the defenders of the status quo, the violent uprisings demonstrated the need for a strong military establishment to maintain law and order. One has to keep in mind that maintaining law and order had long since become an indisputable priority in the value system of Prussian society. It ranked high enough to prevail over any ideological considerations. In 1848, the army assumed the role of permanent guardian of the established order, a function that it had no opportunity to translate into action again until the troubled years following World War I.

Furthermore, the repression of revolutionary uprisings in many German states was equivalent to a continuing demonstration of power capabilities, which paved the way to the unification of Germany under Prussian hegemony. The role the Prussian military performed in leading, organizing, training, or actually protecting many German states assured dynastic stability but at the expense of sovereignty. It also exacerbated the old rivalry between Prussia and Austria, which eventually resulted in the war of 1866. Those German states that sided with Austria were conquered by Prussian troops and forced to join the new confederacy of 1867. The city-state of Frankfurt, the electorate of Hesse-Cassel, the duchy of Nassau, the kingdom of Hannover, and the territory of Schleswig-Holstein were incorporated into the Prussian state (Snell 1976, 163–64).

The defeat of the democratic movement on the barricades and in the National Assembly was followed by a massive exodus of its followers. By the 1830s, there were thousands of political emigrés in France, and of the 180,000 who emigrated to America, a considerable proportion left for political reasons. Following the repression of the uprisings in Baden, about 80,000 emigrated to various American countries (Snell 1976, 56,

123). However, at the same time, emigration for economic reasons rapidly became an established pattern in many regions of Germany, and it seems difficult, if not impossible, to separate political expatriates from emigrants whose move was in no way determined by political motives. At any rate, the forced or voluntary exile of thousands who had been implicated in the revolution of 1848 decimated the democratic elite, depriving the movement of many of its ablest leaders.

On the other hand, the work of the German National Assembly left indelible marks on the political development of Germany. Certain southern states, such as Baden and Württemberg, proved more receptive to democratic principles than did Prussia. Furthermore, the constitution of the German Empire was a slightly changed version of the previous one proposed in 1848, and the newly created federal parliament *(Reichstag)* was elected according to the rules of universal suffrage. It exercised influence but no control over the executive branch of the government, because no party was strong enough to gain a majority and partisan divisions were too deep-rooted to allow majority coalitions. Besides, the Federal Council *(Bundesrat)* was empowered to block any legislation proposed by the *Reichstag* (Snell 1976, 166, 174–75, 218).

In view of subsequent developments, it would be naive to assume that militarism can be contained by constitutional means alone. If, as happened in Wilhelmian Germany, all segments and institutions of a society are pervaded by military modes of thinking and acting, it would be unrealistic to expect a heterogeneous body of elected legislators to form an exception and oppose consistently a principle supported enthusiastically by their own constituencies. As we shall see later, during the most crucial phases of its existence, the *Reichstag* either provided the budgetary resources to finance military developments or refrained from making decisions that might have interfered with military planning.

The consistent failure to bring militarism under parliamentary control can hardly be understood without regard to the profound structural changes that affected German society during the second half of the nineteenth century. When the democratic movement suffered its first major defeats, Prussia and the other German states were still predominantly agrarian. Ten years after the revolution of 1848, all of Germany spent no more than 5 million pounds for its military forces. In the same year (1858), Great Britain spent 23 million pounds, France 19 million, Austria-Hungary 11 million, and Russia 19 million for military purposes. Within a few decades, Germany's relative position changed as the industrial revolution took hold. In 1883, Germany's military expenditures quadrupled, and in 1908, its military budget of 59 million pounds equalled that of Great Britain and exceeded that of all other European nations, except

Russia. Reaching the 100 million level in 1913, Germany outspent by far all other nations of Europe (Vagts 1959, 333).

These figures reflect some of the changes the industrial revolution brought about in the military establishment. They also imply the rise of an entrepreneurial class that owed its growing political power to the control of resources characteristic of an industrial society. This class was composed primarily of industrialists, bankers, merchants, and professionals, and its outlook differed markedly from that of the traditional elite. While the latter proved reluctant to change its preindustrial values and attitudes, the new elite was receptive to, or at least undeterred by, the profound socioeconomic changes following in the wake of industrialism. However, calling the new class a "counterelite," as one sociologist suggested (Speier 1952, 233), seems unwarranted and misleading. The two elites shared too much common ground to justify dichotomizing their relationship. Both were antidemocratic, monarchistic, and utterly militaristic. True enough, antagonisms existed among those members who chose to take extreme positions on either side, but it would be more realistic to represent the relationship between the two classes as a continuum, the broad central section of which implied frictionless coexistence and consensus. In fact, much in the way of life of the traditional elite was attractive enough to stimulate emulation and competition. Quite frequently, members of the new elite sought and attained ennoblement, and intermarriages between the nobility of descent and the nobility of ascent were not unusual. The political orientation of the new elite moved in the direction of imperialistic expansion, challenging the status of the great maritime powers. The traditional elite had little use for imperialistic ambitions and perceived Germany essentially as a land power, potentially threatened by the military might of its neighbors east and west. Yet when Germany actually engaged in building a strong navy, the traditional militarists offered less resistance than might have been expected, undoubtedly because the emperor lent his most enthusiastic support to the naval expansion program.

In subsequent chapters, it will be shown that the militarism of the new elite was rooted in its economic interests as well as in the possibility of structuring the emerging labor force in terms of military patterns of behavior. But whatever the role of vested interests might have been in determining the political orientation of the new elite, one should not lose sight of the fact that they had been brought up in a social environment saturated with military modes of thought and action. The prevailing personality structure of the German entrepreneur was not shaped by his vested interests, but by the family, the school, the community, and the reserve officer corps to which he typically belonged.

Consensus and Dissent

Contrary to the common belief that militarism implies some sort of despotism or dictatorship, it should be noted that, influenced by three victorious wars and the glamour of the newly established empire, the overwhelming majority of the people lent ardent support to the expansion of the armed forces and to further diffusion of military patterns of behavior throughout German society. Liberal opposition to militarism, in Prussia and the southern German states, gave way to acceptance and eventually, toward the end of the nineteenth century, to almost unqualified support (Ritter 1970, 2: 98). Such a degree of consensus must be considered rare in a complex society. A particularly effective sanction of political development may be seen in the rapid industrialization and growing wealth of imperial Germany. The rewards of economic prosperity seemed to reinforce the general conviction that German society was right in pursuing an increasingly militaristic line of politics.

Of course, there were dissenters. The most radical ones were members of the Social Democratic Party (SDP), which steadfastly and openly opposed the militarization of German society. Karl Liebknecht, one of the most outstanding Socialist leaders, was quite aware of the nature of militarism when he defined it as "a system of saturating the whole private and public life of our people with the military spirit" (Liebknecht 1907, 90). Consistent with Marxist doctrine, the Socialists perceived the military establishment as an instrument of capitalist domination and therefore incompatible with the interests of the proletariat.

Organized since 1869, the Socialist movement was considered to be a serious threat to the established order. Following an attempt on the life of the emperor in 1878, the government demanded that the Social Democratic Party be outlawed. Parliament rejected the request and was consequently closed. A second attempt to assassinate the old emperor induced the government to dissolve the *Reichstag* without even approaching it for special legislation. The newly elected legislature acceded to governmental pressure and outlawed the Social Democratic Party. Under the new legislation, which remained in force until 1890, the formal organization of the party was almost totally dismantled, but suppression and persecution stimulated its growth, and when allowed again to participate in elections, the Social Democrats were able to draw three times as many votes as in 1877 (Hintze 1915, 669). From that time, the Social Democratic party was tolerated and allowed to have a freely elected and growing representation in parliament, belying the notion that imperial Germany was ruled by a military dictatorship. As a matter of fact, the military were not allowed to translate their relentless hostility against the Socialists into the sort of suppressive action they had been advocating.

However, to gauge the depth of Socialist dissent, it seems appropriate to refer to two crucial phases of the political process.

First, many Marxist leaders, in Germany and elsewhere, labored under the illusion that the Socialist rank and file, if called to arms in the case of war, would refuse to fight and thus thwart "capitalistic belligerency." This assumption apparently ignored the process of "negative" integration that the Social Democratic workers had been exposed to during several decades preceding World War I. One may argue the appropriateness of the term *negative*, but integration it certainly was that had diverted the Social Democratic Party from its revolutionary course. Whether negative or not, this integration was "characterized by increasing economic improvements and tendencies toward legal and factual equality of rights on the one hand, and by simultaneous refusal of equality in state and society, and continuation of exploitation and oppression, on the other hand" (Groh 1973, 36). The author of this statement plausibly argues that the integrative forces were strong enough to curb the sort of revolutionary action predicted by Marx. He also points out that the tactics of the German labor leaders, substituting the development of labor organizations for labor aggression, reinforced the effectiveness of the integrating factors. "The German Social Democrats were," as Karl Kautsky remarked, "a revolutionary party but not a revolution-making party" (Groh 1973, 36). The same Kautsky also expressed the opinion that there was "nothing more Prussian than Prussian Social Democracy" and that "in Germany the masses are drilled to wait for the command from above" (as quoted in Snell 1976, 301).

When World War I was imminent, the German government skillfully used the construct of "defensive" war to entice the Social Democratic Party to support it. Russia was presented as the aggressor, and the notorious Russophobia of the Social Democrats was "activated" to make the prospective war more palatable. At any rate, the majority of the Social Democrats, who had the largest of all elected representations in the *Reichstag,* allowed themselves to be convinced and to show the same degree of patriotic fervor as everybody else when war actually broke out. The directory of the Social Democratic Party voted 78 to 14 to approve the credits necessary to finance the war, and "nationalistic exaltation" seized almost the entire membership (Groh 1973, 628–29, 663, 692, 706).

The Social Democrats, who for half a century had been treated as enemies of the state, as social pariahs, and as political traitors, encountered a welcome opportunity to demonstrate their political loyalty to the imperiled fatherland and to gain respectability in the eyes of German society.

Second, Germany's defeat and the political ascent of the Social Democratic Party in 1918 afforded a unique opportunity to eradicate militarism once and for all, yet not only did the party fail to carry out what its leaders had preached for decades, it also crushed the uprising of its own radical wing. The chance to carry out a radical reform of the army occurred when, following the revolutionary overthrow of the monarchy, the First German Congress of Workers' and Soldiers' Councils convened in Berlin (December 16–21, 1918) to deliberate on the form of government to be adopted. Social Democratic Party and labor union leaders, members of this Congress, demanded military reforms that eventually were set forth in a seven-point program. "The most important provisions of the plan called for the abolition of all rank insignia, free election of leaders, supreme command in the hands of the Provisional Government . . . and the abolition of the mandatory salute when off-duty" (Herwig 1968, 159). Acceptance of the plan was almost unanimous, and the provisional government was requested to carry out the proposed reform. President Friedrich Ebert, although a Social Democrat, failed to do this. The army command opposed the plan, and the president, recognizing that the stability of the emerging regime depended on the cooperation of the armed forces, repudiated the resolution of the Congress. Yet, beyond the expediency required by a momentary crisis, Ebert, like most Social Democratic leaders of that time, had lost the revolutionary fervor of the genuine Marxists.

They had long since come to terms with the liberal middle class, the enemies of yesterday, who had become allies during the last years of the war. They had accepted not only the bourgeois distaste for violence but also a good deal of nationalist sentiment. August 4, 1914 had clearly shown that the majority of the leaders of the SDP had in practice abandoned Marx' revolutionary teachings and his internationalistic stance, an outlook which the party's attitude in November and December of 1918 reaffirmed rather than reversed (Herwig 1968, 165).

German militarism was thus allowed to survive and to evolve eventually into its most virulent form under Hitler.

The Triple Alliance of Monarchy, Nobility, and Army

The changes of the political structure accompanying the establishment of the German Empire did not affect the focal position of the military system. The alliance of the crown and the officer corps remained intact. Regardless of surviving regionalisms, the armed forces of the various states were unified into a single structure under imperial control. As before, it remained "a monarchical household force rather than an instrumentality of the State" (Ritter 1970, 2: 161). All attempts of parliament to gain fiscal control of the armed forces failed. The federal constitution recognized the supreme military authority of the emperor, a prerogative that was consistently used to frustrate parliamentary interference in matters concerning military developments (Huber 1963, 3: 990). It should be added that public opinion became increasingly favorable to growing military expenditures.

Equally untouched by changes was the position of the Junkers. Inveterate bearers of traditional Prussianism, they reacted to the revolution of 1848 by consolidating their role of "supporters and protectors of the Crown" (Muncy 1944, 30). Out of 1,500 Junkers who had been appointed to influential public office between 1888 and 1914, 698 served in provincial government positions. In 1888, 50 percent of the provincial presidents were Junkers, and 30 percent belonged to other variants of German aristocracy. In 1914, the percentage of Junker presidents belonging to the aristocracy had remained unchanged (Muncy 1944, 68, 163). On the level of the *Landrat*, the traditional power domain of the Junkers, their predominance remained unchanged in the east, but in the western provinces, men of middle-class extraction overshadowed those of aristocratic origin, Junker or not. This, however, did not imply ideological orientations differing from those held by Junker officials. "On the contrary, many of them, although still commoners, were undoubtedly as conservative and as 'feudal' in their outlook as the Junkers and turned to the latter as their models" (Muncy 1944, 192).

While the Junkers were usually involved in conservative party politics (*Kreuzzeitungspartei*), their military peers, like the officer corps in general, were allegedly unpolitical, or at least that is how they considered themselves. If the assumption of an unpolitical army is taken in the narrowest possible sense to mean active participation in party politics, it comes fairly close to the actual situation. Military officers were not allowed to vote; they were often antagonistic to, and contemptuous of, politicians and political parties, but acceptance of the principle that the "army is no place for politics" is, as Obermann clearly recognized, in itself a political decision (Obermann 1958, 104). Carefully obeyed nonparticipation in party politics does not mean, of course, abstention from political decision making, either in imperial Germany or anywhere else. "Group interests and personal interests force every army to be 'in politics' in a larger sense" (Vagts 1959, 295). In its close alliance with the crown, the German army had a legitimate outlet for the exercise of political power. The emperor stood at the apex of the military hierarchy, and his power was, *de jure* as *de facto*, the power of the army. Whenever he made decisions concerning the military, they were implicitly *decisions of the army*. Monarchy and army were integral parts of the same political structure, a circumstance that makes the usual distinction between civilian government and military establishment pointless. There simply was no civilian government in the conventionally accepted sense. The power of the army derived directly from the overruling power of its supreme commander, the emperor, who was also the chief executive of the Reich. To seize power, as military leaders do nowadays in nations of the so-called Third World, would have meant to overthrow the monarchy, a step that would have been totally inconsistent with all interests of the officer corps. Under the prevailing conditions, the military had all the power they could possibly desire.

Monarchy and army were integrated by the nobility, at least to the extent that a substantial proportion of its members controlled virtually all key positions in the military hierarchy, and the nobility, particularly its most conservative core, the Junkers, was fiercely monarchist. It would be difficult indeed to question the political nature of this structural arrangement.

Political action undertaken by military leaders (including the emperor) was designed to implant "desirable" modes of behavior among all ranks of the armed forces and especially to prevent socialism from gaining a foothold in the military system. Under William II, "conservatism was the required world view of the officers, no less than membership in the established churches." Punitive sanctions were inflicted on officers believed to be liberals or Socialist sympathizers (Vagts 1959, 314–15). Criticisms directed against military institutions or against the official version of national history were regarded as incompatible with the principle of military subordination. Even reserve officers "faced the risk of being summoned before a military court of honor for their public statements" (Ritter 1970, 2: 105). The main thrust of political indoctrination by the army was, of course, addressed to the rank-and-file recruits, who had been exposed to strenuous attempts by the Social Democratic Party to attract followers from the working class.

Thus in alliance with the Junkers, the military became the advocates of a particular sociopolitical order. The term *military party*, used in public controversy, does not seem inappropriate because the political process was continuously affected by overt and covert interference of the military hierarchy, partly through its influential voice of conservative doctrine, the *Deutsche Wehrzeitung* (German Military Gazette). Founded and published by members of the officer corps, it was instrumental, for example, in the rejection of a proposed law requiring the military to take an oath on the constitution (Obermann 1958, 109). As before, allegiance was sworn to the king and the emperor instead.

Nationalism as an Integrating Force in German Culture

In regard to the climax of Prussian-German militarism, the question may be raised as to how thoroughly different sectors of a complex culture can be adapted to the mold of a single, highly specialized set of values and attitudes. Certainly, no society can afford to become so militarized that preparation for war, with all its technological and organizational implications, emerges as a nationally approved objective *to the detriment or exclusion of all others*. There were strong cultural traditions in Germany that bore no resemblance whatever to militaristic doctrine or practice. To curtail or destroy those traditions would have been both pointless and counterproductive, because they ranked high in the value system of the middle and upper classes.

At times, the accomplishments of German society in the areas of philosophy, science, fine arts, and literature and, more generally, a strong, continuing emphasis on *Bildung* (the cultivation of intellectual and aesthetic pursuits) have been deemed inconsistent with militarism. How was it possible for a society of "poets and thinkers" (*Volk der Dichter und Denker*) to be, at the same time, a nation of warriors?

If a certain culture complex is thought to be inconsistent with another set of traits, one should look for a third element that may integrate the seemingly incompatible complexes on a more inclusive level. It would seem that nationalism is to be credited with conciliating what otherwise might have proved irreconcilable. Nationalism, as has been pointed out so often, may be defined as "an ideology designed to generate the highest possible degree of solidarity among aggregates of people belonging to different social strata, different local or regional structures, even different ethnic groups." Insofar as such differences may be accommodated or superseded, the capability for concerted action at the national level grows and becomes available for political purposes. Nationalism is a multifarious creed that adapts itself to all political regimes; it seizes on any aspect or sector of a culture, past or present; it thrives on myths or creates its own mythology; and by associating historical events with such geographical features as mountains, woods, or streams, it converts them into sacred places capable of arousing strong collective sentiments. The process we are alluding to is, of course, the creation of symbols that represent the nation as a whole or any of its aspects.

The integrating effect of nationalism is such that apparent inconsistencies between particular cultural traits are reconciled once they acquire the status of national symbols. This means, above everything else, implicit or explicit ascription of basic affinities deriving from a common source or origin, which has been variously named *Volksgeist* (ethnic mind), *Volksseele* (ethnic soul), *Gesamtgeist* (collective mind), *Rassenseele* (racial soul), *Gesamtbewusstsein* (collective consciousness), *Gesamtwille* (collective will), or *Nationalbewusstsein* (national consciousness). No matter how heterogeneous the manifestations of the *Volksgeist* might be, they all were believed to be distinctly German and therefore to belong together in some way. The famous Werner Sombart, an economist with sociological leanings, in 1915 endeavored to reconcile the alleged paradox of German national character in terms of militarism, which he described as "the spirit of heroism elevated to the level of a warlike mentality. It is Potsdam and Weimar in the most sublime association. It is Faust and Zarathustra and Beethoven in the trenches. Because the Eroica and the Egmont overture are the most genuine kind of militarism" (quoted in Obermann 1958, 223).

Although extreme in its formulation, Sombart's view illustrates the integrative role of nationalism. However, it seems doubtful that more than a relatively small sector of German society was aware of possible cultural inconsistencies. The "poets and thinkers," as well as those capable of assimilating the works of Kant, Hegel, Beethoven, and Wagner, for example, were no more than a small though highly influential elite.

To qualify as a symbol of the German national ethos, a work of art, philosophy, or literature did not have to make an explicit contribution to nationalistic ideology. Most of them did not, but some contributed effectively to the creation of a political lore designed to indoctrinate successive generations of Germans. Johann Gottlieb Fichte (1762–1814) may be considered one of the founding fathers of German nationalism. Writing in 1808, he addressed a nonexistent German nation "not recognizing, but setting aside completely and rejecting, all the dissociating distinctions which for centuries unhappy events have caused in this single nation" (Fichte 1922, 3). Fichte attributed immeasurable importance to the potentially unifying forces inherent in a common territory, identical with "the original dwelling places of the ancestral stock," and in the formative power of a common language (Fichte 1922, 54, 62).

The Role of Education in the Transmission of Military Patterns of Behavior

Neither territory nor language, however, could be expected to generate the degree of political solidarity required by a national existence. A new kind of education had to be implanted in order "to mould the Germans into a corporate body, which shall be stimulated and animated in all its individual members by the same interest" (Fichte 1922, 15). In fact, out of a series of reforms emerged an educational system that merits perhaps closer attention than most other spheres of German culture. The almost fanatical belief in the absolute value of the army, in "soldierly virtues," and in militarily oriented patterns of behavior in all walks of life (Obermann 1958, 226) is explainable only in terms of a highly effective system of indoctrination throughout the life cycle of a person. Closely related to this belief was the conviction that the army itself was the greatest educator of the nation. By the time a man was discharged from the army, he was believed to be "stronger in every sense" than he had been at the time he had joined the armed forces. The continuous expansion of the population and its economic system was interpreted as convincing evidence that "military and national progress actually fostered it. Such virtues as method and order, moderation and endurance, solidarity and entrepreneurship" were allegedly acquired in the army and warranted success in whatever occupational career a man decided to embark upon (Jähns 1885, 406–7).

Small wonder then that family and school proceeded to inculcate in the young the military virtues of discipline and boundless respect for authority. The roles of parents and teachers were primarily those of disciplinarians, and their authority to sanction behavior of children and adolescents extended to the adult community at large. There was a tacit consensus among adults that any adult, whether parent or not, should be willing to assume the role of a strict disciplinarian. Doubtlessly, the triple alliance of parents, teachers, and community proved more effective in laying the behavioral foundations of militarism than the annual round of patriotic events with parades and marching bands, the instruction in official history (Bruck 1938, 40), or the military drill that came with physical education. Needless to say, physical punishment was institutionalized and carried over into the lower grades of the secondary school system. Until the end of the past century, there was in each secondary school and college the *Karzer*, a jail room where derelict students were locked up for a short time.

A direct linkage existed between the military complex and the primary school system. Until 1844, retiring petty officers were allowed to become teachers, and while still in the service, they were granted leaves of absence to enroll in teachers colleges. Although the school authorities went to any length to keep the teachers colleges within strictly conservative bounds, King Frederick William IV publicly accused the colleges of having caused the revolution of 1848. He ordered all colleges to be moved from cities to small localities. To prevent "political subversion," they were kept under strict control. Any discussion of political problems was forbidden, and the teachers were told to emphasize religion, national history, and loyalty to the king (Brandt 1981, 172–76). Still, in the second half of the century this ultraconservative orientation of educational policy continued. By 1880, the "free" teachers' associations were charged with fomenting "particularistic tendencies," and teachers were discouraged from attending meetings of their professional organizations. All civil servants, including teachers, were urged to "represent the politics of the royal state government in elections." Bismarck too opposed all attempts to develop the primary school curriculum beyond instruction in religion, reading, writing, and arithmetic (Meyer 1980, 273–74, 280).

At first glance, it seems difficult to reconcile the humanistic tradition, kept alive by the *Gymnasium* (secondary school) with its heavy emphasis on classical languages and literature (nine years of Latin and six years of Greek), with the pragmatic implications of a premilitary education. However, the selection of original texts to be read clearly reflected a preference for writers steeped in Greek and Roman versions of militarism. Out of the pages of Caesar, Livy, Sallust, Virgil, Xenophon, Homer, and Herodotus, history was reconstructed as a long sequence of wars that lent themselves to the apotheosis of the heroic warrior who dies for his fatherland. Inculcated in the mind of the adolescent was the Roman motto *Dulce et decorum est pro patria mori*. Consistent with this principle was the initial sentence of the welcome address with which the headmaster of a famous military academy received freshman classes: "This is the place where you will learn how to die."*

In secondary schools and in colleges, the subjects most amenable to manipulation were history, philosophy, and the social sciences. Far from being unpolitical, the faculties of the German universities succumbed, with some exceptions, to the lures of a militant nationalism. The enthusiasm with which numerous professors embraced the ideology of a militaristic state is perhaps not unrelated to the profession's rise from the rather low social and economic level characteristic of eighteenth-century institutions to the enviably high status the German professor came to enjoy in the nineteenth century.

The political stance of some German philosophers during the Wars of Liberation presaged later trends. For example, Fichte conceptualized the nation as the society of the future held together by coercive education and the force of the state (Flitner 1957, 81), and Hegel referred to war as the "steel bath of the peoples" (Obermann 1958, 224).

*Personal communication from Herbert Baldus.

Among those who proposed annexation of French territories after the victorious war of 1870–71, the German historians were well represented. Of the eight names mentioned by Schleier, the most illustrious were Sybel, Duncker, Mommsen, and Treitschke (Schleier 1965, 110). In fact, Treitschke ranked high among the most ardent advocates of the militaristic state. Believing that "the reputation of invincibility means one half of the power of a militaristic state," he did his utmost to build up the myth of invincibility of the German army (Schleier 1965, 113). His lectures at the University of Berlin in the 1890s drew large, enthusiastic audiences from among students and army officers. "The state," Treitschke taught, "is carried by the organized physical force of the nation which is the army," and the army he regarded as "the most real and effective bond of national unity, certainly not, as one had hoped earlier, the German Reichstag." Venting his contempt for the *Reichstag*, the federal legislature of imperial Germany, he referred to it as "a source of mutual hatred and calumny" (Treitschke 1898, 2: 355–56).

Perhaps nobody had ever exalted war as extravagantly as Treitschke. He wrote,

We have learned to recognize the moral majesty of war precisely in those of its characteristics which to superficial observers seem brutal and inhuman. That for the sake of the Fatherland the natural sentiment of humanity is to be suppressed. . . . this at the first glance is the terrible side of war, but it is at the same time its grandeur. It is not life alone that man is called upon to sacrifice but also the natural and most profoundly justified emotions of the human soul. He is to sacrifice his entire ego to a great patriotic idea. That is the morally sublime element in war (Treitschke 1898, 2: 361–62).

It was Treitschke who praised universal military service as "the foundation of political liberty and training in blind discipline as the finest school of character and described the Prussian generals as an elite of open-minded men of character" (Ritter 1970, 2: 99).

The interest that German industrialists as a class took in the militarization of education deserves special attention. Nobody put it more clearly than Goetz Briefs, a well-known social scientist of the Weimar Republic:

There is no doubt that in Germany barracks and primary school created social categories that affected the formation of relationships within the corporative enterprise. Military discipline turned out to be a valuable asset in the rise of German industrialism. A residue and reflection of feudal and military conceptions of the seigneurial order encroached upon the managing directorates via the reserve officer institution, the college education of the upper and the student corporations. High-ranking military officers were and still are found among the leading executives of industrial enterprises. The German entrepreneurs collectively, particularly the high ranks of managing directorates, were increasingly attracted by the military pathos of leadership, by standoffishness and the sort of command that demands unhesitating obedience. The military model formed the entrepreneurial leadership from the top of the hierarchy down to the level of the foreman, a process that met less and less resistance as migrant populations with Slavic admixture joined the labor force of the industrial cities. Many German enterprises exacted a degree of dependence and submission from their employees which went far beyond the objective demands of the production process and which tended to intrude upon the private life of their personnel. The strictly liberal property concept which perceived the industrial plant as an expanded household and dealt with the labor force from the vantage point of the lord of the house, often combined with the ideology of military leadership and command generating a "managerial militarism" which proved effective, yet bound to produce attitudes of protest and mental resistance (Briefs 1931, 47).

Obviously, the industrialists considered militarism to be a means of shaping a docile labor force that could be manipulated and would not succumb to the lures of socialism. It can be argued that in the end "managerial militarism" turned out to be counterproductive insofar as it contributed to the revolution of 1918.

As German politics assumed an increasingly imperialistic stance toward the end of the nineteenth century, and the pressure of public opinion induced the political parties to shun no sacrifice to support the rapid buildup of a powerful navy (Ritter 1970, 2: 98), economists lent support to the conquest of overseas markets and the acquisition of colonies.

It should not be assumed that those members of the German professoriat who did not join the panegyrists of the militaristic state constituted some kind of political opposition. Following the philosopher Friedrich Paulsen, who taught that "scholars cannot and should not engage in politics" (Paulsen 1906, 255), they adopted a rather disdainful attitude toward party politics. On the whole, they put no strain on the political consensus of the bourgeoisie to which they belonged.

At the outbreak of World War I, the German professoriat was called upon to guide the "mobilization of the minds" and to provide ideological support for the cause of the nation. The professors enthusiastically accepted the challenge, although their attitudes were far from homogeneous. Outright defense or even extravagant extolment of militarism was common. By some, militarism was equated with "heroic mentality" and "highest perfection of German consciousness of duty." In public addresses and pamphlets, the professoriat almost unanimously proclaimed that "the union of the German mind and militarism was indissoluble." A threat to militarism was widely believed to be the equivalent of a threat to German culture (Schwabe 1969, 24–25).

Much of the ideological effort of the professors tended toward injecting meanings into the war. There was a revival of Hegel's idea that war had a cleansing effect on society. Unselfish service to the fatherland, particularly the sacrifice of one's life, was thought to exalt the individual morally. Collectively, war "appeared as a regulator of the entire historical process, as an arbiter of good and evil, of what was politically, culturally and even economically worthy or unworthy of survival and thus serving human progress" (Schwabe 1969, 39). Also, the meaning of technological progress was defined in terms of the contributions it was making to a more effective conduct of war. A religious or mystical meaning was attributed to war by those who believed it to be a "crusade," a "holy war," or a "metaphysical awakening" (Schwabe 1969, 38–39).

Incapable of recognizing anything but partisan fanaticism and mindless, squabbling factionalism in the political pluralism of prewar Germany, the professoriat interpreted the consensus characterizing the early phase of the war as a "melting down process" in which the "disparate elements" of German society, especially political parties and social classes, would blend into a unified, monolithic structure. The integrative function of the war was hailed as "internal conquest," paralleling external conquest east and west.

Along with the academicians of the extreme right, a number of more liberal professors interpreted the rejection of Western political traditions as "a rejuvenation of Germany and a revival of its vitality" (Schwabe 1969, 40–44).

More numerous than their moderate opponents, the "annexationists" took it for granted, as did many intellectuals elsewhere, that military conquest legitimized permanent control over occupied territories. In fact, a petition to annex huge territories in the east and the west, addressed to the imperial chancellor in 1915, bore the signature of 352 college professors, the largest single group among the 1,347 supporters of German imperialism who signed the document (Grumbach as cited in Thayer 1917, 60–66).

The behavioral model set up by the military elite found its most fervent emulators among the student associations, such as the so-called *Corps* whose educational ideals centered on the concepts of honor, discipline, obedience, courage, and determination (Obermann 1958, 194). The sword was very much in evidence on formal occasions, and the student "commander" (*Fuchsmajor*) used it like a gavel to underline his orders. Numerous public events required "color-wearing students" (*Couleurstudenten*) to wear a uniform with high cuirassier boots and sword. "An aggressive demeanor and instant readiness to fight a duel were widely copied attitudes in academic circles" (Ritter 1970, 2: 102).

Laws against duels had been on the books for a long time, but military officers, as well as dueling student corporations (*Schlagende Verbindungen*), were allowed to flout the law with impunity. Except among the Catholics and the Socialists, the duel was widely approved, even by such "liberal" philosophers as Friedrich Paulsen: "The ability to defend his [the student's] honor, if necessary with a weapon in his hand, is a demand which his fellows make first and foremost" (Paulsen 1906, 270). "Even so enlightened a thinker as the sociologist Max Weber firmly supported the principle of dueling" (Lowie 1945, 62). Bearing the scars of duels on one's face was regarded as a mark of distinction and a source of pride. To accentuate the visibility of scars, the wounds left by a rapier, sword, or saber were sometimes tampered with.

Dueling was permissible only with adversaries of equal or higher social status. A man's honor could not be touched by someone ranking below his own social level, and challenging such a person would have irreparably debased the challenger. If a member of a dueling corporation (or a military officer for that matter) felt his honor had been questioned, the first step was to determine whether or not the offender's social rank made dueling admissible. Since situations calling for such contests did not occur often enough to satisfy the fighting spirit of the student corporations, the *Mensur* (duel) frequently became a command performance in which the adversaries were designated by corporate authority.

The dueling student corporation was designed to instill in a military officer the personal characteristics he was expected to possess, often including the snarling, insolent tone of contempt used in contact with one's social inferior. Of course, it was every student's ambition to become an officer in the reserves, if possible in one of the more prestigious regiments, and many of them refused to commission *any* officer who had not fought at least one duel.

The Militarization of Civilian Society

Since the founding of the empire, the institution of the reserve officer had gained immensely in prestige. Often accused of arrogantly shunning association with "civilians," the professional officer corps was nevertheless besieged by emulators, mostly sons of the new plutocracy who were irresistibly attracted by the social nimbus surrounding the military nobility. To surmount the social barrier separating the military from the bourgeoisie, a reserve officer's commission was a *conditio sine qua non*, but it symbolized more than a ploy for upward social mobility. The reserve officer corps tended to assimilate the middle strata of German society to the aristocratic and monarchistic value system of the militaristic state. In fact, this so-called feudalization process transformed the German bourgeoisie into a mainstay of militarism and thus contributed decisively to its stability. It also presented a more pragmatic aspect insofar as it satisfied the growing demand for officers, which the professional officer corps was unable to supply.

The reserve officer was expected to exhibit the demeanor usually associated with that of a professional officer. At all times, the reserve officer was to assume a stiff, ramrodlike posture, his voice was to convey clipped incisiveness and authority, and the saluting ritual vis-à-vis a social equal or superior was to be accompanied by a bow and a clicking of the heels (*Hacken zusammenschlagen*). No word characterizes the posture expected of the military officer more aptly than *Schneid*. Its meaning is more comprehensive than "dash." *Schneid* not only denotes the external aspects of military bearing but also implies courage in personal confrontations and valor in battle.

The desire of the bourgeoisie for social ascent was strong enough for many of its members to emulate the exclusiveness of the conservative nobility by establishing social boundaries designed to keep persons of Jewish ancestry and of leftist leanings out of the corps. Only under exceptional circumstances did the sons of peasants, artisans, laborers, and shopkeepers or, more generally, men married to lower-middle-class women have a chance to get commissions in the reserve officer corps (Ritter 1970, 2: 102).

Ubiquitous in the professions and in high-level positions in the civil service, in industry, in banking, and in big business, the reserve officer tended to shape social relationships in terms of the drill ground. "This spirit of prompt obedience extended from the army to industrial life. The local units responded to the least word from headquarters. The giant industrial plants, large savings banks, local branches of the social democratic party, and even the trade unions, functioned through men of the type of captains or non-commissioned officers" (Bruck 1938, 39). Not only were there formal rank differences among reserve officers, but branches of the armed services were informally stratified according to the degree of prestige they carried. Men in the legal professions and the highest echelons of the civil service sought commissions in elite regiments whose officers belonged to the nobility. To the extent that high professional status was associated with wealth and adherence to political conservatism, formal ennoblement was not out of reach. At the turn of the nineteenth century, a substantial proportion of the German nobility was new, including some outstanding military commanders such as von Kluck, von Mackensen, and von Lietzmann (Vagts 1959, 255), apart from the many naval officers to be mentioned elsewhere.

What the reserve officer endeavored to do at the higher level of the social structure, the noncommissioned officer, retired from active service and entitled to subaltern positions in all branches of the civil service, strove to accomplish at the lower levels of the social pyramid. After twelve years of service, the petty officer was even more inured to military patterns of behavior in his sphere of action than the reserve officer. Reputed to be reliable, honest, and obedient to his superiors and a stern disciplinarian to his inferiors, the military aspirant (*Militaranwärter*) was a common figure in all branches of public administration, in the postal and national railway systems, and in the police force. The power of these former petty officers was such that they were capable of acting as a public pressure group.

The militarization of "civilians" was reinforced by a variety of voluntary associations encompassing most sectors of German society. Two generals, Friedrich von Bernhardi, an extreme advocate of imperialistic expansion, and Kolmar von der Goltz, reputed to be a partisan of preventive war, created a paramilitary youth organization, the *Jungdeutschlandbund* (Young Germans' League), which had a membership of 750,000 in 1914. Highly influential at the village and small town levels were the *Kriegervereine* (Warriors' Associations) and the *Deutsche Kriegerbund* (German Warriors' League). In 1909, 16,533 Warriors' Associations with 1,439,145 members were counted in Prussia alone. A constituency of 19,625 local associations was affiliated with the German Warriors' League, whose total membership amounted to 1,687,990 in 1909. All Warriors' Associations were integrated into the *Kyffhäuser Bund* (Kitchen 1968, 103–135). As an organization of former service men, the *Kyffhäuser Bund* proposed to keep alive the military spirit: "Love of and fidelity to Kaiser and Reich, Sovereign and Fatherland, will be cherished by its members, put into action and strengthened, national consciousness will be enlivened and strengthened, the ties of comradeship, even in civil life, will be preserved and cherished by its members" (Kitchen 1968, 129).

In 1912, the *Wehrverein* (Defense League) was established, and the Association of Soldiers' Friends endeavored to support the militaristic state by distributing propagandistic literature among the armed forces. Between 1897 and 1907, 589,518 free books and magazines were handed out to soldiers (Vagts 1959, 337). Founded by Prince Wied and Alfred Krupp, the armament magnate, and strongly supported by heavy industry, the *Deutsche Flottenverein* (German Naval League) enjoyed immense popularity in those years of burgeoning imperialism. And the Colonial League, with 20,000 members in 1897, intensively propagated, with thousands of brochures and pamphlets, Germany's claim to a colonial empire (Herwig 1973, 7).

Although not directly an offspring of militarism, the numerous Riflemen's Associations or Guilds *(Schüzenvereine)*, the origin of which can be traced to the Middle Ages, not only fit the system but also performed the specific function of fostering interest in and familiarity with firearms on a competitive basis. The Riflemen met on weekends at their firing range for target shooting, and the annual competition was part of the normal round of village festivals. The best marksman was crowned "king" *(Schützenkönig)*, and the uniformed members of the corps participated in public parades along with other associations. In Catholic regions, Saint Sebastian often was the patron saint of the Riflemen's Guild, which constituted a kind of religious brotherhood. Since possession and use of guns were strictly regulated, these organizations afforded virtually the only opportunity, outside the army and police, to acquire experience in the use of firearms. The idea that a citizen might have a constitutional right to bear arms was totally alien to German (and most European) societies.

The Church as an Instrument of the Militaristic State

The extent to which a church may become involved in the pursuits of the state depends, above all, on whether or not it is structurally dependent on the polity. The fact is that the Reformation was carried out by the heads of several German states, and the German Evangelical Church remained under state authority until the nineteenth century, when the Protestant churches succeeded in achieving partial autonomy. Until then, the church administration was part of the state bureaucracy. To the present time, however, the Protestant and the Catholic clergy have received their income from a special tax, collected and disbursed by the state. In other words, a militant state had the power and the opportunity to recruit the clergy, particularly the Protestant clergy, to perform ideological services supporting given political objectives.

Political support by a church may assume different forms. The church may pursue the general strategy of defending the state and what it stands for. Frederick the Great, for example, was quite pragmatic about the duties of his field preachers, who were expected to indoctrinate the soldiers in the belief that "obedience to God and obedience to the ruler were one and the same thing" (Höhn 1963, 174). Since 1849, the alliance of Protestant orthodoxy, monarchy, and officer corps has defined the ancillary role of the church. Protestantism was tantamount to conservatism and orthodoxy, a combination intended to keep all the king's subjects in a state of submissive obedience *(Untertanengehorsam)* (Kitchen 1968, 87).

The belief "that the monarchy is the divine world order," that "the emperor was instituted by God and that therefore he was empowered to command unconditional obedience," was maintained in the face of the antireligious preachings of the "godless" Socialists (Höhn 1963, 236). In a proclamation to the German army of the east, in 1914, the emperor claimed divine support for his role as supreme commander: "Remember that you are the chosen people! The Spirit of the Lord has descended upon me because I am the emperor of the Germans! I am the instrument of the Almighty. I am his sword, his agent. Woe and death to all those who do not believe in my mission! Woe and death to the cowards! Let them perish, all the enemies of the German people! God demands their destruction, God who, by mouth, bids you do his will!" (Thayer 1917, 4).

Although the German Protestant churches maintained what was widely believed to be an unpolitical position, the preachings of individual clergymen invoked supernatural sanctions to support militarism. A typical exponent of the alliance between orthodox Protestantism, monarchy, and political conservatism was Adolf Stoecker, preacher at the imperial court and the *Dom* (Cathedral) of Berlin. In a futile attempt to co-opt the urban masses, particularly the Social Democrats, he founded the Christian Social Labor Party in 1878. His ultraconservative message held little appeal for the working class, but he proved more successful, at least temporarily, in mobilizing the bourgeoisie of the capital against what he called "Jewish liberalism." His movement collapsed in 1890.

In many a clergyman's homilies, the German army became an "Instrument of God; wars were ordered by God to decide peoples' destinies, and the German army had been entrusted with the task to fight for the greatness of Prussia and Germany" (Höhn 1963, 231). Individual preachers would attack pacifists and all those (mostly Socialists) opposing the appropriation of funds for the expansion of army and navy (Höhn 1963, 234). There were even attempts to instill the belief in supernatural rewards for the brave warrior who sacrificed his life in battle for the greatness of the fatherland (Höhn 1963, 185).

On the other hand, the army chaplains were not free to speak out against what they perceived as violations of morality. Any hint at the "sins" of officers and soldiers was interpreted as an attempt to subvert military discipline (Kitchen 1968, 171).

The political militancy of the Protestant churches of the eastern provinces was not unrelated to the influential role of the Junkers in the ideological orientation of the clergy and the faithful.

The Catholic church was reluctant to support a state that had been pointedly Protestant since its very inception. In the 1870s, the allegiance of the Catholic minority to the government was put to a severe test when Bismarck spared no effort to bring the Church of Rome under the control of the state. The so-called *Kulturkampf* (culture struggle) was accommodated, however, and most Catholics were carried away by the nationalistic wave that swept Germany during the two decades preceding World War I. However, the Catholic population of western and eastern Germany proved less amenable to militarization than the Prussians of the eastern provinces.

The Economic Tenets of Militarism

The beginnings of Prussian militarism were contingent on a reorganization and centralization of the fiscal system, which made it possible for the king to control the allocation of surpluses for military expenditures (Lamprecht 1913, 3: 684). There is no point here in repeating what has been said about the political processes that, after many hesitations, resulted in a definite shift of fiscal power from the estates to the crown. Taxation was heavy enough to cause substantial redistribution of resources, curtailing the economic development of the cities and seriously weakening the peasantry. Although the power of the nobility to participate in high-level decision making had been considerably reduced, the landed aristocracy was able to reap substantial economic rewards. The surplus allocated to the military created a market for agricultural and manufactured commodities as the monarch succeeded in increasing the standing army. In fact, agricultural producers, manufacturers, and traders developed a vested interest in a continuous expansion of the military establishment.

Concentration of fiscal authority in the crown was but one aspect of the mercantilistic economic system, a creation of the absolute state and its cameralists, the learned servants of the ruler's "camera" who designed and carried out a policy of state interference and state monopoly (Bruck 1938, 36). While other European countries rid themselves of cameralism, Prussia and the German Empire pursued an economic policy that incorporated the changes caused by the industrial revolution, but "without deflecting it from the ancient cameralistic aim of making the most of the nation's resources for the dynastic purpose of the state" (Veblen 1939, 175). This modern version of cameralism was intended to serve the state "in the sense of a coercive war power." As an economic policy, it was "pursued with an eye single to the enhancement and husbanding of the resources of the State as a warlike power" (Veblen 1939,

211–12). Further emphasizing the militaristic nature of the close association of polity and economy, Veblen noted that it was "with a view to the fighting capacity of the State, and indeed with no other view," that "the economic system of the country has been controlled wherever control was conceived expedient for this purpose" (Veblen 1939, 214).

A reciprocal dependency between the economy and the military establishment developed long before the industrial revolution changed the technology of warfare. The agrarian nobility found a profitable market for its increased production in the many garrison towns that dotted eighteenth-century Prussia; the substantial increase of the standing army under Frederick the Great would not have been possible without the growing productivity of agriculture (Büsch 1962, 111). As the army expanded and equipment became costlier, more complex, and more specialized, the military establishment became more dependent on economic development. There was no spontaneous industrial entrepreneurship in the eighteenth century, but the military demand for certain products induced the Prussian kings to further the development of textile and metal-working industries. Independence from foreign import was the objective of this policy, which was never entirely successful, although the state subsidized such industries and acquired their whole output. Each regiment was ordered to procure its supplies in a specific city (Schwieger 1980, 180–81).

In the second half of the nineteenth century, capital investment in armament industries reached a level unprecedented in history, and the dependency of such industries on a continuing demand for their products reached a point at which it overruled any consideration opposing the current armament policy. What appeared to be preparation for war on the level of international politics was protection of huge capital investments and an increasing demand for profit on the economic level. As imperial Germany was competing with its neighbors for military supremacy, one felt justified in raising the argument that only from a position of great military strength could the nation expect to reach any kind of international understanding about armament. To emphasize the point, there were recurrent waves of "modern terror created by the dread of insecurity" (Vagts 1959, 361–64). The pattern has since become so familiar that it need not be discussed in detail.

In addition to the impersonal relationships joining the economy and the military arm of the polity in mutual dependence, industry and the army were linked by personal relationships. Many sons of wealthy entrepreneurs gained access to the *noblesse d'epée* (Ritter 1970, 2: 101), and these new officers tended to promote the spirit of bellicosity untrammeled by traditional restraints that had kept the old nobility in line.

However, there was an even closer association between the army and the armament industry. The Krupp Concern, the largest manufacturer of armaments, employed "hundreds of officers, on leave or inactive, at high salaries, for doing nothing much. To some families Krupp was a great sinecure providing jobs for nephews and poor relations of officers who had great influence in the army" (Vagts 1959, 368). Thus the interpenetration of the army and industry on the personal level tended to reinforce the impersonal alliance based on structural interdependence.

Advocated by prominent German bankers and industrialists in prewar days, the imposition of Germany's hegemony on central Europe, implying conquest, annexation, and the creation of peripheral satellite states, was espoused by Chancellor Bethmann-Hollweg at the beginning of World War I. At the same time, plans to establish a vast colonial empire, including the Portuguese colonies, the Belgian Congo, and French Equatorial Africa, were proposed and discussed by other members of the government (Fischer 1962, 107–8, 110).

The degree of consensus achieved among the largest and most powerful economic associations with regard to the imperialistic objectives of German militarism was reflected by a document requesting the emperor to annex parts of France, the Baltic provinces (Lithuania, Latvia, and Estonia), and other eastern territories. Formulated in 1915, when victory in World War I seemed within reach, the request was endorsed by the Central Association of German Industrialists, the Union of Industrialists, the Farmers' Association, the German Peasant League, the Middle Class Association of Imperial Germany, and Christian Associations of German Peasants (Craig 1955, 309).

The Navy: The Epitome of German Militarism

The sudden expansion of the navy deserves special consideration, mainly because it epitomized various facets of German militarism. Two parallel realities were discernible in the evolution of German militarism: conservative or traditional patterns of thought and action on the one hand, and the tendency toward innovation and change on the other. Both characterize the development of German maritime power.

It was not the mere existence of a navy but the decision of 1898 to transform it into a powerful battle fleet that ought to be considered a major change. Far more than the addition of a vast arsenal of recent technology to the existing war potential, the creation of a large, modern navy implied a radical reorientation of German militarism. Traditionally, the military were concerned with possible threats from west and east, most notably with the problems of a two-front war, but the new political trend was clearly imperialistic and directed primarily against the maritime power of Great Britain. The kaiser, strongly supported by Admiral von Tirpitz, his state secretary of the Naval Office, intended to create a battle fleet larger and stronger than the British navy, one capable of supporting overseas expansion in competition with Great Britain and other nations. The navy symbolized the new role of a "world power," which Germany was about to assume under William II, "and if in the future Great Britain should refuse to yield to this pressure, Tirpitz was willing to stake Germany's fate on a single, decisive naval battle in the North Sea" (Herwig 1973, 15).

Possible internal opposition was circumvented by the leading role the kaiser assumed in the process of expanding Germany's battle fleet. The emperor made full use of his personal power to carry through one of the most radical changes in the history of militarism. His power, like that of his royal ancestors, rested on the close alliance between monarchy, nobility, and officer corps. As indicated earlier, this association bore the characteristics of an extreme conservatism in its ideology of feudal retainership and in its political party orientation. The use of such an ultraconservative structure for the adoption of radical changes seems rather unusual. In the case of German maritime imperialism, an additional problem arose because the construction of a rapidly growing fleet required the creation of a totally new officer corps. It was in the solution of this problem that the traditional mechanism proved its practical value. The marine officer corps was considered a personal creation of the kaiser, and therefore felt closely bound to the monarch. Many of its officers were ennobled by the kaiser, replacing those members of the older nobility who showed little enthusiasm for the imperialistic reorientation of German foreign policy.

The process of translating the imperial initiative into reality afforded the opportunity to utilize a novel way of harnessing popular support for the construction of a large battle fleet. With the approval of the kaiser, "Tirpitz upset all previous notions of how a military government agency should conduct itself by turning his Reich naval office (Reichsmarineamt) into a political intelligence and propaganda agency, systematically campaigning in support of his navy bills in a fashion never before seen in Germany" (Ritter 1970, 2: 137). Anticipating future patterns of military propaganda, Tirpitz's agency used every means of converting the people to the kaiser's naval doctrine. The response was truly impressive. Not unexpectedly, heavy industry backed the naval construction program and also lent generous financial support to Tirpitz's propaganda campaign. A newly established Navy League (Flottenverein), attracting almost a million members within a few years, carried the message to all sectors of German society. So effectively was the institutional structure permeated with the novel idea of Germany's becoming a great naval power, "so foreign to Prussian tradition," that most opposition ceased (except for that of the Social Democrats), and even parliament was carried away to the point of committing itself "to extremely high appropriations for a period of seventeen years" (Ritter 1970, 2: 138). Perhaps most relevant in this connection was the stand taken by numerous university professors who strongly backed Germany's naval rearmament. Among the so-called fleet professors (Flottenprofessoren) were quite a few distinguished scholars, such as Lujo Brentano, Hans Delbrück, Otto Hintze, Hermann Oncken, Gustav Schmoller, Werner Sombart, and Max Weber (Herwig 1973, 7). Given their extraordinary prestige, the impact of their widely publicized support on the bourgeoisie can hardly be overestimated. In fact, national consensus about Germany's new role as a maritime power was clearly concentrated in the growing middle class, a phenomenon that by itself may be considered a novum. The militaristic wave sweeping the country around the turn of the century finally succeeded in co-opting the majority of the German liberals.

Interlaced with conspicuous strands of technical and organizational innovation, traditional structural elements were borrowed from the Prussian army to integrate the naval forces into the military establishment. The old disciplinary system was transferred unimpaired, not as it was in 1900 but as it had been before 1872, meaning that flogging continued to be used as a means of punishment (Herwig 1973, 66). Reflecting the structure of German society, the naval officer corps was rigidly stratified. The top rank was represented by the executive officers, the middle range was allotted to the naval engineer-officers, and the lowest rank was assigned to the deck officers.

Because they were overwhelmingly of bourgeois extraction, the executive officers were, by then-current standards, at a social disadvantage in comparison with army officers. To compensate for such "shortcomings," they sought equality with the military nobility by formal ennoblement and by adopting "the aristocratic way of life of the Prussian army officer corps, ranging from the issue of the duel to the practice of officer elections, in order to preserve the exclusiveness and homogeneity of the executive officer corps" (Herwig 1973, 69). Indeed, "feudalization" by ennoblement continued a tradition that had originated in the eighteenth century. At least twenty-two of the highest ranking naval officers were admitted to the aristocracy, and in 1913 the process of ennoblement by the kaiser was regulated to prevent admission of "undesirable" elements. Usually after completing active service, an executive officer was allowed to approach the crown for admission to the nobility. The entire cost (over four thousand marks) had to be borne by the applicant (Herwig 1973, 273–74).

The rigorous selection of naval cadets contributed to the desired exclusivity of the corps. Applicants from Social Democratic, trade unionist, or Jewish homes had no chance of being admitted to cadet school, and generally a lower-middle- or lower-class background was an almost insuperable barrier. The high cost of cadet training acted as a (plutocratic) criterion of selection that kept the underprivileged strata out of the contest (Herwig 1973, 54ff.).

The transfer to the navy of the time-honored prejudice against technical specialization must be regarded as part of the feudalization process. Professions that would have been perfectly respectable within the cultural milieu from which most executive officers came were felt to be "bourgeois" and therefore incompatible with the newly acquired status of the officers. Up to 1914, the executive officer corps consistently rejected "education and technical ability as *determinants* of military and social status" (Herwig 1973, 35).

The creation of a large, modern navy not only increased the complexity of the military establishment and military planning but also reflected the increasing differentiation of German political ambitions. An immensely attractive new focus of German militarism was added to the existing ones: British maritime power was to be challenged and eventually destroyed in a war that, according to the customary posture of militarism, was considered inevitable.

Liabilities of the Tradition

Germany's defeat in World War I suggests significant flaws in the customary interplay of tradition and innovation in the evolution of militarism. Although the past seemed to justify the expectation that all new forms could be grafted successfully on traditional structures, the fate of the German navy, for example, clearly belies such an assumption. Long before the new fleet could be tested in battle, the structural weaknesses of the officer corps had become rather noticeable. Actually, there was an untested element in the very hierarchy that had been introduced in the navy. While those sectors of the army involving technical specialization (artillery, engineering corps, and so on) constituted *separate* branches, they belonged to the *same* hierarchical structure in the navy. Informal prestige differentials attributed to diverse branches of the army became formal ranking criteria in the navy, and what might be considered a relatively minor irritant in the army generated widespread discontent in the navy. The men were confined to the narrow space of the naval vessels, and the social isolation of the executive officers in their own messes and their lack of social intercourse with the lower-ranking officers repeatedly called to mind an invidious distinction the engineer-officers refused to accept. Conscious of their vital function on board the modern warships, they strove for social parity with the executive officers, but they were equally concerned with keeping their distance from the deck officer corps (Herwig 1973, 132–33).

Nor were the deck officers satisfied with their ranking on the same level with the petty officers and ratings. They strove for recognition as a distinct officer category, but like those of the engineer-officers, their social ambitions were consistently thwarted by the high command.

The significance of these manifestations of nonconformity seems to be that they continued throughout the decade preceding the outbreak of World War I. The navy was then riding the crest of popular enthusiasm, support was virtually unlimited, and unconditional subordination, at least within the military establishment, was still taken for granted. Yet the persistent demands for structural changes the engineer-officers and deck officers presented cannot be reconciled with the principle of unquestioning obedience. These first cracks in the traditional authoritarian structure began to widen after 1914, when the hope for a short and victorious war had faded.

However, another factor added fuel to the smoldering fires of discontent. Contrary to the extravagant expectations of the nation, the role of the battle fleet during the war remained minimal. Far from challenging the British navy in daring strikes, the German fleet spent most of the war years in demoralizing idleness. From being the "darling of the nation," it became the butt of public ridicule and contempt (Herwig 1973, 196). No matter how many battleships the Germans built, the British built more, and their naval superiority remained unchanged. Any major strike against the British navy would have resulted in senseless defeat, perhaps annihilation, of the German naval forces.

At any rate, the prolonged inactivity of the battle fleet undermined the discipline of officers and ratings: It contributed to the mutinies of 1917 and 1918 when the crews of three or four battleships refused to sail against the British fleet (Herwig 1973, 257). In the fall of 1917, "the various groups within the naval hierarchy—executive officers, engineer-officers, deck officers, petty officers and ratings—established positions of 'splendid isolation' vis-à-vis one another. The fragmentation of the naval grades was complete, with each group suspicious of the other and looking for future opportunities to redress grievances" (Herwig 1973, 209).

The breakdown of the traditional authoritarian system began in the navy before it affected the army. Of course, other factors may have been involved in the gradual deterioration of the disciplinary system. Naval recruits often came from industrial cities, and throughout the years of service, they had frequent contact with the population of the port cities where the ships were stationed or overhauled. In other words, the crews were almost constantly exposed to "subversive" ideas and thus were disinclined to accept unquestioningly the rigors of traditional military discipline. Furthermore, the staffing of the large submarine fleet drained the navy of many capable, reliable men who were frequently replaced by recruits of politically "subversive" background (Herwig 1973, 201).

A full understanding of the structural weaknesses of the German navy seems to be possible only within the context of the military establishment as a whole. There is no question that in World War I Germany's naval policy turned out to be a military failure of "immense consequences" (Ritter 1970, 2: 150). In retrospect, the creation of the second largest battle fleet in the world bears the hallmarks of an almost fanatical manifestation of German militarism. Yet far from becoming an effective instrument of its imperialistic objectives, the navy proved unable to assume any initiative of consequence in the North Sea. It became a focus of disintegration and discouragement instead. One may also argue that German militarism would have been more effectively served if the enormous human and economic resources that went into the creation of a huge battle fleet had been available to the armies fighting a two-front war. What had been thought of as the crowning achievement of German military effort actually contributed to its downfall.

To cast some light on the almost unbelievable discrepancy between expectations and strategic realities, several factors have to be taken into account. First of all, experiences with modern naval warfare were very limited in 1914, and the Germans had none at all. The technology available for constructing armored, steam-driven battleships was in sharp contrast to the uncertainty about their military effectiveness. The range of the German fleet, particularly of the torpedo boats, depended on the availability of coaling stations, and the Germans had none outside their own territorial waters that could be relied on in the case of war (Ritter 1970, 2: 154–55). Thus, the German fleet proved unable to break the blockade that the British navy had set up in the English Channel and in North Scotland. The impossibility of engaging in long-distance action, added to the numerical superiority of the British navy, was a major determinant of inaction.

Second, the German naval complex had remained outside the sphere of the General Staff. On land, the war proceeded more or less according to long-established plans, but no such clear-cut strategy existed for the navy (Herwig 1973, 176). In other words, the military leadership proved incapable of integrating the navy effectively into the military complex.

Third, obsolete military traditions seem to have influenced the role assigned to the navy. The German fleet had been built "for swift decision at sea," and the idea of "a single, decisive naval battle in the North Sea" always remained at the back of German military thinking. In fact, after four years of inactivity, the navy "attempted in October an eleventh-hour, single-handed effort to alter the course of the war," to "gamble away, in one throw, the fleet so painstakingly created by Tirpitz ever since 1898" (Herwig 1973, 231).

It would seem that this idea of a naval strike—opposed by the more realistic admirals—was based on the traditional model of the "dash and dare" sort of military action in which a combination of surprise, swiftness, and personal bravery would inflict defeat even on superior enemy forces. In a sense, it was comparable to the traditional cavalry charge, reinterpreted in terms of naval warfare.

Fourth, the extravagant expectations associated with the development of the German navy were not counterbalanced by critical judgment. A combination of authoritarianism and nationalism prevented Germany from producing civilian experts on military strategy allowed to follow the example of the British specialists who often scrutinized official naval policy. "The absence of public discussion concerning military strategy and naval construction was inherent in the German constitution—Bismarck's most fateful legacy—which allowed the Kaiser virtually free hand in determining Germany's military and foreign policy" (Herwig 1973, 16).

The survival of nonadaptive elements of military tradition was by no means limited to the navy. Apparently, it was difficult to retire the image of the knight embodying, to the highest degree, the virtues of the traditional warrior. Nor is it surprising that the Junker nobility adhered to the idea of knighthood: The Knights of the Teutonic Order provided the glorified historical model. From its ranks came many families of the ancient Prussian aristocracy. When the Junker nobility was induced to assume military leadership in the seventeenth and early eighteenth centuries, the chivalry complex *(mutatis mutandis)* made a comeback. Since the image of the knight was inseparably associated with the horse, the lance, and the sword, it is hardly surprising that the cavalry became the main bearer of knightly traditions. Eventually, the cavalry came to be considered the most prestigious branch of the German armed forces, a position it maintained until World War I. Its officer corps, like that of the imperial guards, was open only to members of the nobility. Among the officers of these elite regiments of hussars and dragoons (light cavalry), of uhlans and cuirassiers (heavy cavalry), the faith in their own military value contrasted sharply with the low esteem in which they held the technically specialized branches of the armed forces. In 1914, the German army contained 110 cavalry regiments, a total of 55,000 men. Parading through the streets of many garrison towns, the colorful cavalry, preceded by blaring martial music, provided the theatrical ingredient of militarism, the significance of which should not be underestimated. In fact, the kaiser's well-known love of dashing military display emphasized the role of the cavalry, and the furious charges of "his" hussars and cuirassiers tended to convert the great annual military maneuvers into theatrical shows. In retrospect, it seems unreal that the mounted soldier armed with lance and saber should still be around in an age in which the battlefield was dominated by the machine gun and shrapnel.

In bygone times, the public display of military forces was intended to be pageantry *and* demonstration of martial power capabilities. In the Wilhelmian era, the cavalry parades and, as it turned out later, the glamorous naval reviews were designed to gain and maintain the popular support militarism thrives on. They also created an impressive appearance of military might that was only tenuously related to the actual capabilities of conducting war. Much military pageantry of those times actually widened the gap between expectations and reality regarding modern warfare.

Horse and sword characterized not only the cavalryman but also the whole officer corps, except those of the lowest ranks. Yet all, including sergeant-majors *(Feldwebel)*, went to war wearing the long, straight sword. The only concession to modernity was the automatic pistol these contemporary knights were allowed to carry.

A study of other aspects of the military system seems to indicate that the exclusiveness of the German officer corps became, during the Wilhelmian era, a crippling liability. As long as the nobility had little or no competition from other sectors of Prussian society, its exclusive control of the officer corps, associated with status privileges, could not have diminished the survival chances of Prussian militarism. Yet exclusiveness did not come about at once, nor was it a spontaneous initiative of the corps itself. It was at the insistence of King Frederick II that the officers began to refrain from social intercourse with members of the bourgeoisie *(Militärgeschichtliches Forschungsamt* 1964, 51). Just as the nobility had previously been enticed to assume the role of a military elite, so it was later coerced into the odious social isolation that eventually contributed to the disintegration of the Wilhelmian type of militarism. True enough, bourgeois officers had to be admitted in growing numbers, but there was considerable ambivalence among their aristocratic peers, many of whom assumed an attitude of distrust concerning the ideological reliability of their bourgeois confreres. In fact, there was a tendency among the most conservative officers to keep the army small in order to prevent bourgeois (and presumably liberal) officers from becoming more numerous (Kitchen 1968, 31).

Furthermore, virtually insurmountable barriers kept people of working class background out of the officer corps. Especially abhorrent to the military elite was the thought of ideological "contamination" by Socialists and Jews. The latter were believed to be physically unfit and politically unreliable. The dreaded specters of socialism and liberalism always loomed large in the mind of the military. By the time of the war of 1870–71, sixty Jewish officers still served in the Prussian army, but their sons were unable to secure commissions. By 1878, not a single Jewish officer was left, yet Christian sons of Jewish parents were allowed to join the officer corps. The fact that baptism was deemed appropriate to overcome the barrier erected by the military suggests that specific racial ingredients of an otherwise virulent anti-Semitism had not yet been fully developed. In World War I, however, Jewish officers were again accepted and found worthy to die for the fatherland that had previously rejected their services (Kitchen 1968, 38–47).

One has to admit that the deliberate exclusion of large sectors of German society from its most prestigious professional group was detrimental to the cause of militarism, as the events following World War I clearly indicate.

Why were elements of the German militaristic system allowed to become liabilities? One may argue that such changes from functional to dysfunctional, from adaptive to nonadaptive, are incompatible with what militarism is all about, namely, the tendency to maximize preparedness for war. For example, it would seem rather obvious that the cavalry did not stand a chance against rapid-fire weaponry, but before 1914 this was far from obvious to military experts. The question was raised, of course, but the perception of obsolescence (or lack thereof) was not the only problem. The question of why the cavalry outlasted its strategic usefulness is inseparable from the power position of the nobility, which monopolized its officer corps. Any project to abolish or transform the cavalry could not possibly have prevailed against the intransigent opposition of the most influential stratum of German society. And one could always point out that *all* the European armies had cavalry corps and that the nation should not relinquish a means of defense that was highly valued by its potential enemies.

In other words, far from being a model of rationality, the German militaristic system was a composite of contradictory elements, some of which clearly prevented the nation from maximizing the development of its military resources. The structural determinants of these liabilities meant that there was no way to avert their impact, short of a major transformation of German society. Structural changes indeed occurred with the revolution of 1918 and the assumption of power by the National Socialists in 1933. No traditional forces were allowed to interfere with the rearmament of National Socialist Germany, but the regime established by Adolf Hitler eventually became another military liability of catastrophic proportions, culminating in the most crushing defeat Germany ever suffered at the hands of its enemies.

The Rhetoric and the Reality of Belligerency

Among the many encomiasts of war the Wilhelmian era produced, none took a more radical position than Friedrich von Bernhardi. His book *Germany and the Next War*, published in 1913 and translated into several languages, left a profound impression on European political opinion. The sensation caused by the book was in part attributable to the fact that the author had formerly been a member of the German General Staff, although nothing indicates that he acted as a spokesman for that powerful organ of the military establishment.

Like so many of his contemporaries, Bernhardi wrote under the influence of social Darwinism, which uncritically transferred the concepts of "struggle for survival" and "survival of the fittest" to human societies. Struggle for survival, Bernhardi proposed, is simply the "universal law of nature," and struggle acts as a creative force since it eliminates the unfit. Human societies have the right and duty of self-assertion, which implies more than "mere repulse of hostile attacks." Self-assertion implies conquest, and "the right of conquest is universally acknowledged" (Bernhardi 1913, 19–21). "Might is at once the supreme right, and the dispute as to what is right is decided by the arbitrament of war. War gives a biologically just decision, since its decisions rest on the very nature of things" (Bernhardi 1913, 23).

Paraphrasing rather familiar thoughts, Bernhardi asserted that long periods of peace have "stunting" effects upon the citizenry while petty personal interests and selfishness prevail, and luxury and money acquire an "unnecessary and unjustifiable power." Though accompanied by "material and mental distress," war "evokes the noblest activities in the human nature." Even "defeat may bear a rich harvest" because it leads to "healthy revival" (Bernhardi 1913, 26–28).

Since, according to Bernhardi, peace leads to "degeneration," efforts intended to abolish war are branded as "foolish," "absolutely immoral," and "unworthy of the human race." Also, those who think that war should be postponed as long as possible "do an immense disservice to their country, because under certain circumstances it becomes the duty of the statesman to bring about war." Like Frederick the Great, a statesman must assume the role of the aggressor to prevent the enemy from developing his war potential. "Wars that have been provoked by farseeing statesmen have had the happiest results" (Bernhardi 1913, 35, 45).

Reflecting ideas expressed before, Bernhardi believed that acts of the state cannot be judged by the standards of individual morality. No moral duty ranks higher than that of increasing the power of the state. Often the "threat of war" suffices to achieve political objectives, yet the decision to wage war is not always a matter of comparing cost with possible benefits. In certain cases, war must be engaged in simply as a point of honor "whether there is a prospect of success or not," for it is preferable "to die sword in hand than to conclude a degrading peace" (Bernhardi 1913, 45–52).

Like many German militarists before and after him, Bernhardi was in favor of "crushing French power once and for all," although he regarded Great Britain as Germany's "archenemy." In accordance with militaristic doctrine, he suggested that international treaties should be respected only insofar as they coincide with national self-interest. Germany, so he urged, should make a supreme effort to strike at any moment (Ritter 1970, 2: 115).

If national self-interest makes war necessary, one could argue, its avoidance is equally dictated by national self-interest. Not even the most intransigent militarist could deny that war constitutes the highest possible risk a society may assume. When a country is under the threat of actual or alleged aggression, war is believed to be a means of national survival, but at the same time it gravely imperils the survival it is supposed to secure. Actually, we are dealing here with a built-in antinomy that characterizes the use of violence whether organized or not. However, the concept of survival calls for further clarification. There was a time when the biological existence of a society was not really imperiled by war. As high as the casualty rates may have been, even prolonged and extensive fighting did not result in the total extermination of either one of the warring foes. As long as war was limited in scope and scale, the risk was perceived as commensurate with conceivable gains in terms of territorial conquest, population increase, or economic resources. Not to survive then meant to be conquered, partitioned, enslaved, or otherwise to lose political sovereignty or cultural identity. Only in the present century has annihilation of the enemy rather than mere defeat of its military forces become not only technologically feasible but strategically acceptable. With the advent of atomic warfare, the mutual extermination of warring nations has indeed become possible.

To be sure, much highly destructive weaponry had already become available prior to World War I. In fact, the flowering of German militarism coincided with an unprecedented technicalization of warfare. It is not surprising that the growth of military might and the rhetoric of belligerency fed on each other. Not even the cataclysmic experience of World War I and the development of air forces, armor, and chemical warfare put an end to the fantasies of social Darwinism. In the 1930s, for example, Major E. Suchsland suggested that bombing raids on cities favored the survival of the fittest because the bombs would kill more poor people in the most densely settled districts. Since poverty was, in the major's opinion, an indication of "racial inferiority," the bombs would eliminate the least desirable (Vagts 1959, 447).

Before World War I, the political reality was in marked contrast to the rhetoric of belligerency. Although the notion of preventive war against presumptive enemies enjoyed considerable popularity among the militarists, Germany refrained from translating it into action. Russia's crushing defeat in the war against Japan, combined with subsequent revolutionary attempts to change the czarist regime (1904–1905), reduced the country's military capabilities to such an extent that it would have been unable to defend itself effectively against a powerful enemy or to assist its Western allies in case of war. The situation offered a unique opportunity for Germany to break the dreaded "encirclement" and to remove the specter of a two-front war for years to come. But Germany did not take advantage of the situation. Oddly enough, for all its militaristic exaltation it enjoyed one of the longest periods of peace in its history.

The high value attached to war and the actual avoidance of war seem less paradoxical if one takes into account the nature of the arms race and the complexity of the society that had to be mobilized to support the use of massive violence. The risk involved in waging war was such that the powerholders of the German state could not afford to rush headlong into battle without exploring possible alternatives. The German General Staff was not a band of swashbucklers and fanatics. The prevailing patterns of training had transformed most staff officers into what Janowitz has called "military managers," who were increasingly concerned with the "scientific and rational conduct of war" (Janowitz 1968, 23). Their planning of future campaigns was intended to minimize risks, such as the risks of a two-front war. It proved to be a never-ending task, because existing plans had to be continuously readjusted to a changing technology and to the development of the military capabilities of presumptive enemies. This proved extremely frustrating, because of the way innovations spread through international trade channels irrespective of political considerations.

The point here is that the mechanism of diffusion of military technology never ceased to impose restraints on belligerency. It was the perception of enemy strength that prevented the warmongers from gaining the upper hand. Germany's attempt to strengthen its own position by concluding the Triple Alliance with Austria and Italy (1882) was neutralized by the Triple Entente including France, Great Britain, and Russia. The alliance of three presumptive enemies seemed to convert the threat of political and military encirclement of Germany into a dreadful reality, which suggested further restraints in warlike intentions—at least until the implicit threat could be met by additional military strength.

As a rule, militaristic societies are unlikely to accommodate differences by compromise. When Great Britain approached Germany with the intention of reducing the naval arms race, she was rebuffed by Kaiser William on the grounds that such an attempt was an insolent invasion of his sovereign rights (Ritter 1970, 2: 162–63). Although compromise was felt to be "humiliating weakness," negotiations did take place, and the fact that they did suggests internal opposition to the German naval office and its many supporters. In Great Britain and in Germany, voices were heard demanding an Anglo-German detente. Negotiations were conducted between 1910 and 1912, but in the end Germany refused to change its naval policy and Great Britain remained adamant in its resolve to maintain its maritime superiority (Ritter 1970, 2: 162–63, 168ff.).

Although unsuccessful in the long run, opposition to unrestrained belligerency probably delayed the outbreak of major conflicts for several decades. Ambivalence toward war derived, to a considerable extent, from the fact that the German military establishment was not a monolith. Janowitz's somewhat rough division of the officer corps into "heroic leaders who embody traditionalism and glory" and the "military managers" trained to conduct war in a "scientific and rational" fashion certainly applies to the German officer corps prior to World War I (Janowitz 1968, 231), but there are many indications that the managerial type was still in its incipient phase, striving to reconcile the behavioral concomitants of technicalization with traditionalism.

In spite of growing international tensions and antagonisms, the fissures within the German military establishment remained. In 1906, the war minister rejected the chancellor's plan to modernize the armed forces. The war minister's worries concerned an altogether different matter. He repeatedly complained about the scarcity of "suitable" officer candidates, meaning candidates of noble extraction who could be relied on to remain stalwart supporters of the throne. "What would become of the aristocratic traditions of the officers' corps if it took large numbers from the lower middle class? What would become of the unshakable noncom loyalty if working-class youths from a socialist milieu rose to noncommissioned rank side by side with the peasant sons from Brandenburg and Pomerania, who formed the hard core of the army?" (Ritter 1970, 2: 211). The tendency to apply socially selective criteria to recruitment procedures thus acted as a restraining force on the full use of the human resources a large-scale war seemed to require.

Whatever the significance of such restraints may have been, they were counterbalanced by the prevalence of the "heroic leader" type among the German officers. The persistence of the traditional warrior image was genetically related to the dominant role the nobility was allowed to play in the filling of commanding military positions. Since first called on to serve in the army, the Prussian nobility had considered themselves members of a land-holding aristocracy. Their cultural identity developed into an ideological bulwark of political conservatism, which predisposed them against the technological and social changes of the industrial revolution. Class prejudices prevented them from fully grasping the role industry was performing in the evolution of warcraft. One may assume that the "military managers" of the General Staff were sufficiently well informed to realize that the war of the future would be quite unlike any war of the past. On the whole, however, the German military, like their counterparts in other European countries, "failed to attain a competent understanding of the potentialities inherent in the forces they represented." Sufficiently diffused knowledge of the technical realities might have curbed belligerency, but as it happened, World War I began on the assumptions that it would last two or three months and that about three battles with three hundred shells per gun would decide its outcome (Vagts 1959, 344, 365–66).

The circumstances attending Germany's entrance into World War I somewhat reflected the inconsistencies that had marked its militarism since the days of Bismarck. It has often been said that the assassination of the successor to the Austrian throne in Serbia on June 28, 1914, "triggered" World War I. The word *trigger* suggests mechanical and immediate effects, but it took the Austrian government a month to declare war on Serbia. In spite of the "elemental outburst of passions" in the streets of many Austrian and German cities where the masses clamored for revenge and nothing less than a punitive war against Serbia, the great powers refrained from rushing into a war, the virtues of which the ideologists of militarism had been extolling for so long. Austria's bellig-erency and the threat of Russian intervention led to a bewildering sequence of diplomatic initiatives intended to temporize, to settle the conflict by mediation or, at least, to prevent it from becoming a general conflagration. It seems a herculean task to find one's way through the maze of messages, demarches, telegrams, declarations, rumors, as-sumptions, and misunderstandings that preceded the actual outbreak of hostilities (see, for example, Albertini 1957, Chapters 1, 2, and 4). There seems to be no suggestion of insincerity in the attempts at mediation, but while monarchs and ministers endeavored to save the peace, one nation after another proceeded to mobilize its armies.

If an exceptionally difficult decision, such as the declaration of war against an alliance of powerful adversaries, depends as it did in Ger-many on the judgment of a single ruler and his immediate advisers, the leadership qualities of those men suddenly become crucially important. Clearly, the situation put a tremendous burden on the kaiser, his chan-cellor, and the chief of staff, and none of them measured up to the task. Unstable and impetuous, the monarch wavered between "wrathful out-bursts," temporizing, euphoria, and apprehension. His telegram to the Austrian emperor proclaiming his willingness to start war against Russia and France "at once" singularly contrasted with the "immense relief, indeed something close to enthusiasm" with which he and his chancel-lor received the British premier's offer to "save the peace of Europe at the last hour" by seeking French neutrality (Ritter 1970, 2: 264, 268).

In spite of his bellicose moods, the kaiser was reluctant to sign the mobilization order. His relationship with Chancellor Bethmann-Hollweg was not one of complete confidence. At times, neither one was fully informed about what the other was doing. In fact, the monarch failed to maintain the close contact with his immediate advisers the situation seemed to require. In his dealings with the military and the Austrian government, the chancellor proved "faint-hearted, irresolute and be-wildered" (Albertini 1957, 5). While the chief of staff insisted on mobi-lization, Bethmann-Hollweg temporized, but in the end he lost control to the generals (Albertini 1957, 5, 12, 14). Perceiving the situation in purely military terms, Moltke, the chief of staff, demanded immediate mobilization. "If we linger over mobilization, our military position will become every day more unfavorable and may have the most disastrous consequences for us, should our probable adversaries go on making their preparations unmolested" (Albertini 1957, 25). Usurping the powers of the chancellor (to use Albertini's words), Moltke encouraged Austria to mobilize and declare war on Serbia, as indeed it did on July 28, 1914. The following day, the czar, at the insistence of the military, reluctantly decreed the mobilization of twelve army corps to be deployed against Austria and Germany. And finally succumbing to the pressures of his generals, the kaiser declared war on Russia six days earlier than Austria, for whose sake Germany entered the conflict in the first place. It was, of course, not by chance that Austria and Russia were the first nations to mobilize their armies, for they saw the war as a unique chance to shore up their credibility as great powers vis-à-vis the Balkan nations. In addition, Conrad von Hötzendorf, the Austrian chief of staff, harbored the peculiar belief, supported by Moltke, that participation in a European war was the last recourse to preserve the integrity of the Austrian Empire. Under the pressure of the leading German, Austrian, and Russian generals, all militarists to the hilt, the existing system of alliances, created primarily to discourage aggression and thus to avert war, began to propel one nation after another into a major conflagration.

Although bound by the stipulations of the Triple Entente, France and Britain were in no hurry to declare war on Germany, and Germany in turn, squeamish about being branded as an aggressor, hesitated to carry out the long-standing plan to invade neutral Belgium in order to gain strategic advantages over the French forces. Finally, on the ground of dubious and unreliably reported "border incidents," the German General Staff assumed that a *de facto* state of war justified the invasion of Belgium and a formal declaration of war on France. In view of the invasion of Belgium and France, Britain entered the conflict without knowing what kind of war it would have to fight (Albertini 1957, 502).

In the many and often confused attempts to accommodate the spreading conflict, the ultimatum played a rather conspicuous role. Divested of its diplomatic trappings, the ultimatum may be defined as "a patterned attempt to extort, by threat of war, certain concessions from an antagonistic nation." Whether preceded by fruitless negotiations or not, it may induce a weak adversary to surrender. If addressed to a powerful opponent, however, the ultimatum is bound to be rejected and both nations feel "honor-bound" to fight. Often enough the terms of an ultimatum are such that acceptance would imply intolerable humiliation and loss of international status. This was certainly the case with Germany's ultimata to Russia and France. The German government demanded no less than the temporary occupation of the fortresses of Toul and Verdun as guaranty of French neutrality (Albertini 1957, 40–41)!

To the extent that the ultimatum, implicitly or explicitly, threatens the use of violence, it obviously plays into the hands of the militarists. In contrast with undisguised aggression, however, the ultimatum proclaims the willingness of the aggressor to forgo war if the adversary yields to the demands of the proposal. The German leaders understood the unacceptability of their demands, but apparently they hoped to shift the responsibility for the imminent war to their adversaries.

"The German people went into the First World War with a clear conscience convinced that a multitude of enemies all about were swarming over them without warning" (Ritter 1970, 2: 275). The "clear conscience" of the German people is understandable only in terms of a cultural hermetism that effectively excluded all doubts and uncertainties. Indeed, it was successful to the point of providing ideological elements designed to rationalize the defeat of 1918 and to prepare the ground for the revival of militarism under Adolf Hitler.

The Impact of World War I on the Traditional Political Structure

World War I subjected Germany's political structure to a crucial test. Created by Bismarck, that structure was based "on the personal authority of a popular monarch and his successful Chancellor" (Ritter 1972, 3: 447). The monarch was expected to assume two simultaneous and potentially conflicting roles: He was the supreme military commander and the chief executive. It must be admitted that an adequate performance of these two roles required unusual capabilities, particularly in times of war that put the very survival of the nation in jeopardy. Indisputably, the emperor's personality did not measure up to such a difficult task. As "Supreme Warlord," he lacked the professional expertise and the moral stamina of a top commander. "Rather helpless in the face of great challenge—a task indeed to daunt anyone—of maintaining a sound balance between military and political authority," the emperor gradually faded into the background, virtually withdrawing from the leadership that tradition and constitution had assigned to him. The integrative function the monarchy had performed since the inception of the Prussian state thus came to an unexpected end. In other words, the unifying power of the monarchy failed at a time when it should have reached the highest possible level. No political leader or institution was prepared or allowed to cope with the problems of the power vacuum created by the emperor's withdrawal. Irresolute and passive, the *Reichstag* never seriously endeavored to gain control over the conduct of the war. Thus, everything was left to the military, who proceeded to fill the power vacuum by default rather than by design. This happened at a time when victory on the western front seemed rather remote and the German people experienced increasingly severe food shortages because of the Allied blockade. Two years of military stalemate generated growing war-weariness, demands for democratization of the regime, and ominous revolutionary rumbles on the radical left. An extraordinary concerted effort seemed necessary to gear the nation to the needs of the war, and to accomplish this, Paul von Hindenburg and Erich Ludendorff, the victorious generals of 1914, were appointed to head the High Command. Of the two, Ludendorff was the more aggressive, and he immediately made demands on a weak government. Of course, his bold attempt to establish the ascendancy of the military over the civilian authorities counted on the unconditional support of the conservatives and the German bourgeoisie in general. Without violence or threat of violence, without taking over the office of the chancellor or any other top position in the government, Ludendorff succeeded in launching a *de facto* military regime that tightened the authoritarian grip on German society (Bracher 1960, 12–13).

As staunch conservatives, Hindenburg and Ludendorff did not think of themselves as bound by constitutional restrictions, yet nothing was farther from their way of thinking than the idea of subverting the established political order. Their ideological position was clearly expressed in a letter Hindenburg addressed to Chancellor Hertling, almost at the close of the war: "Because of our position, which has developed without our conscious efforts, we feel responsible to the German people, to history, and to our own consciences, for the form of the peace settlement" (Kitchen 1976, 47).

The last hurdle in the way of a military regime was Chancellor Bethmann-Hollweg, who tried to conciliate the demands of Ludendorff and the High Command with those of the opposition. To Ludendorff and his supporters, the quest for political reform in the midst of a war was tantamount to high treason. They were incapable of discerning the proposed democratization of Prussian electoral law, for example, as a way of achieving the kind of political consensus that rigid resistance to change could never attain. Bethmann-Hollweg had to go, and with him the last chance to reconcile conflicting political ideologies that were rapidly becoming irreconcilable. In fact, Ludendorff forced the dismissal of the chancellor "in whom William II only a few days earlier had expressed absolute trust" (Ritter 1972, 3: 457; 1973, 4: 120).

Ludendorff's approach to political control was openly criticized as a *military dictatorship* by some members of the *Reichstag*. The term has since been used sporadically by various analysts of German military leadership during World War I. Unless one wishes to use the term *dictatorship* in a rather loose sense, its suitability in this case seems questionable.

First of all, has a dictatorship ever been known to put up with a parliament and political parties unless they can be forced to pledge unconditional support to the dictatorial regime? Most of the time Ludendorff ignored the *Reichstag*, but he did not have the power to silence an often vociferous opposition, the most radical wing of which openly advocated a Socialist revolution. In 1918, the Spartacus group (later the German Communist Party) "distributed leaflets and posters calling for mass strikes as a weapon of revolutionary rebellion, to prevent the great western offensive and creating a 'German People's Republic' on the Russian model" (Ritter 1973, 4: 124).

Political compromise with the opposition cannot possibly be regarded as a hallmark of dictatorship. What Ludendorff and the High Command wanted was "total" war by increasingly harnessing German society to military imperatives. The lengthy negotiations preceding the enactment of the Patriotic Auxiliary Act (December 5, 1916) would have been unthinkable under a dictatorship. Total mobilization of the population for economic purposes, as intended by Ludendorff, was opposed by labor unions and the liberal bourgeoisie. Eventually, a compromise version was accepted with 235 votes against 14, which made all male Germans aged seventeen to sixty-one, who were not serving in the armed forces, liable to "patriotic auxiliary service" (Ritter 1972, 3: 356). More likely than not, a dictator would have imposed his own version of such an act without concessions to his opponents.

Ludendorff forced important decisions on the emperor by threatening to resign, but as soon as rumors of his impending resignation were allowed to seep into the media, "there was an instant furor in nationalistic circles and a flood of telegrams implored the Kaiser not to dismiss Ludendorff the hero" (Ritter 1973, 4: 95). Making continuance in office depend on the will of a superior authority, with or without the supportive intervention of a multitude of hero worshipers, sharply contrasts with the ways a dictator tends to secure his position. In fact, no submission or deference, however reluctant, to superior authority seems compatible with genuine dictatorship. Ludendorff's usurpation of power remained incomplete. The institutional structure of the imperial government, of Prussia, and of the other states was not changed by the military. Unlike what happened in most dictatorships, Ludendorff and his fellow generals did not usurp political or administrative positions alien to military affairs. Furthermore, the *de facto* transfer of power to the High Command did not imply a violation of the German constitution. Article 68 of the *Reichsverfassung* entitled the emperor to declare a "state of war" if the public safety of any federal territory was imperiled. In such cases, the Prussian law on the "state of siege" was to be applied, which gave executive power to the military commanders and made them almost independent of the civil government and the legislative bodies (Kitchen 1976,

50). Under the state of siege, most civil liberties could be suspended, but the authority to decide which rights were to be suspended had been bestowed on the individual commanders by a formal declaration of the emperor at the beginning of the war. The only permissible appeal had to be directed to the emperor himself. The "Supreme Warlord" never concerned himself with coordinating the actions of the individual commanders, who were thus allowed to build their own fiefdoms, virtually without any control at all (Kitchen 1976, 52, 54). Although the constitutional norms regarding the state of war and the state of siege were open to different interpretations, the ascendancy of the military over the civilian authorities was clearly established.

Yet Ludendorff and his cohorts in the High Command were not known for leaning on constitutional sanctions to exercise the authority deemed necessary to attain the objectives they had in mind. They were able to mobilize ample support among the most powerful sectors of German society. Their closest and most influential allies were Germany's industrialists, particularly the ones that produced weapons, ammunition, and equipment indispensable to the conduct of the war. As pointed out earlier, the industrial and financial elite of Wilhelmian Germany had fully committed itself to a program of imperialistic expansion in Europe and overseas. Their role went far beyond that of mere profiteers; they fancied themselves heirs of the British Empire, and as such they demanded everything possible to "knock Britain out of the war" (Kitchen 1976, 114). Their alliance with the military resulted in plans for total mobilization and militarization of the economy. In 1915, the idea of an "Economic General Staff" was debated without concrete results, but as the war went on and a considerable increase in industrial output became a vital priority, Ludendorff agreed with the leading industrialists that if such objectives were to be attained labor productivity would have to be drastically increased. One might have expected some kind of rational plan to determine the real needs of industry, yet no such project ever materialized. Nevertheless, Ludendorff and the High Command, incapable of visualizing a solution except in militaristic terms, intended to impose strict discipline on labor by reducing the free movement of workers, by increasing working hours, and by employing women and children. The assumption was that maximum interference with the economic process would ensure the desired maximum output of war materials (Kitchen 1976, 68–75). Much of what the generals and industrialists intended to do was inevitably perceived as exploitation by the Marxist sector of the working class.

Political opposition was strong enough to thwart, to some extent, Ludendorff and the industrialists, who eventually accepted the toned-down version of the Patriotic Auxiliary Act. Although a compromise solution, it was still essentially a repressive law that reduced the workers' freedom of movement and greatly strengthened the relative position of the industrialists (Kitchen 1976, 78).

The regimentation of labor was not limited to German workers. In areas under military control, French workers were forcibly recruited and used, with considerable ruthlessness, for a variety of purposes related to the logistics of the war. The idea of "opening up the great reservoir of manpower" in occupied Belgium met the enthusiastic support of German industrialists. Since attempts at voluntary enlistment had been rather unsuccessful, forcible recruitment was debated and eventually authorized. In violation of international law, the deportation of Belgian workers began in October 1916. In many places, it was carried out "with great brutality," conveying the impression of "regular slave transports." Early in 1917, about 61,000 Belgians had been removed to Germany, and many for whom no jobs could be found were forced to remain in camps. Eventually, the failure of the whole project became so obvious that it had to be abandoned (Ritter 1972, 3: 361–69).

Strictly in accord with the patterns of militarism, Ludendorff responded to a wave of strikes in key industries by imposing an "emergency state of siege" and the threat of court martial. Certain industrial plants were "militarized," that is, the workers were drafted into the army and coerced to resume work under military supervision (Ritter 1972, 3: 125). Increasingly concerned about the diffusion of Marxist ideology, Ludendorff imposed censorship on the armed forces and insisted that "patriotic indoctrination" be carried out by specially appointed propaganda officers (Kitchen 1976, 59). Demanding unconditional support of the nation's effort to win the war, Ludendorff branded any deviation from the established course of action as treason. A peace initiative of the *Reichstag* was called "shameful," and the legislators in favor of the proposal were decried as "traitors" (Ritter 1973, 4: 16).

The fact that political suppression did not assume more violent forms during World War I may be attributed to the peculiarities of the power structure. Neither Ludendorff individually nor the High Command collectively commanded the political support necessary to crush the opposition by applying the sort of violence that was to become standard procedure under Hitler. In spite of their rigid authoritarianism, the German generals lived by a code of honor that precluded terror, torture, and assassination as tools of political suppression.

A sample of German imperialism may be seen in the Treaty of Brest-Litovsk with defeated Russia. Signed in March 1918, at a time when victory over the western Allies was hardly more than a forlorn hope, it signified a clear triumph of the German High Command, already reflecting the state of alienation from political realities that characterized the last few months of the war. In addition to one million square kilometers of territory and fifty million inhabitants, Russia was to lose 90 percent of its coal mines, 54 percent of its industry, 33 percent of its railway system, 32 percent of its agricultural land, and most, if not all, of its sugar beet, cotton, and oil production (Kitchen 1976, 183). The Treaty of Brest-Litovsk was a convincing demonstration of what the defeat of Germany's enemies would entail. It sent shock waves through the Western world and certainly reinforced the resolution of the Allies to persist in their effort to win the war.

Ludendorff's relentless pursuit of military victory was combined with an almost total lack of political skills. His ideology moved within the narrow confines of three concepts: leadership, obedience, and nationalistic indoctrination foreshadowing, as it were, some tenets of the yet unborn Nazi ideology. Like his associates in the High Command, Ludendorff rigidly opposed democratization and thus, implicitly, any reform program that might have relieved some of the tensions characterizing the German political system, particularly since 1916.

A realistic appraisal of the military situation, two years after the war had broken out, would have raised some doubts about the chances of Germany's winning the war. A more balanced political leader might have considered the advisability of a negotiated peace before escalating the conflict. Not so Ludendorff. When he declared unrestricted submarine warfare, the United States entered the conflict, thus further reducing the chances for a German victory. Undeterred by a steadily deteriorating military situation and civilian morale, Ludendorff and his cohorts, strangely dissociated from reality, formulated grandiose plans of annexation of territories, east and west. They relentlessly pursued the idea of total war until the Allies crushed the last military offensive of the German armies in France in the summer of 1918.

Not unlike their military leaders, the German people refused to face reality. "Misled by an unending sequence of victory reports, unshaken—at least so far as the middle class was concerned—in their national pride and confidence, [they] stubbornly refused to entertain the idea that a war waged at such sacrifice, with such heroism, and with so many battlefield triumphs could end in defeat" (Ritter 1973, 4: 235). Although the war did end in defeat, the myth of Germany's invincibility persisted, as we shall see.

When Germany's military position on the western front had clearly become untenable, Ludendorff suddenly reversed his stand, demanding not only the opening of peace negotiations but also the immediate democratization of the regime. In a stormy session with the emperor, Ludendorff "demanded in extremely brusque tones to be relieved" of his functions (Ritter 1973, 4: 367). The general's resignation suggests that he had usurped power, "because in the widespread confusion since 1916 no other power group, no constructive political principle could possibly have prevailed in a responsible fashion" (Bracher 1960, 13).

Ludendorff's reversal did not convince either the Allies or his internal adversaries. Within days, the western front collapsed, and no individual leader, no party, group, or institution seemed capable of stemming the tide of the Socialist revolution in Germany. But neither the fall of Ludendorff nor the revolution ended the political role of the military. The failure of the emperor to assert his constitutional authority precipitated the assumption of power by the generals. The failure of the victorious revolutionaries to carry through a military reform allowed an unreconstructed General Staff to remain in power, thus setting the stage for the political role the military were to assume in the Weimar Republic.

The concept of total war was probably Ludendorff's most significant legacy, particularly in view of the strength it was allowed to gain in Hitler's Germany. The concept was not new, of course. Clausewitz and some of his predecessors had advocated the *Vernichtungskrieg* (war of extermination), and Moltke pursued it by proposing to carry the war against France to the point of complete annihilation of French resources. To accomplish this, Moltke admonished, the "war machine must maintain complete independence of action in regard to the political leadership" (Ritter 1969, 1: 195).

Thus, total war was a concept that applied almost exclusively to the enemy. Ludendorff, however, saw it as a process of harnessing all the nation's resources to gain victory. Since technological developments had extended warfare from the front lines to the whole national territory and to the entire population of the belligerent nations, a far-reaching adaptation of the economic system to the exigencies of war appeared inescapable. But total participation of the population in the war required specific skills to keep morale high at home and to undermine it among the enemy. Thus, psychological warfare became important to Ludendorff. He recognized the need for the strongest possible form of social cohesion to maximize the nation's war effort. Mere drill and external discipline were not enough to sustain morale. Ludendorff believed that certain forms of religion might provide the degree of social solidarity necessary to win a war. In his opinion, Japanese Shintoism was the most effective agent of social integration.

Ludendorff thought it necessary that all authority be turned over to a single supreme commander. There was no place for civilian statesmen in the conduct of total war, yet unlike the Nazi doctrine of total war, Ludendorff's conception lacked any ideological content (Speier 1952, 285). However, he espoused the National Socialist doctrine and played a leading role in the early days of the Nazi movement. He participated in Hitler's failed attempt to seize power, and with Hitler he stood trial in Munich. Although Ludendorff greatly contributed to the preservation of Germany's militaristic tradition, he changed his mind about the *Führer*. When President Hindenburg appointed Hitler chancellor of the Reich, Ludendorff addressed the following letter to his former comrade in arms: "By appointing Hitler chancellor of the Reich you have surrendered our sacred German fatherland to one of the greatest demagogues of all times. I solemnly prophesie to you that this wretched man will plunge our Reich into the abyss and bring unspeakable misery to our nation. Further generations will curse you in your grave for this act" (Deuerlein 1968, 418).

6

From Disorganization to Restoration

The Aborted Revolution and the Survival of Militarism

Viewed in evolutionary perspective, German militarism underwent its most radical change in the wake of World War I and the revolution of 1918. With the abolition of the monarchy, the Junker nobility and the officer corps suddenly found themselves deprived of their main source of power. The traditional triple alliance of monarchy, nobility, and officer corps had disintegrated, and for the first time since its inception, the survival of German militarism seemed doubtful.

The impact of this structural breakdown was reinforced by the political pressure of antimilitaristic groups and the severe restrictions imposed by the Treaty of Versailles, which had reduced the German military complex to a fraction of what it had been before 1918. Thus, the end of an agelong tradition seemed imminent. Yet German militarism did not succumb to its internal and external foes. A unique concatenation of circumstances contributed to its survival, even though at the expense of traditional elements often judged to be inseparable from its very essence.

What saved militarism from oblivion was the reaction of German society to the defeat of 1918 and the establishment of a republican regime. It was the reaction of a thoroughly militarized society that endeavored to solve its internal conflicts by using organized violence as a matter of course. There certainly was no explicit intent to salvage militarism. The idea was not popular at all, but the underlying pattern of conflict solution persisted and came to the fore in ideology and action.

As pointed out before, the republican powerholders lacked the revolutionary élan to carry through the radical changes that, according to Marxist precepts, would have overturned the traditional class structure and destroyed the foundations of militarism. Actually, many sectors of German society remained almost untouched by the revolution. The bureaucracy, the judiciary, the police forces, and the educational system successfully resisted changes. Civil servants, particularly those in key positions, judges, police officers, and secondary school teachers had been carefully selected during previous decades for their political conservatism and loyalty to the monarchy. By refusing to replace them with persons expected to be loyal to the new regime, President Ebert decisively contributed to the eventual downfall of the Weimar Republic. It has been suggested that ingrained reverence for knowledge, experience, and professional expertise prevented the republican government from enacting the structural changes necessary to consolidate its own position (Carsten 1972, 45–46). Far from supporting the new state, its own servants made little effort to disguise their contempt for the new leaders, whom they either ridiculed as parvenues or denigrated as "Bolsheviks and traitors." Their strong emotional ties to the older order were shared by millions of Germans. Although the monarchy had been abolished, the belief in the superiority of the monarchical regime continued to be widespread, most notably in eastern Germany. The myth of the invincibility of the army was maintained by interpreting Germany's defeat in World War I as a "stab in the back," as a treacherous subversion of the traditional order by the Socialists and the founders of the republic (Fried 1942, 37). The new state generated more hatred and contempt than support, at least among the middle and upper classes. The Republic of Weimar was held responsible for the military surrender, for the "disgraceful" peace treaty, and for a monetary inflation that wiped out large sectors of the German bourgeoisie.

One major weakness of the Weimar regime may be seen in the deep split within the Social Democratic Party, whose radical wing (later the Communist Party) intended to erect a Marxist state by revolutionary means if necessary. To avert the danger of subversion by violence, the government depended on the army (*Reichswehr*), whose leaders were known to oppose the republic. Their public utterances left little doubt about their strong feelings against the armistice and peace treaty, particularly against a government that had "dishonored" the nation by signing those documents (Carsten 1966, 62). Hans von Seeckt, the supreme commander of the new army, thought it was impossible to collaborate with the Social Democratic Party because it "repudiated the idea of *Wehrhaftigkeit* (military preparedness)" (Carsten 1966, 117).

The vulnerability of the new state did not lie in the lack of consensus alone. The constitution itself, expected to inaugurate for the first time in history a democratic regime in Germany, contained elements that lent themselves to undermining the very foundations of the regime it was supposed to protect. Traditional patterns of political organization proved to have a firm hold on the architects of the first republican charter in German history. There was a rather strong aversion to bestowing supreme legislative power upon an inexperienced and internally divided parliament. The recognized need for a strong head of state instead may be regarded as a survival of the monarchic tradition. Even a representative democracy apparently could not do without an *Ersatzkaiser* (emperor substitute), though legitimated by popular vote. And Article 48 of the Weimar constitution vested almost dictatorial powers in the president of the republic whenever serious threats to the maintenance of law and order seemed to warrant the use of such "emergency" powers (Bracher 1960, 47–48, 52). The use and abuse of Article 48 played a crucial role in the final phase of the Weimar Republic, providing a transition from representative democracy to the dictatorship of Adolf Hitler.

From the very beginning, the Weimar Republic had to fight for its survival. In December 1918, a division of the People's Army rebelled against the government, and in January 1919, a radical Socialist faction attempted to seize power by violence. The army, in combination with irregular units of the extreme right (Free Corps), rescued the regime after heavy fighting (Görlitz 1950, 303). Following the suppression of insurgency, the two most outstanding Socialist leaders, Karl Liebknecht and Rosa Luxemburg, were assassinated while "trying to escape." Of course, the armed forces were prompted by hatred of the "Bolsheviks" rather than by loyalty to the established government. At any rate, to satisfy the demand for "order" and "discipline"—high-ranking priorities in the traditional value system—President Ebert appointed Gustav Noske, a Socialist member of the federal parliament, as chief of army affairs. Known for his "toughness," Noske was willing to play the role of "bloodhound" to reestablish discipline, and he and the Prussian minister of war, a member of the General Staff of the imperial army, became the "fathers" of the *Reichswehr* (Görlitz 1950, 303). Conspiracies and actual insurgencies among radical factions of the left and right prolonged the dilemma of the republican government for several years, and the need to compromise prevented it from imposing effective control upon two parallel developments, namely, the organization of a new army, limited to one hundred thousand men by the peace treaty, and the formation of the so-called Free Corps, irregular troops recruited by ex-officers among the demobilized soldiery.

The army itself had managed to salvage its leadership tradition by transferring, during World War I, many regular officers to staff duty. The power of the military was such that this surviving nucleus could be used to build the *Truppenamt*, actually a disguise of the old General Staff, forbidden by the Treaty of Versailles. This was done without giving any consideration at all to the political loyalties of the officer corps, which represented, to a man, the traditional value system of the imperial army. According to Demeter, 36 percent of all officers were still members of the nobility in 1931, while Carsten refers to an increase of noble officers from 20.5 percent to almost 24 percent in 1932 (Demeter 1965, 49–55; Carsten 1966, 216), but the officers of middle-class extraction proved to be as conservative and nationalistic as their aristocratic confreres.

Perhaps the most crucial device the military succeeded in salvaging from the imperial army was the prerogative of the regimental commanders to select their own officers. By relinquishing the right to select an officer corps loyal to the state and constitution, the German republic compromised its own future (*Militärgeschichtliches Forschungsamt* 1964, 87).

In addition to being able to reorganize the army along traditional lines, totally inconsistent with the existing regime, the military succeeded, against the opposition of the government, in pursuing a rearmament and training policy that violated the stipulations of the peace treaty. General Von Seeckt concluded secret agreements with Russia, arranging for the production of armaments and the training of aviators (Carsten 1966, 143–45). To maintain Germany's leading position in military technology, the army reached an understanding with the Krupp industries, which acquired control of plants in Sweden, Holland, and Spain where weaponry research and experimentation could be conducted without directly infringing the Treaty of Versailles (Craig 1955, 406–7).

The Emergence of Private Armies

The evolutionary trend prevailing from 1918 to 1933 may be interpreted as a power contest between mutually exclusive factions that ended with the victory of National Socialism and the restoration of a militaristic state far more virulent than any of its preceding versions. Although recourse to constitutional devices played no minor role in this contest, its origin, development, and final outcome were linked to the role private armies of different parties, factions, and political movements were allowed to play. By *private army*, we mean any military association serving the political interests of ideologically disparate groups that arise in competition or cooperation with, or opposition to, the regular army.

The formation of numerous Free Corps, associations of returning combatants, paramilitary units, and party militias, may be interpreted as a dispersive dislocation of fighting capabilities from the core area of the military complex to the periphery and to other sectors of German society alien or inimical to the republican regime. Almost completely out of control in the beginning, these groups reflected an unusual degree of social disorganization, as well as the tendency to settle their conflicts by the use of violence. By 1920, an estimated total of 85 Free Corps had somewhere between 120,000 and 400,000 members (Fried 1942, 177–78). The Free Corps were gradually superseded by larger and more stable organizations, some of which represented the military arm of certain political parties.

The militarization of political parties, totally inconceivable by traditional standards, may be interpreted as a rather ingenious way of assuring the continuity of militarism, albeit under precarious conditions. The most powerful of these militias was the *Stahlhelm* (Steel Helmet), originally, like most of these groups, a league of ex-combatants that tended to become a youth organization of the extreme right and to keep alive the "spirit of the front soldier." It repudiated the "swinish revolution," the Weimar Republic, and democracy with its attendant party system and demanded restoration of the monarchy or, at least, the leadership of "a great and strong man." A rather isolated league in the beginning, the *Stahlhelm* developed into a genuine political power, almost a militant state within the state. The heads of the regular army encouraged it because they considered the *Stahlhelm* to be instrumental in perpetuating the "traditional military spirit" imperiled by the strictures of the Treaty of Versailles. Von Hindenburg himself deliberately protected the *Stahlhelm*, of which he had become an honorary member (Fried 1942, 151; Bracher 1960, 134–37). In 1928, the organization claimed a membership of one million, a figure that has been considered too high. At any rate, the *Stahlhelm* had demonstrated its capability of mobilizing thousands of uniformed members for frequent street parades in most German cities.

In opposition to the Free Corps, the political parties supporting the regime founded the *Reichsbanner Schwarz-Rot-Gold* (Banner of the Republic Black-Red-Gold), a military organization designed to protect the state from subversive violence. Since it was difficult to elicit more than lukewarm support for the Weimar Republic, the *Reichsbanner* proved relatively ineffectual.

Far more combative than most other private armies was the *Rote Frontkämpferbund* (Red League of Front Soldiers), the military arm of the Communist Party. It was involved in countless street and beer hall fights with Nazi troops, but obscure manipulations imposed by party line strictures prevented it from reaching its full power potential (Bracher 1960, 143–44).

The ex-combatants who were members of the Free Corps found the return to civilian life difficult and unrewarding. Many of them had "internalized the spirit of combat for combat's sake"; they fought not so much "as the result of political commitment as from the primitive joy of conflict and destruction" (Weingartner 1968, 142). During World War I, many of these soldiers had served in "storm" or "shock" squads, a tactical innovation introducing a pattern of infantry combat that was going to play an important role in future wars. "Youthful, self-confident, glorying in battle, and utterly ruthless, the storm troops were commanded by officers whose leadership was based less on formal authority than on personal example and charismatic attraction" (Weingartner 1968, 141).

The most articulate exponent of this "chaotic warrior spirit" was Ernst Jünger, erstwhile storm troop commander, who had been seriously wounded fourteen times. Yet he survived four years of the most exhausting and inhuman combat experiences with his warrior's morale unscathed and strengthened in his conviction "that the war, for all its destructiveness, was an incomparable schooling for the heart" (Jünger 1980, xii). Battle was perceived as "a magic delight," a "magnificent show of destruction," yet meaningful nevertheless, for "life has no depth of meaning except when it is pledged for an ideal," and "there are ideals in comparison with which the life of an individual and even of a people has no weight" (Jünger 1980, 316). Although references to the "fatherland" inject some specific meaning into Jünger's idealism, his writings convey the distinct impression that he felt fighting *as such* was an exalting experience: "What is essential is not what we fight for, but the way we fight," and "What could possibly be more sacred than a fighting human being?" (Jünger 1980, 78). These (as many other) remarks suggest that Jünger regarded fighting as something that constitutes a value in itself, independent of any political cause.

Less elaborate versions of the "storm troop mentality" served as common denominators of the Free Corps, the *Stahlhelm*, and the Nazi SA *(Sturm Abteilung)*. A number of National Socialist leaders, under the influence of Jünger's writings, recognized the advantages such a fighting force offered in the struggle for political power (Höhne 1967, 169f.; Weingartner 1968, 143). As a matter of fact, the ruthless fighting capacity of the SA, particularly during the late twenties and early thirties, must be considered a major determinant of Nazi success. On the other hand, fighting for fighting's sake no longer met the needs of the Party once Hitler had assumed the chancellorship of the Reich. As we shall see later, the so-called Röhm *Putsch* provided opportunity for a "blood purge" in which SS units *(Schutzstaffel)* "liquidated much of the upper leadership of the SA," which "had become an acute embarrassment to Hitler" (Weingartner 1968, 143).

In the years following World War I, the Free Corps fought against radical leftist groups, as well as against Polish irregular forces invading certain areas of eastern Germany that they considered irredenta territories claimed by Poland. In 1919, the Free Corps took it upon themselves "to eliminate the power of the workers' and soldiers' councils in one town after the other" (Carsten 1972, 64). It seems that in Bavaria, following the bloody repression of the so-called *Räterepublik* (Soviet Republic), several paramilitary leagues and corps, involved in the assassination of persons suspected of political opposition or supposed to be "traitors" to the national cause, proceeded with the approval of leading members of the Bavarian government. Also, "part of the judiciary legalized killing as a political means" (Nusser 1973, 142).

Beginning in 1923 or thereabouts, the first National Socialist troops marched in the streets of many German cities. Although most Free Corps disappeared, the Nazi paramilitary organizations gained in strength and eventually outdistanced the *Stahlhelm* in numbers and aggressiveness. In the end, the *Stahlhelm* was left no choice but to merge with the National Socialists.

The emergence of private armies, composed of demobilized soldiers and led by professional officers, should not be confused with the rise of paramilitarism. Both phenomena were new in the evolution of German militarism, but while the Free Corps were composed of ex-soldiers and participants of World War I, the paramilitary organizations recruited youths for definite political causes requiring the kind of training the regular army was not allowed to provide. Initially, there was no clear line of demarcation between these two organizational types, but as the years went by, the Free Corps dissolved, became inactive, or gradually developed into paramilitary groups as they succeeded in attracting increasing numbers of younger men who had no previous military experience. Politically indoctrinated against the parliamentary system, their uniformed members had access to (clandestine) weapons, and their actions, characterized by violence or threat of violence, were those of persons who had surrendered their individuality to a mass movement (Williams 1975, 142–47). Germany was by no means the only country in which paramilitarism throve, but nowhere else did it play such a crucial role in the reintegration of militaristic traditions and the eventual establishment of a militaristic state of totalitarian origin. Obviously, the paramilitary organizations frustrated the intentions of the peace treaty, as well as the domestic opposition to a revival of militarism.

The Power of the New Army

The relationships between the *Reichswehr* and the Free Corps were ambivalent. Von Seeckt's adverse attitude was related to the fact that the existence of private armies threatened the military monopoly of the regular army, something without precedent in Prussian-German history; on the other hand, the Free Corps were needed to fight the Polish insurgents. Barred from actually interfering in the conflict, the *Reichswehr* nevertheless provided covert assistance to the Free Corps, and later, after these had been dissolved, secret military training to such ultranationalistic organizations as the *Heimatverbände, Landbund, Jungdeutscher Orden, Wiking,* and *Stahlhelm* (Carsten 1966, 154). Eventually, Von Seeckt reached an agreement with the paramilitary *vaterländischen Verbänden,* whose members declined to merge with the regular army. These groups should be "at the disposal of the Reichswehr as a defence against attacks of foreign armies" (Carsten 1966, 157).

Maintenance of order rather than support of the domestic regime was foremost in Von Seeckt's mind. To him, the greatest threat to the established order came from the left, and it was communism that the *Reichswehr* was trained to perceive as the internal enemy, quite in contradiction with the often proclaimed precept that the *Reichswehr* "should stay out of politics." Von Seeckt's inconsistency was merely a repeat of the struggle the allegedly apolitical imperial army sustained against the Social Democrats *(Militärgeschichtliches Forschungsamt* 1964, 91–92).

In 1923, Von Seeckt reached the peak of his power. Under the pressure of increasing political turmoil, the federal government decreed the state of emergency transferring supreme executive powers to Von Seeckt, who thus became a kind of constitutional dictator (Görlitz 1950, 350; Carsten 1966, 187). Members of influential political circles of the right, including military leaders, urged him to establish a permanent authoritarian government or dictatorship. Von Seeckt did not yield to pressure and continued to defend the unloved Weimar Republic against conspiracies, subversion, and open rebellion, including Adolf Hitler's attempt to proclaim a "national dictatorship" (Görlitz 1950, 352).

Hans von Seeckt chose not to avail himself of the opportunity to become the first military dictator in German history. To judge from his own utterances, he was not averse to dictatorship per se, but he was apparently unable to cast himself in a role that was basically incompatible with his cultural background. He was seemingly willing to accept and perhaps support the "right man"; his interest lay in reestablishing national sovereignty in military matters and in finding a "liberator" capable of dominating the masses, but he declined to assume that role (Görlitz 1950, 353).

To understand the charismatic role Von Seeckt played within the armed forces, some consideration has to be given to the impact the demise of the monarchy had on the military hierarchy. Throughout the centuries, the extraordinary power of the military had been derived directly from the power of their supreme commanders, the Prussian kings and the German emperors. The sudden elimination of that source of power was tantamount to an ideological and structural "decapitation" of the military hierarchy, which experienced great difficulty in adapting to the uncertainties of parliamentary control and general political instability. Small wonder then that Hans von Seeckt, with his striking personality and his emphasis on Prussian traditions, should perform the function of filling the void created by the abdication of the emperor. He became a sort of substitute for the monarch, at least within the army (Carsten 1966, 107).

From Survival to Revival of Militarism

With the election of Field Marshal Paul von Hindenburg to the presidency of the republic in 1925, the influence of Von Seeckt declined. Von Hindenburg, the national hero of World War I, provided a far more powerful symbol not only for the military but also for a very large segment of the German people. He became the *Ersatzkaiser* (substitute emperor), as some of the less monarchically minded Germans used to call him. Von Hindenburg represented the state, and following the monocratic traditions of Germany, the military leaders redefined their loyalty to the state as loyalty to the field marshal and national hero (Carsten 1966, 249).

Nothing could have been more indicative of a militaristic revival than the election of Von Hindenburg, a prominent member of the Junker nobility and a victorious general of World War I, to the highest office of the land. No longer could there be any doubt that the transition from the Weimar Republic to the Third Reich indeed proceeded on "a broad basis of consensus." Most remarkable in term of consensus was Von Hindenburg's reelection to the presidency, which was accomplished with the support of the Social Democrats and the Catholic *(Zentrum)* party, two political bodies whose ideological stand seemed irreconcilable with the revival of militarism.

Among the ideological developments that led to "revolutionary nationalism," and eventually to the National Socialist brand of militarism, the most influential perhaps was Moeller van den Bruck's doctrine of the Third Reich. Actually, the idea of a "Third Reich" came to be the focus of a rather amorphous movement, for various versions of the concept were proposed in forty-six books by different authors published during the 1920s and early 1930s (Goedecke 1951, *passim*).

Writing in 1923, Moeller van den Bruck presented a nonpolitical version of the Third Reich ideology, whose roots have been traced to early Christianity (Schwierskott 1962, 103–4). Assuming an attitude of nonconformism with Germany's defeat in 1918, Van den Bruck visualized a Pan-German Third Reich, including Austria and "the young peoples of the east." In his political trilogy, the medieval Sacred Roman Empire was followed by the Second Reich founded by Bismarck, but vitiated by political doctrines leading up to the disaster of 1918. His Third Reich, of course, lay in the future, and the prelude to Van den Bruck's esoteric idea of the future German Reich encompassed a radical condemnation of virtually all political orientations of the Wilhelmian era: Marxism, liberalism, parliamentarism, the "reactionary" trend favoring a restoration of the monarchy, even the revolutionary doctrines inspiring the French Revolution, the Russian revolution of 1917, and the German revolution of 1918. Apparently, he saw himself as the authorized judge of a superior court called "conservatism," which "places itself above the parties, which refuses to be either party or opinion, not even a historical movement, but which presents itself as a 'cosmic vision of space,' of geopolitical space above everything else" (Tazerout 1936, 69).

Highly abstract and vaporous, Van den Bruck's ideology pleaded for a "conservative-revolutionary nationalism" to replace the monarchy and a sort of socialism that "begins where Marx ends." In 1923, he advocated a revolution, even a war if necessary, to implant the Third Reich. "There are problems in our history," he wrote, "which would never have been soluble without war and without a revolution. Let us make the War and the Revolution the means of solving them" (Moeller van den Bruck 1931, 38, 248, 254; Schwierskott 1962, 103, 104, 109).

Van den Bruck's brand of messianism predicted the appearance of a great leader, whom he called interchangeably *Führer* or *Retter* (Savior) (Tazerout 1936, 88). The author of *The Third Reich* never joined the then-fledgling Nazi movement. In 1925, long before Hitler came to power, he committed suicide, but *The Third Reich* became a kind of bible for the National Socialists, who showed their reverence in countless manifestations of ideological homage, at least before 1933.

In his own way, Moeller van den Bruck contributed to the trend, among the middle and upper strata of German society, toward a liberation from the "shackles" of the peace treaty and a reintegration of militarism, not as it had been prior to World War I but as it was perceived by certain military leaders and writers who viewed their own roles as those of "reformers" or even "revolutionaries." Obviously, their writings were influenced by Ludendorff's concept of total war. What they had in mind may be summarized as follows:

1. In view of the changes in the methods of warfare experienced in World War I and even more radical ones to come about in the future, it was deemed necessary that the state put the whole economy at the service of war in planning as well as in action in the case of belligerency.

2. The technological advances of armaments had obliterated the distinction between combat zone and "homeland" *(Heimat)*, between military and civilian participation in acts of belligerency.

3. It was found impossible to wage a "rational" war, one that could be adapted to well-defined political objectives, in terms of Clausewitz' treatise. In the long run, the dividing line between war and peace would become blurred. Eventually, a permanent state of war could prevail, merely varying between "hot" and "cold" cycles (Hillgruber 1974, 38).

The foregoing premises seemed to justify the need for a thoroughly militarized state, to be achieved either through the assumption of political functions by the military or through the "mental" militarization of statesmen and all leading groups of administration, diplomacy, and economy. The armed forces were perceived as only one war organization among others within a militarized state. War itself was regarded as a *Naturgewalt,* a natural force, and consequently "unavoidable." There should be, it was argued, a "central point of convergence," a single supreme "leader-commander" *(Führer-Feldherr)* capable of holding the nation in a state of permanent war (Hillgruber 1974, 39).

The Road to Total Power

The National Socialist German Workers' Party (Nazis) succeeded in recruiting a large following, first among the farmers and, shortly thereafter, among the impoverished sectors of the bourgeoisie and, increasingly, among the millions of unemployed workers. The epithets "Socialist" and "Workers" were incorporated in the official designation of the Party in the (correct) assumption that no political mass movement could possibly succeed without a token concession to the leftist leanings of an industrial proletariat that, for several decades, had been exposed to intensive Marxist indoctrination.

In the late 1920s and early 1930s, the confrontations between the paramilitary organizations of the Nazis and those of the Communists became more frequent and violent. Those street and beer hall battles performed the double function of affording opportunities to gain combat experience and, at the same time, to demonstrate available means of physical coercion or "power capabilities" (Anderson 1964), which, in conjunction with thoroughly militarized mass assemblies, proved highly effective in determining the final outcome of the power contest.

However, after the unsuccessful uprising in 1923, Hitler did not stage a coup d'etat to seize power. If National Socialism was indeed carried to victory on a "broad basis of consensus," one would expect the movement to win through democratically organized elections. As a matter of fact, Hitler gained his first great electoral victory in 1930 when the Party's representation in parliament jumped from 12 to 107 (Carsten 1966, 310). The second, overwhelming success came in the general elections of July 1932, which more than doubled the Nazi representation in the *Reichstag*. A total of 13.7 million voters, corresponding to 36.7 percent of all ballots, elected 230 deputies, making the NSDAP *(Nationalsozialistische Deutsche Arbeiterpartei)* the largest party by far. However, in the November elections of 1932, the NSDAP lost 2 million votes and 34 deputies in the *Reichstag*. For the first time, 17 percent of all ballots favored the Communist Party, whose representation in parliament rose to 100 (Domarus 1965, 142). Yet, this implied increasing polarization of political forces rather than a victory for the government, whose supporters did not exceed 10 percent of the population (Domarus 1965, 142). The success of the Communist Party actually played into the hands of Hitler, who was able to capitalize on the "red peril" threatening to engulf Germany. Yet, the results of fifteen national and local elections indicated that the Nazis could not count on a decisive electoral victory in the immediate future.

On the other hand, the support structure built by the Nazis and the pressure brought to bear on the government, its official and unofficial advisers, were such that access to power at the cabinet level seemed possible. The contest required the total mobilization of Hitler's persuasive and organizational resources.

He, who for years had been ridiculed as a puny party leader and unsuccessful rebel, became socially acceptable *(salonfähig)* in 1932. The president of the *Reich* received him several times. Ministers in office and former ministers, business leaders, former generals and active officers of the *Reichswehr* had meetings with him; party leaders from the German National Party to the *Zentrum* (Catholic party) asked to be received by him. Some endeavored to join him, others wanted to co-opt him with unimportant ministerial positions. He had served well enough as a "drummer" of the national uprising (as Hitler had called himself), but they did not wish to relinquish the exercise of power (Domarus 1965, 58).

Needless to say, as a power contender Hitler proved far superior to his rivals. Defying the legitimate government, he converted the Party into a state within the state and publicly claimed that he and the Party, rather than the government, represented the German people. His regional and local leaders behaved as if they were ministers and governors. Party offices issued statements about public affairs and actually interfered with public policies. Delegates of the Party were sent as observers to international conferences, and the *Reichspressechef* of the NSDAP held press conferences as if he were the spokesman of the actual government. Everywhere uniformed members of the SS assumed police functions during street demonstrations, and SA battalions held military parades in numerous former garrison towns (Domarus 1965, 58). These astute political rehearsals performed various functions simultaneously. As demonstrations of power capabilities, they were probably more effective than all previous ones. Designed to intimidate foes and to encourage partisans and sympathizers, they also exposed the weaknesses of the government. Furthermore, they provided opportunities for the future politico-administrative elites to familiarize themselves with the roles they were going to assume once the *Führer* was securely installed in the highest office of the land.

Under constant political and economic pressure, the constitutional government opted for a line of action that proved to be self-destructive. In 1930, to override parliamentary opposition to proposed emergency legislation, the chancellor dissolved the *Reichstag,* and invoking Article 48 of the constitution, he initiated "government by decree." President Von Hindenburg signed the emergency decrees, adding the following justification: "I acted in accord with the good, old principle of the Prussian *Felddienstordnung* (field service regulation) which says that a mistake in the choice of means is not as bad as the omission of any action at all" (Bracher 1960, 340, 344).

Once chosen, the trend toward an antiparliamentary "strong state" proved difficult to reverse. In 1930, the *Reichstag* convened ninety-four times. The following year, the number of sessions was down to forty-one, and in 1932, it dwindled to thirteen. Divided by irreconcilable differences and torn apart by violent confrontations, the *Reichstag* was no longer capable of resolving its own conflicts (Bracher 1960, 422).

The functional viability of a democratically elected parliament is based on two assumptions: (1) implicit consensus about the regime it represents and (2) legislative decision making by mutual accommodation of conflicting interests. Ideological ambivalence and intransigence had always been a major problem of the German *Reichstag*. During the last three years of the Weimar Republic, the increase of the National Socialist and Communist delegations, both totally opposed to representative democracy, eventually paralyzed legislative activity by uncompromising opposition. In fact, systematic obstruction was used to discredit, if not to destroy, the legislative institution itself.

In the meantime, the executive engaged in futile attempts to formulate convincing ideological tenets to justify government by decree. Actually, by doing what it did, it cleared the way to a National Socialist takeover (Bracher. 1960, 538). The crucial decision in the power contest came in January 1933 when Hitler was appointed chancellor of the Reich by President Von Hindenburg. There was nothing unusual about appointing the leader of the largest party representation in parliament to high office in the government, but Hitler was invited to assume the chancellorship of a cabinet that was constitutionally authorized to run the country "by emergency decrees" without previous approval of the legislature (Domarus 1965, 186). The military, the only power that might have prevented the fateful event, did not raise serious objections (Bracher 1960, 723).

Hitler took the fullest possible advantage of his emergency powers to void, by decree, a number of constitutional provisions that might have retarded or obstructed the monopolization of power by the NSDAP. After imposing Nazi satraps on all states of the federation, he proceeded to abolish all labor unions, political parties, and other politically oriented organizations. In July of 1933, the NSDAP became, by decree, the only permissible political party in Germany.

Since Hitler shared with other contemporary dictators a craving for popular acclaim, the German people were given the opportunity, on November 12, 1933, to express their attitude by answering yes or no to the following question: "Do you, German man, and you, German woman, approve the politics of your government, and are you prepared to declare it to be an expression of your own reasoning and of your own will, and solemnly to acknowledge it as your own?" A total of 40,500,000 votes, or 95.1 percent of all votes, was allegedly found to be favorable to the new regime. At the same time, the Germans voted for a new *Reichstag* composed exclusively of Nazi representatives, thus setting up the usual rubber stamp parliament, an expedient device few contemporary dictatorships seemed to be able to do without.

The final step in Hitler's ascent to total power was taken when the office of the president of the republic was combined with that of the Reich's chancellor. On August 1, 1934, Hitler's cabinet decreed the merger, transferring all powers of the president "to the *Führer* and Reich's Chancellor Adolf Hitler." Since the octogenarian Von Hindenburg was dying, the office was to become vacant, but the actual merger was ordered one day before the president's death (Domarus 1965, 420). On August 19, 1934, the Germans were allowed to vote on the merger, and "only" 89.9 percent of all voters approved the act. Since Hitler and his cohorts showed considerable concern about the results of the plebiscite, one may assume that the ballot boxes had not been tampered with. Thereafter, however, balloting was closely monitored, and the percentage of discordant votes never surpassed the 1 or 2 percent that became so characteristic of totalitarian regimes (Domarus 1965, 44–45).

The fact that the German army refrained from preventing Hitler's ascent to absolute power did not suggest "civilianism triumphant," as one author put it (Huntington 1957, 113). It did not in any way change the militaristic structure of the NSDAP, nor did it prevent the Nazi government from extending its control to the armed forces. In fact, the appointment of Hitler to the chancellorship of the Reich provided an occasion for a giant display of military might in Berlin, which lasted three and one-half hours; numerous battalions of the SA, SS, and the *Stahlhelm* paid homage to Hitler and Von Hindenburg, the new and the old symbols of German militarism (Domarus 1965, 188–89).

What the victory of National Socialism actually meant was a new way of merging civilian and military rule. The function of merging the "two rules," which, prior to 1918, had been performed by the monarchy and the nobility, was now carried out by the *Führer*, the Party, and its own militia. Formerly, the German soldier swore allegiance to the emperor; now his oath bound him to Adolf Hitler. The formula clearly reflects the fusion of the two rules: "I swear by God this sacred oath that I will render unconditional obedience to the Führer of the German Reich and people, Adolf Hitler, supreme commander of the armed forces, and that I, as a brave soldier, shall be willing, at any time, to give my life for this oath."

Two approaches are discernible in the way Hitler built the "broad basis of consensus" that carried him to power. As a populist leader and demagogue, he gradually succeeded in marshaling mass support, reflected by the growing number of Party members and Party representatives elected to serve in the *Reichstag*. Hitler's ascent was doubtlessly contingent, to a very large extent, on the militarization of his own Party. Continuous display of his private army intimidated foes and attracted many of those who believed that only government by force could save Germany from political and economic chaos. The elections of 1932 and 1933 suggested that the rise to power by gaining an absolute majority at the polls seemed too uncertain and much too slow to suit Hitler's plans. Direct support at the top of the political hierarchy opened up more promising prospects, however. The actual and would-be powerholders could not afford to ignore the aggressive demands of a leader whose party had the largest representation in parliament. The demonstration of strong popular support, implicit in Hitler's electoral victories, was directly related to his assumption of the chancellorship at the invitation of President Von Hindenburg. Subsequently, events at the two levels reinforced each other: Support gained at the executive level consolidated Hitler's position among the masses, and growing mass support attracted more and more followers, fellow travelers, and opportunists, few of whom seemed to pay attention to the distinction between constitutional government and usurpation of power.

Public endorsement of Hitler and his regime by such personalities as the former crown prince and the son of President Von Hindenburg further broadened Hitler's base of support. On the eve of the plebiscite of August 1934, a few weeks after the death of the president, his son, Colonel Oskar von Hindenburg, addressed the German people over public radio with the following words: "My late father himself considered Hitler as his successor as head of the German Reich, and I am acting in accord with my father's intention when I summon all German men and women to vote for the transfer of my father's office to the *Führer* and Reich's Chancellor" (Domarus 1965, 444).

Support from academic quarters was influential in winning over the educated sectors of the middle class. The philosopher Oswald Spengler, who had gained worldwide fame with his opus, *Der Untergang des Abendlandes (The Decline of the West)*, openly acclaimed Hitler's "national revolution," confessing that he detested the "sordid revolution of 1918, for it was the betrayal by the inferior part of our people of that strong, live part which had risen up in 1914 in the belief that it could and would have a future" (Spengler 1934, ix).

Even more outspoken was Martin Heidegger, a highly respected philosopher and university professor. He emphasized the *Führerideal* (leadership ideal), rejected the traditional academic freedom, and wanted to transform the German university into a *Kampfgemeinschaft* (fighting community) of students and professors (Messerschmidt 1969, 15).

An equally extreme, though more comprehensive, view was set forth by Werner Sombart, who revived the doctrine of divine right, formerly reserved for kings, extending it to anyone presumably chosen by the Divinity:

The leadership principle we believe in culminates in the acceptance of a supreme will of the leader who receives orders, not like the lower-ranking leader from a higher-ranking one, but only from God, the "leader" of the world. Those who completely understand and earnestly accept the leadership principle must believe in continuing revelation. Without this faith in revelation, the leadership principle lacks basis. The leader of the state thus receives his mandate from God which, in the ultimate analysis, is meant by the saying: "All authority comes from God." He does not have to pay attention to the "voice of the people," unless he recognizes it as the voice of God, that anyhow never talks through the fortuitous and varying totality of all citizens, much less through a majority of those citizens (Sombart 1934, 213).

Not content with postulating this version of divinely inspired political absolutism, Sombart applies it to a proposed economic order, which he called "German socialism":

Side by side with "private initiative" stands the "leadership principle". . . . The "leadership principle" signifies that group behavior is determined by order of a leader (opposite: the majority decision), and that the leader does not derive his competence from the will of his subordinates, but rather from orders of his superior leaders. The essence and scope of the leadership principle are best explicated by comparing it with the organization of a modern army at war. Here, the order passes from leader to leader until it arrives at the level of the squad leader. Its point of origin, however, is the High Command of the army, the supreme authority for all individual decisions, while the general military code still ranks above the High Command: For example, a colonel cannot introduce corporal punishment in his regiment. Now what in the economy corresponds to this organization? Here the laborer receives his orders from the foreman, he in turn receives them from his supervisor who receives them from the managing director, and the managing director gets them from the general manager who (perhaps) receives them from the president of the board. And he? In individual enterprises, the end of the hierarchy is reached earlier, namely at the level of the private entrepreneur. From whom does he receive his orders? Is he already the High Army Command? And do the many thousands of "leaders of the economy" confront one another as independent powers, as powers that do as they like battling with each other and marching off in different directions?! I should say that the entrepreneur's rank at best compares with that of the commander of a battalion or regiment, who himself must obey the orders of the High Command, but at least he is allowed a certain strategic and tactical autonomy. What powers then should the capitalistic entrepreneur be allowed to exercise? (His authority would be commensurate with that of the director of a public establishment.) To leave the ultimate decision to each individual would be tantamount to the disintegration of the army. Obviously, in the economic system too there must be something like a supreme command, over and above the individual "leader of the economy," something comparable with the High Command of the army. It is exactly the "leadership principle" that heads, with absolute necessity, toward a planned economy, namely socialism (Sombart 1934, 307–8).

Evidently, if the leadership principle rests on unappealable divine revelation, then its economic derivative must be divine by itself, or at least it must submit unconditionally to the divine mandate of the supreme political leader.

Gaining Control of the Military by Ideological Attrition

The central problem confronting Hitler was the relationship between the NSDAP and the *Reichswehr*. The army, which under the Weimar Republic had become "a state within the state," was the only organized force powerful enough to challenge the *Führer* and his cohorts. Many traditionalists among the officer corps watched, with misgivings and distrust, the meteoric ascent of the former army corporal to the position of chief of state and supreme commander of the armed forces. It had taken the *Reichswehr* years to neutralize the private armies that had sprung up in the wake of the revolution of 1918, only to see Hitler's private militia, the *Sturm Abteilung* (SA), develop into a more dangerous rival under Ernst Röhm. Indeed, Röhm, whom Hitler had appointed chief of staff of the SA in 1930, advocated a "second revolution," which would transform the SA into the nucleus of a People's National Socialist Army designed eventually to absorb the *Reichswehr*.

Hitler was well aware of the latent antagonism between the army and the Party, and since the ultimate success of his political pursuits depended on the consensus of the military, he developed a skillful strategy intended to win over the officer corps of the *Reichswehr*. Understanding that any attempts to rush changes in the structure of the military establishment might compromise his plans, he acceded to the request of a few generals and leaders of the NSDAP to take action against Röhm. Röhm and a number of SA officers were arrested and then killed on the grounds that they had been involved in a *Putsch* against the government. The SA thus ceased to be a threat to the army, at least temporarily, and at the same time Hitler had gotten rid of the only Nazi leader who might have become a rival contender for power within the NSDAP.

To carry out a gradual rapprochement between the Party and the army, Hitler availed himself of those ideological elements he shared with the military. His contempt for political parties, parliamentary democracy, and the republican form of state he had in common with the officer corps. The National Socialist doctrine preached a militant nationalism, which seemed hardly different from what had been a military tradition since the Napoleonic Wars. Exactly like the army, Hitler insisted on the restoration of national sovereignty and the repudiation of all restrictions imposed by the Treaty of Versailles. The heart of the ideological "common ground" of the Party and the army was *Wehrhaftmachung* (militarization) of the German people in general (Messerschmidt 1969, 12, 22).

The attempts of the Nazi leaders to consolidate the ideological basis of movement went far beyond immediate concerns. Emphasis on tradition, for example, led to the claim that National Socialism was identical with Prussianism. Before the seizure of power, this alleged identity served to integrate divergent groups within and outside the Party. Since the Nazi elite did not belong to the bearers of Prussianism, it was deemed particularly important to legitimate the movement and give it historical validity. Frederick the Great was represented as the person-ification of Prussianism. His unyielding strength in apparently hopeless situations and his tendency to risk everything in war made him, in the eyes of the Nazi leadership, a model for the Germans of the twentieth century (Schlenke 1981, 256–57).

Although the army seemed determined to preserve its autonomy vis-à-vis the Party, there was no agreement among the generals on how to react to the claim of the NSDAP to become the exclusive and undisputed political integrator of German society. If, as Nazi ideologues affirmed, the state and all that it stood for were conceivable only as functions of the Party, the army would inevitably gravitate into the orbit of a totalitarian organization, a dismal and profoundly disturbing prospect to many con-servative officers (Messerschmidt 1969, 22).

To dispel the doubts of the generals, Hitler's rhetoric, steeped in care-fully chosen military vocabulary, stressed the need to preserve the pro-fessional and unpolitical character of the army. He placed much emphasis on the army's obligation to remain loyal to "state" and "father-land," expedient abstractions that could mean different things to dif-ferent people. To win support, the Party engaged in an endless succession of public demonstrations, parades, and consecrations of flags in which the army invariably participated. In fact, the Nazis developed the theatrical aspects of their military parades to the fullest possible ex-tent, and the expected rewards in terms of popular support did not fail to materialize.

The renaissance of German militarism implied, of course, rearma-ment on a large scale, including a rapid expansion of the army. This was exactly what the officer corps of the *Reichswehr* had been hoping for, but at the same time, the induction of several hundred thousand new sol-diers seriously threatened the relative homogeneity of the *Reichswehr*, particularly its capability to resist the alluring approaches of the Nazis. An unknown but certainly large proportion of the new soldiers had been converted to the National Socialist cause prior to conscription.

The fact that the officer corps of the *Reichswehr* failed to muster stronger resistance against Nazi control was due, at least in part, to an ideological rift within its own ranks. While the older officers adhered primarily to traditional Prussianism, most of the younger ones sup-ported Hitler's tenets. Their position was immensely strengthened after 1933 by the recruitment of twenty-five thousand new officers, many of whom sympathized with, or were actually members of, the NSDAP.

Although the rapid expansion of the armed forces was tantamount to an ideological subversion "from below," a similar but more subtle pro-cess was under way at the top level of the army command. In April 1934,

Defense Minister Von Blomberg decreed that the army should present itself in public as the *sole* bearer of arms of the nation, but absolutely loyal to Hitler's regime and well educated in National Socialist thought (Messerschmidt 1969, 34). Von Blomberg's decree thus implied a compromise: To preserve its military monopoly, the army accepted the regime and acquiesced in political indoctrination of its personnel. Recognition of the army's claim to remain the nation's sole bearer of arms was certainly incompatible with Nazi doctrine and policy, something that the military elite fully understood only after control over the armed forces had been taken away from them.

The relentless pressure Hitler brought to bear on the military establishment gradually sharpened internal antagonisms within the officer corps. In 1938, Hitler's growing power vis-à-vis the army enabled him to exploit openly the dissension among the generals. He surrounded himself with a military entourage sympathetic to the regime and willing to cooperate, while a number of high-ranking officers known to oppose the *Führer's* plans of conquest on ideological or professional grounds were removed from the active ranks of the armed forces.

Several facets of the power contest between Hitler and the army have to be considered to understand how the dictator was able "to impose upon the army a control more rigid than any of its long existence, and to compel the obedience of its officers even to commands which violated their historical traditions, their political and military judgement, and their code of honor" (Craig 1955, 469).

With the merger of presidency and chancellorship, Hitler assumed the president's constitutional position of supreme commander of the armed forces. As such, he autocratically ordered all military personnel to swear allegiance to him. This was, of course, a reversion to the personal oath of allegiance to the monarch, an institution that had deep roots in Prussian military ideology. In the Weimar Republic, Von Seeckt and President Von Hindenburg provided informal substitutes for the dethroned emperor and thus allowed relationships of personal allegiance to continue until Hitler was able to formalize the existing pattern.

Although the development of the storm troops (SA) was held in abeyance, the *Schutzstaffel* (SS) rapidly evolved into Hitler's praetorian guard, ready to carry out any order to secure compliance with Nazi policies. At this point, the army was unable to prevent the growth of an armed force that was intended to constrain possible adverse military reactions to Hitler's power monopoly. In fact, young men were allowed to serve in the SS without going through the army. The circle of control was completed by the total control the SS established over the German police (Messerschmidt 1969, 123). Finally, in 1938 Hitler assumed the position of chief commander of the armed forces. By that time, all significant resistance to nazification of the military establishment had ceased.

Initiated by Defense Minister Von Blomberg, the education of the army was based on the rallying motto, "rebirth of Germany through National Socialism." It meant thorough politicization of officers and enlisted men. The new military ideology was totally opposed to the traditional isolation or, perhaps, alienation of the officer corps from the rest of society. The new "German People's Army" was expected not only to accept the dominant role of *Führer* and Party but also to "awaken" the *Wehrgedanke* (military spirit) in the German people. Party ideology was interwoven with Hitler's *Kriegsvorbereitungskunst* (the art of preparing for war), and the impact of this combination on the younger officers proved "overwhelming" (Messerschmidt 1969, 154, 160, 162). Widespread approval of Hitler's military ideology did not come from disinterested sources, of course, for the rapid expansion of the armed forces created excellent chances for fast promotion and advancement of military personnel *(Militärgeschichtliches Forschungsamt* 1964, 101).

If to be a National Socialist meant to be a soldier, and to be a soldier meant to be a National Socialist, or, in other words, if the army and the Party were to coalesce, the emergence of a "political soldier" was only to be expected. Hitler himself was such a political soldier, and so were "General Field Marshal" Hermann Göring and other prominent Nazis appointed by Hitler. The political soldier was a paradox in an era of growing professionalism and technical specialization of the military. The anachronism inherent in this reversal of vital priorities would hasten the ultimate defeat of the German armies.

The traditional pattern of military discipline, principled by a code of honor, failed to satisfy the totalitarian demands of Nazi ideology. Since the concept of the soldier was inextricably connected with ethical norms tempering conduct in the face of the enemy, the Nazis attempted to substitute *Kämpfer* (fighter) for soldier. Following the SS model, the relationship between leader and follower was elevated to an absolute principle implying "blind obedience" to *any* order emanating from a leader, even the one that violated the traditional moral code. Acts of violence, defined as atrocities and punishable as crimes according to previous military codes, became standard procedures, at least in the SS. The army proved less receptive to Nazi attempts to subvert the moral conventions of the past (Messerschmidt 1969, 160–62, 211, 213, 218). In the Nazi code of "ideological morality," "injustice, crime, brutalities satisfying the necessities of ethnic life, were raised to the level of useful behavior, and scruples or opposition against these new meanings were considered faults punishable with death" (Messerschmidt 1969, 422).

It was primarily against Russia that these principles of unrestrained warfare were carried out to the fullest possible extent. The Soviet Union was perceived as the "Jewish-Bolshevist" enemy. By Nazi standards, no trait or combination of traits could be more abhorrent than the alleged alliance of the Soviet state, its political intelligentsia, and Jews, who supposedly were playing the leading role in this complex. Nothing less than complete annihilation of the Soviet state, its armed forces, and ideologues could satisfy Hitler and his cohorts. All political functionaries and commissars captured by the German armies were to be executed without the benefit of legal process. The rejection of generally recognized international norms of warfare, implicit in these acts of violence, produced occasional protests from individual field commanders but no unified opposition. Some commanders acted in accordance with such orders, but others ignored them (Messerschmidt 1969, 400, 413). The most relentless executioners in Hitler's extermination campaign were the SS, whose atrocities at home and in occupied territories rivaled, or perhaps surpassed, the great purges in Stalinistic Russia.

Hitler's control over the armed forces brought increasingly draconic sanctions for behavior judged to be inconsistent with Nazi ideology. During the war, any officer who saw his own orders disobeyed was supposed to execute the insubordinate soldier immediately. The death penalty could be inflicted on anybody attempting to destroy or paralyze military morale, to induce another to refuse military service, or to desert the army. A soldier trying to defect to the enemy would forfeit his life and property, and even his relatives could be made responsible for his act. During World War II, approximately 16,000 military personnel were sentenced to death, and about 90 percent of the sentences were actually carried out. An estimated 475,000 persons were sentenced by military courts during the entire war (Messerschmidt 1969, 363, 369, 380). In the final phase of the war, "political education" of the army was entrusted to National Socialist *Führungsoffiziere*, a kind of replica of Soviet commissars, but time was too short for these "educators" to have any measurable impact upon the deteriorating morale of the German armies.

The Changes That Made Militarism Totalitarian

In determining the role of the National Socialist Party in the reintegration of German militarism, one notes new elements that were, with varying degrees of success, blended with surviving traditions. Novel, of course, was the idea of a thoroughly militarized political party. Certainly the aftermath of World War I, with its available Free Corps of soldiers fighting for various rightist causes, provided a fertile recruiting ground for the organization of the NSDAP whose *Sturm Abteilungen* (SA), or storm troops, were joined by parts of the *Ehrhardt Brigade* of former soldiers (Schäfer 1957, 7). The NSDAP was definitely designed to fight, in a literal rather than a metaphorical sense. First, it fought its internal enemies of the left, and once in control, it fought to reestablish Germany as a great power by engaging in the conquest of territories felt to be necessary to the survival and expansion of the German "race." The paramilitary and military cadres of the SA and SS were as essential to the development of the Party as the rank-and-file members. On innumerable occasions, *all* could be seen in uniform, marching in formation to the martial music of brass bands. The NSDAP had indeed become a "fighting machine," and the political scene closely resembled an "open state of war," in which the power contenders were allowed to feed on the weaknesses of the Weimar Republic, "the stillborn product of civilian degeneracy" (Obermann 1958, 270–71).

Within the military superstructure of the Party, the SS merits special attention, not only because of its privileged position as Hitler's praetorian guard and personal police force designed to eradicate dissent, but also because it was supposed to embody the most desirable qualities of national socialism. Step by step, Heinrich Himmler, supreme commander of the SS, developed it from a small group of 200 men in 1929, to 2,727 in 1930, and to over 250,000 in 1939 (Höhne 1967, 57, 148). After Hitler's assumption of the chancellorship, the SS were besieged by countless thousands who wished to join the ranks of the new military elite. Rather indiscriminate admission of many who failed to meet Nazi standards led to a purge of 60,000 men found to be opportunists, alcoholics, homosexuals, "racially suspect," or otherwise undesirable (Höhne 1967, 134).

Himmler's ambition to free the SS from the tutelage of the SA, and to transform it into an autonomous body within the Party, was sanctioned by Hitler in 1934. The process of differentiation within the military structure of the Party had thus begun. There were now two militias performing different functions, but Himmler pushed hard to add stratification to division of labor: He undertook every conceivable effort to raise the SS to the level of what he assumed to be an elite, distinct form, well above the SA, the "plebeian mass of brown foot soldiers" (Höhne 1967, 125). Radical changes in the social composition of the SS reflected Himmler's success, as well as a stratification pattern that had survived the postwar changes of German society. Formerly composed of Free Corps combatants, "Party veterans" of lower-middle-class extraction, and individuals whose professional training had been disrupted by the economic depression, the SS now attracted numerous members of the old nobility, the educated middle class, and the peasantry. In 1938, 60 percent of the six highest-ranking positions in the SS officer corps were held by noblemen (Höhne 1967, 127).

Under the Weimar Republic, Germans had little opportunity to wear uniforms and thus to satisfy a yearning rooted in a long military tradition. Skillfully playing up to this need, Himmler created a startling black uniform and a complex set of symbols to emphasize the uniqueness of the SS and to stress internal differences in rank and merit. In view of the destiny awaiting the SS, the death's head insignia, worn on the cap, turned out to be a prophetic choice. The "honor sword" became a special token of distinction bestowed on SS officers of the higher ranks.

Himmler apparently thought the Jesuit Order provided the most desirable model of obedience and efficiency to use in dealing with groups perceived as enemies of the regime. Just as the Jesuits endeavored to stamp out religious heresy, so the SS proceeded to annihilate political heresy attributed to certain individuals and categories of people. "The similarities between the two bodies was startling indeed: both constituted highly privileged orders, free of any secular jurisdiction, protected by severe rules of admission, held together by an oath of absolute and blind obedience to a supreme lord, called pope there and Führer here." Like the Jesuit Order, the SS was under the authority of a general assisted by several counselors (Höhne 1967, 135).

The Knights of the Teutonic Order served as another model inspiring some of Himmler's theatrical extravaganzas. Like the Grand Master of the Order, he chose a medieval castle as the "spiritual" center of the SS where, in the company of his highest officers, he was going "to forge the ideological tools" of his military order. Himmler carried his historical fantasies to the point of playing the role of King Arthur, inviting to his round table twelve SS generals reputed to be his "bravest knights" (Höhne 1967, 142–43).

Far more consequential than this freewheeling symbolism were the extrajurisdictional privileges Himmler was able to secure for all sectors of the SS. No court of the German jurisdictional system was considered competent to judge an SS man; not even the courts of honor of the SA were allowed to extend their jurisdiction to the SS. Like noblemen of former times, members of the SS could be judged only by their peers. To complete the analogy to aristocratic traditions of bygone eras, the duel was revived with Himmler's order that "each SS-man has the right and duty to use arms in order to defend his honor." Yet the decision as to whether a duel was justified in any particular case was left to higher authority, and the details of the dueling procedure were pedantically regulated in a special order issued by Himmler. SS men who had been condemned to death by a peer court might be allowed to expiate their crime by committing ritual suicide in an equally regulated fashion (Höhne 1967, 140–41).

The revival of these age-old traditions suggests a cultural inconsistency. How could institutionalized status privileges possibly be reconciled with the National Socialist doctrine of *Gleichschaltung* (uniformization) and total control of all institutional manifestations of German society? It could be argued, somewhat speciously, that formerly jurisdictional privilege had emanated from, and was maintained by, the nobility itself, while now it was bestowed on the SS militia by high Party authority, which was identical with the state, according to Nazi doctrine. The SS Peer Court would thus be just another state court, although the question as to the grounds on which the state would grant such privilege remained unanswered. Actually, the privileged position of the SS was justified by emphasizing the extraordinary responsibility of the SS man to sacrifice his life to protect the *Führer* and the Party (Höhne 1967, 140). Since all soldiers of the regular army took an oath assuming exactly the same duties, there really was no difference between the SS and the army so far as responsibilities were concerned. Jurisdictional privilege could not possibly be dispensed with if the SS was to destroy, by application of unrestrained violence, those who were considered enemies of the regime. Without exemption from regular judicial process, countless SS men would have run afoul of the law and thus risked court trials, which might have exposed practices the Nazi leaders wished to conceal from the public.

As the power domain of the SS expanded, internal differentiation proceeded in several directions. In 1934, there already was a General SS in contrast to various *Sonderformationen* (special units). The *Sicherheitsdienst* (security service) became an increasingly powerful police force. Reinhard Heydrich, a former naval officer, was appointed chief, and under his command it developed far beyond the conventional role of the police to defend the state. Heydrich endeavored to transform it into an attack force determined to detect and capture enemies of the state even before they were able to engage in subversive action. By purging German society of all "undesirable ideas," by "eliminating all energies alien and therefore destructive" to the ethnic purity of the people, the SD was determined to perform the role of the nation's "educator" (Höhne 1967, 162–63).

The Gestapo: Institutionalized Terror

The urge to gain total power caused the Nazi potentates to institutionalize terror in the form of the *Geheime Staatspolizei*, or Gestapo (secret state police). This, as well as other initiatives intended to expand and redefine the controlling functions of the SS, did not follow any systematic line of development, but came about rather haphazardly as personal enterprises of ambitious men like Göring, Himmler, Heydrich, and others vying for power, often against the resistance of other sectors of the Party. Eventually, in 1936, Himmler emerged as the chief of the German police, which was subdivided into two major divisions: the former SD, encompassing the Gestapo and detective force under Heydrich, and the *Schutzpolizei*, gendarmerie, and local police under SS General Daluege (Höhne 1967, 182).

As an attack force, the Gestapo transformed the nation into a battleground. Sniffing out often unsuspecting "enemies" and striking in small raids, preferably at dawn, SS men killed some of them on the spot, but most were taken prisoners and put into concentration camps. Who were these enemies of the regime? All those who "actively oppose the people, the Party and the state, their ideological foundations and political actions." Or in more concrete terms: "Communists, Marxists, Jews, politicizing churches, Freemasons, political grumblers, members of the National Opposition, reactionaries, followers of the Black Front, economic saboteurs, habitual criminals, abortionists, homosexuals, and traitors" (Höhne 1967, 172). So many were these categories and so flexible and comprehensive some divisions that almost anyone incurring the displeasure of the Gestapo could be imprisoned, tortured, or murdered. Since the Gestapo were given the prerogative of taking anyone, and for indefinite time, into "protective custody," there was no recourse against arbitrary imprisonment, nor was there any way of controlling the treatment given inmates of concentration camps.

The Gestapo campaign against an alleged enemy, who was neither armed nor organized and who, more often than not, was totally unaware of his own wrongdoings, represented a new stage in the evolution of militarism insofar as it turned a substantial proportion of armed partisan forces against the nation's citizenry. It was not a civil war because the "enemy" was unarmed and totally defenseless; yet, he was treated with the implacable ferocity usually reserved for a mortal enemy who prefers death to surrender. The only parallel that comes to mind is the great purge in Stalin's Russia.

There was another enemy the Gestapo could not liquidate in the usual way. Within the judicial system, some public prosecutors, either members of the Party or sympathizers of the regime, attempted in 1933 and 1934 to investigate cases of homicide and torture inflicted on inmates of concentration camps. A few members of the Gestapo were convicted and sentenced to penal servitude (*Zuchthaus*). In 1934, Hitler himself was approached by Nazi lawyer Frank and Minister of Justice Gurtner with the request that all concentration camps be abolished. Needless to say, such efforts caused men like Göring, Himmler, Heydrich, and others to mobilize their defense so effectively that Hitler refused the request and thereafter lent his full support to the penal system organized and enforced by the Gestapo.

Attempting to cut through the ideological verbiage the Nazis generated to justify their policies, one detects a major objective, namely, a concentrated effort to establish national consensus by all available means, including genocide. The most elementary knowledge of how a large, complex society is put together might have convinced less fanatical leaders that such a goal is virtually unattainable. And relative consensus, providing sufficiently strong support of Hitler's plans of military conquest, might have been achieved without the extreme forms of violence the Gestapo inflicted on its countless victims.

Internal specialization within the SS produced a number of sections. Some (*Junkerschulen*) were entrusted with the education of SS officers; others performed administrative functions. The *Totenkopfverfbände* (Death's Head Units) were in charge of the concentration camps, and the so-called *Verfügungstruppe* (Disposal Troops), originally subdivided into three regiments, was "to act as an armed reserve for the defense of the regime in time of peace while preparing itself for combat employment in wartime" (Weingartner 1968, 21). In fact, it developed into a veritable army in World War II.

In the early years of the Nazi regime, the problem of how to defray the ever-increasing cost of maintaining the growing SS militia was solved by Himmler's extracting large subsidies from Germany's wealthiest industrialists, financiers, and businessmen. It is a matter of conjecture whether these men were motivated by political conviction or opportunism. Apparently, those who joined the "Circle of Friends" of the SS *Reichsführer* (Himmler) did so for diverse reasons. Some were genuine Nazis, others perceived the Party militia as an effective assault force against the "Communist peril," and still others wished to buy protection against actual or threatened harassment by Nazi agencies. Even disguised adversaries of the Party were said to be among Himmler's wealthy patrons (Höhne 1967, 131–32). Whatever the motives, their generosity provided the needed financial support to build up organized terror. Supporters who did not wish to be too closely identified with SS procedures were allowed to join the nearly anonymous Promoting Members organization (FM). Each member of the SS was expected to recruit at least one FM willing to make an annual monetary contribution without incurring any other obligation to the Party. In 1932, 13,217 Promoting Members contributed 17,000 Reichsmarks (RM). After Hitler's assumption of power in 1933, the FM membership jumped to 167,272 paying 357,000 RM, and in 1934, there were 342,492 persons who contributed 581,000 RM. Along with genuine followers of National Socialism, enough "promoters" were keenly aware that the FM insignia bought protection from the very same forces their monetary contributions helped to develop (Höhne 1967, 132–33).

The Militarization of German Society Under the Nazi Regime

The military organization of the NSDAP eventually developed into a "second army numbering by 1944 twenty-five or thirty divisions, virtually all of them armored, mechanized, or airborn (sic)" (Huntington 1957, 118). Since the 1930s, the SS had tended to militarize the internal structure of the Party, especially those sectors concerned with foreign relationships (Schäfer 1957, 49, 55).

· Further evidence of militarization is to be seen in the way the Corps of Political Leaders and the youth organizations were compelled to acquire military skills. By 1935, 1,250,000 youths between fourteen and eighteen years of age had already been trained on the firing range (Klöne 1960, 29). A substantial number of them had also acquired specialized skills related to the navy and the air force, to motorization and communication (Klöne 1960, 19). At the age of eighteen, the members of the *Hitler Jugend* (Hitler Youth) were expected to join the SA or SS (Klöne 1960, 36).

The principle of blind obedience played a paramount role in the training program of the Corps of Political Leaders. Within the party structure, complaints and requests signed by members of subordinate sectors and directly addressed to the *Führer* were considered "mutiny" and dealt with as such (Schäfer 1957, 66–68).

In contrast to traditional Prussian-German militarism, which had been engineered by the ruling dynasty in close alliance with the nobility, the militarism of the NSDAP was conceived and carried through by people of the lower social strata of German society, particularly by the "proletarized" segments of the lower middle class. In 1930, the composition of the Party showed that the urban working class, with 26.3 percent of the membership, was heavily underrepresented, while the white-collar workers, constituting 24.4 percent of all members, went far beyond their proportion in the general occupational structure. By 1932, however, the proportion of blue-collar workers had risen to 32.5 percent, while that of white-collar workers had sunk to 20.6 percent of the total membership (Schäfer 1957, 19).

The predominance of the lower social classes is even more obvious in the composition of the Hitler Youth. Before the enormous surge of new members in 1934, 69 percent of the Youth were young workers and apprentices (Klöne 1960, 11). There was a definite emphasis on egalitarianism and a militant opposition to such traditional institutions as the Student Corporations. In fact, the campaign conducted by the National Socialist Youth Organization contributed to the disbandment of the Corporations for being "feudalistic and hostile to workers" (Klöne 1960, 77).

In the previous stages of militarism, whole sectors of the culture were left virtually untouched, but the attempted restructuring of German society in terms of totalitarianism implied the elimination of anything or anybody felt to be at variance with National Socialist ideology. Unlike imperial Germany, the Nazi regime did not tolerate political opposition or any intellectual or aesthetic endeavor that failed to conform to official doctrine. Before World War I, militarism had been carried by national consensus, and any dissent was handled without major deviations from the established course. In the wake of military defeat, the "unfinished" revolution of 1918, the fall of the monarchy, and the political turbulence of the postwar years, no such consensus could be expected to emerge spontaneously. Organized violence, which characterized the political ascent of the National Socialist Party, was used with ever-increasing frequency to silence the opposition and eventually to exterminate any individuals or groups felt to be a threat to the power monopoly of the Party or at variance with the basic tenets of Nazi ideology. The Jewish minority was assumed to be biologically incapable of participating in the moral and political order envisioned by Hitler and therefore condemned to annihilation.

If far-reaching consensus was actually achieved, it was due perhaps not so much to the never openly admitted practice of police terrorism and genocide as to the demonstration effect of early victories won virtually without bloodshed: Rearmament was carried out at a rate surpassing all historical precedents; the new army reentered the demilitarized Rhineland; Austria was invaded and became an integral part of the incipient Third Reich, while Czechoslovakia, abandoned by Chamberlain in 1938, surrendered to the German army invading its territory.

"Independence" was bestowed on Slovakia, while the rest of the country was transformed into a German protectorate. Equally successful was the political pressure brought to bear on Lithuania, which surrendered the port and district of Memel to the Germans. All these events met no more than verbal opposition from the former allies responsible for enforcing the Versailles treaty. Obviously, the success of these aggressive acts suggested that the remilitarization of Germany and the use of military power in international politics were indeed appropriate to redeem the nation from the infamy of defeat and the "ignominy of Versailles," and to vindicate Germany's international status as a great power.

Victories Turning into the Final Debacle

The invasion of Poland met with strong resistance, and a war of conquest ensued, the dimensions of which surpassed by far any military enterprise Europe had ever seen before. Within three years (1939–1942), the German armies were in control of most areas of continental Europe and North Africa. A combination of technological achievement and high military morale generated results that could be matched only after extraordinary and time-consuming efforts on the part of the powers actively involved in containing the Germans. Although the outbreak of actual warfare failed to arouse the enthusiasm the German people had shown on previous occasions, a rapid succession of major victories apparently convinced the skeptics, unified the German people, and disposed them to accept the exigencies of total war (Carroll 1968, 250). Indeed, the extraordinary success of Hitler's campaigns could be considered the crowning achievement of three centuries of German militarism if they had not been followed by the most crushing defeat Germany ever suffered.

Territorial conquest was, from the very beginning, one of the avowed objectives of the war, primarily in the east. To secure control of the occupied areas and to prepare them for the satellite role they were supposed to play in the structure of the emerging Third Reich, appropriate policies should have been developed to gain the support of the conquered populations. Actually, the Nazi warlords and their storm troops antagonized the Poles, the Russians, and most other peoples under their control by the widespread use of the most brutal forms of violence. The patterns of police terrorism and genocide, transferred to the conquered territories, not only contributed to sabotage and partisan warfare behind the German lines but also reinforced the decision of the Allies to continue the war until the German armies surrendered unconditionally.

German militarism reached its historical peak in World War II, but it was out of step with the realities of the political process. Not only was conquest accompanied by gross mismanagement of violence, but the war itself was conducted as if economic, technical, and human resources were inexhaustible. Neither Great Britain nor Russia proved amenable to the pressures of total war, and as soon as the United States entered the conflict, it was only a matter of time before the position of Germany became untenable. Far from realizing the hopelessness of the military situation, the Nazi elite increasingly seemed to lose touch with reality as the war went on. Notwithstanding crushing defeats, appalling casualties, and wholesale destruction of German cities, fighting continued until the Allied armies totally occupied the country.

The Junker nobility, the main bearer of German military traditions, was almost wiped out. The war had taken an extremely heavy toll of lives, and following the attempt on his life, Hitler ordered the execution of many aristocratic officers whom he suspected of involvement in the conspiracy. The advancing Russian armies captured and deported many others; quite a few died while trying to defend their estates against the enemy; and many committed suicide (Görlitz 1950, 689–90).

The End of German Militarism

The greatest triumph of German militarism turned into its ultimate rout. Miscalculations about what militarism in peace or war may accomplish have not been rare in history. Such errors of judgment resulted in the defeat of the Prussian armies in 1806, and a few years later (1812) the French armed forces suffered a similar fate, as they did again in 1871. In World War I, the tremendous military effort of the German Empire could not prevail against the combined power of the western Allies and Russia, but none of those gross miscalculations brought about a reversal of the militaristic tradition. On the contrary, defeat appeared to revivify and reinforce militarism, to prepare the nation more effectively for future wars assumed to be as ineluctable as solar eclipses or earthquakes. In France the lost wars of 1812 and 1871 caused drastic changes in the political structure, but no such changes occurred in Germany prior to 1918, and even then the new regime proved unable to marshal the support indispensable to its own continuity. The surviving forms of militarism played into the hands of the National Socialists, who succeeded in establishing themselves, by popular placet, as the new political elite and the protagonists of a new militaristic state. It should be added that in World War I Germany was neither devastated nor fully occupied by the Allies, who attempted, however, to impose and enforce a peace treaty the stipulations of which supplied ample ammunition to all groups and parties advocating the remilitarization of Germany.

None of these conditions existed after World War II. For the first time in three centuries, the chances for a revival of the militaristic tradition were nil, at least in West Germany. In a discussion of determinants of such a radical reversal, the following would seem to be crucial:

1. There could not be the slightest doubt in any German's mind that defeat was definitive and total. No invincibility or stab-in-the-back myth could possibly arise in the midst of an utterly devastated country, totally dominated by the enemy.

2. It seems reasonable to assume that the enormous casualties inflicted on the German armies annihilated a very large proportion, probably the majority, of the most ardent supporters of militarism.

3. The political division of Germany may be considered the most relevant factor in the disruption of established patterns of behavior, insofar as irreconcilable ideological and structural commitments prevented the two German states from restoring and pursuing any common political tradition. Most significant in this context is the fact that large areas of East Germany, the traditional bulwark of Prussianism, fell to Poland and Russia, while the remainder became a satellite state of the Soviet Union. The structural changes imposed on the eastern territories not only eliminated the Junker nobility but also made it impossible to pursue an independent line of international politics.

7

The Cross-cultural Dimensions of European Militarism

No more than a few observations of the most general kind have been offered so far about militarism in other European societies, which at one time or another interacted with and influenced, in different ways, military developments in Prussia and the German Empire. In its formative state, Brandenburg-Prussia borrowed numerous organizational and technological elements from such diverse nations as Spain, Switzerland, Holland, Sweden, and France, whose military establishments were, in some respects, further advanced than that of Prussia. Much later, particularly during the nineteenth century, the process was reversed, and Germany increasingly performed the role of the donor society with regard to things military. However, it was not so much the process of diffusion as the competition and antagonistic interaction between Germany and its neighbors that seem relevant to the understanding of the events that generated the wars of the nineteenth and twentieth centuries. Just how militaristic were these neighbors? Were they as determined as Germany to go to war to resolve international differences? And if they were, did their military establishments, as well as the structural and moral support they could count on in their respective societies, measure up to Germany's military preparedness and its national consensus about war?

The militarization of German society, the wars it won or lost, occurred within an ever-changing international context, the major components of which were constituted by France, Great Britain, and Russia. Thus, a brief characterization of French, British, and Russian military developments should cast some light on the revolutionary direction of German militarism, not only its flowering but also its survival in the Weimar Republic and its revival under the Nazi regime.

Furthermore, the comparative nature of this inquiry will test the assumption that Prussian-German militarism was unique in some basic aspects and that its growth constituted a process of special evolution not paralleled or repeated anywhere, at least not in modern Europe.

France

Certain developments in prerevolutionary France resembled those that contributed to the rise of militarism in early Prussia. In the sixteenth century, poverty drove many noblemen from their castles and forced them to join the army, first as apprentices and later as officers. As in Prussia, they were initially allowed to monopolize the officer corps, but they had to conform to certain disciplinary and educational standards. The French *hobereaux* of the eighteenth century have been compared with the Prussian Junkers. In fact, we are told that five hundred impecunious *hoberaux* of "old race" were enrolled in the newly founded *École Militaire*. As in Prussia, the nobility merged with the military establishment. By 1776, there were military colleges in the provinces, but their graduates were sent to the *École Militaire* to complete their professional training. A further similarity may be seen in the early creation of a standing army. Yet to a larger extent than in Prussia, members of the French bourgeoisie were allowed to join the officer corps, usually through the purchase of a title-bearing government office implying ennoblement of its holder. By 1750, there were about four thousand officers of "common" origin, but they were denied access to the higher levels of the military hierarchy. The military aristocracy despised the bourgeoisie, but the split was never allowed to grow as deep as in Prussia (Vagts 1959, 52–61).

Under Louis XIV, French imperialism, combined with strong emphasis on the development of military technology—Vauban's siege techniques come to mind—bears certain features of militarism, but at no time did the "military spirit" prevail in French society as it did in Prussia under Frederick William I. Nevertheless, voices advocating a more thorough militarization of French society could be heard long before Napoleon revolutionized warfare. In fact, some of his innovations were already proposed in Comte de Guibert's *Essai de tactique générale* (1773). He recognized nationalism as an integrative force, capable of turning armies into more effective and less expensive fighting forces. It should be added, however, that the manpower reservoir of eighteenth-century France was much greater than that of its neighbors and that, consequently, the need to hire alien mercenaries was virtually nil. Guibert indeed suggested a "popular" or "national" army. He also advocated intensive physical training that would make it possible to accelerate the marching rhythm from 70 to 120 paces per minute. This is exactly what happened under Napoleon, whose armies outmarched those of his foes. Among other things, Guibert suggested the introduction of "divisions," or autonomous army corps, which were indeed adopted in 1793 as part of a general army reform (Vagts 1959, 82–83).

Seen in a comparative perspective, the French Revolution was notable for at least three reasons. First, its occurrence, including the execution of the king and the abolition of the monarchy, clearly indicated that the integration of army, nobility, and monarchy was infinitely weaker than in Prussia. In 1789, the armed forces were so divided between defenders of the status quo and adherents of subversive ideas that they were unable to save the monarchy, or even the life of the king. Countless aristocrats shared the monarch's fate, and many saved their lives only by fleeing the country. In other words, what happened was exactly what the concept of revolution implies: a sudden and radical structural breakup, which "unleashed energies" (to use Clausewitz' expression) that changed the current patterns of warfare almost beyond recognition. It is needless to observe that no such event ever befell Prussian or German society.

Second, the belligerency of the revolutionary government shifted power from civilian to military leaders. Napoleon's military successes eventually destroyed the ruling revolutionary institutions, and his role as consul in the government was merely a first step toward absolute government. The French army eventually requested that he assume the emperorship. In other words, what is often believed to be an invariant characteristic of militarism actually occurred in the wake of the French Revolution: A general, supported by his army, formally assumes the government by a peaceful coup d'etat. Of course, no such thing ever happened in Prussian-German history (Vagts 1959, 116ff.).

Third, the French Revolution lasted long enough to set a pattern of political unrest and instability that haunted French society throughout the nineteenth century. The dread of another revolution was instrumental in redefining the role of the armed forces, which from that time would be expected to protect the French bourgeoisie from subversive violence. Equally appalling was the possibility of another military dictatorship. Napoleon had left a "heritage of shock" that took French society a century to overcome. Not only was the army purged, with considerable brutality, of Napoleonic officers, but it was also isolated from civilian life and expected to serve as an institutional safeguard against coups. To the extent that militarism survived the Napoleonic era, it was thus deflected, to a considerable degree, from external to internal objectives (Ritter 1970, 2: 10–15).

Again, comparison with Prussia reveals profound structural differences. The Prussian army required no safeguards to remain loyal to the established regime. The monarchy commanded the total loyalty of the officer corps, and usurpation of power by a general would have been unthinkable. Only once during the nineteenth century was the military temporarily deflected from its objective to serve as an instrument of foreign politics: It was used to suppress the revolution of 1848.

If one wishes to look for overall differences between French and Prussian militarism since 1789, the most striking one perhaps lies in the discontinuity of French developments in contrast to the continuity of Prussian-German military evolution. The first and most radical manifestation of discontinuity was the army reform Napoleon succeeded in carrying through by cleverly using the social upheaval created by the revolution. Neither universal conscription nor the opening of the military career to talent rather than status would have been conceivable under the *ancien régime*. Yet Napoleon's *levée en masse*, the renowned national army or, as it were, the "nation in arms," was not an instantaneous success. To supplement the voluntary contingents, thousands had to be rounded up and forcibly inducted like prisoners. Only the demonstration effect of a series of stunning military victories made it possible for Napoleon to marshal enough popular support and to tap nationalism, the "great energy source of war" (Vagts 1959, 109ff.). It was precisely the widespread popular support of war and everything related to war that transformed French society, at least temporarily, into a militaristic nation. It could be argued, of course, that the predatory nature of Napoleon's wars acted as a strong determinant of popular support. Eagerness for decisive battles was not just sound strategy from a military standpoint; it also accelerated the pillage of the vanquished country's resources. The army directly participated in the plunder to the extent that loot was allocated to officers and soldiers. Besides, heavy taxes were imposed on conquered territories. It has been estimated that, between 1805 and 1809, 743 million francs were extracted from defeated enemy countries (Vagts 1959, 123–24).

Napoleon's mass armies dwarfed everything his adversaries were able to muster. The first *levée en masse*, in 1793, amounted to 300,000 men. Between 1804 and 1813, 2,400,000 men were drafted, in addition to 50,000 volunteers, seamen, and *gardes d'honneur*. Casualties were disproportionately high, even in relationship to France's population of nearly 29 million. Of these, 1,700,000 perished before 1806, but diseases took a larger toll than battles (Vagts 1959, 125–27).

In sharp contrast to the style of eighteenth-century warfare, Napoleon's wars were known for the utter ruthlessness with which he pursued the complete annihilation of the enemy. In spite of his disregard for human lives, Napoleon enjoyed considerable popularity among his soldiers. Whenever expedient, he showed personal concern for the rank and file, and the soldiers, we are told, were moved to the point of protesting their willingness to die for him. The fact is that in 1815 a military revolt among the subaltern ranks brought Napoleon back to the throne and encouraged him to engage in a hopeless war against all of Europe (Ritter 1970, 2: 10).

The way French society reacted to the final defeat of Napoleon was the exact opposite of what happened in Prussia following the military debacle of 1806. The defeat of the Prussian armies generated a revival of militarism that became more virulent, relentless, and persistent than any of its preceding forms. In France, however, militarism entered a long-lasting decline. Conscription was abolished in 1814, and the army became a corps of professionals. The draft was reinstituted only when too few volunteers were available, but one could always escape military service by paying for a substitute. Neither social status nor financial rewards made the officer's career particularly attractive, and throughout the nineteenth century the military aristocracy gradually lost interest in the army career (Ritter 1970, 2: 12–15).

On three occasions, the French army found opportunity to live up to the expectations of the bourgeoisie, which was becoming very powerful indeed. When Charles X dissolved parliament in 1830, students and workers revolted, and street fighting broke out in Paris. The last Bourbon king abdicated, and Louis-Philippe of Orléans, *le roi citoyen*, acceded to the throne. In 1832, the opposition, showing the red flag for the first time, grew more violent until muted by military repression.

The second and far more serious manifestation of political instability was the revolution of 1848, which forced Louis-Philippe to relinquish the throne. In temporary control, the workers proclaimed the republic and proposed some Socialist reforms. Troops under General Cavaignac, "chief of the executive power," suppressed the workers' rebellion, and shortly thereafter Louis-Napoléon was elected president of the republic. Yet the new president did not consider himself committed to the republican regime, nor did he sympathize with the parliamentary system. In 1854, the legislative assembly was dispersed by the army, and once Louis-Napoléon had assumed discretionary powers, political repression became widespread and virulent. Close to twenty-six thousand opponents were taken prisoners, and several thousand of them were exiled to Algeria. A year later, a plebiscite restored the empire, and Louis-Napoléon assumed the throne. Again France became an authoritarian monarchy supported by the army.

The third political uprising occurred in the wake of the lost war of

1870–71. Following the deposition of the emperor, the Communards of Paris rose against the monarchistic assembly convening in Versailles. The civil war between the Commune and the army ended with the reconquest of Paris and the summary execution of numerous Communards (Seignobos 1969, 291–304).

The fall of the Second Empire and the adoption of a republican regime, combined with a parliamentary democracy, intensified the dilemma of the French military. How could they possibly build up loyal relationships with the state if no form of state seemed to have much permanency? A succession of widely different regimes had been punctuated by popular rebellions that the army was called to suppress, but in the name of powerholders whose credentials seemed suspect to the conservative officer corps. Napoléon Bonaparte had been extremely adept at eliciting strong feelings of loyalty from his officers and enlisted men, but none of his successors was able or allowed to establish strong ties with the military. On the whole, the officer corps retained a preference for the monarchy, and Louis-Napoléon obviously capitalized on that preference to become emperor. During the nineteenth century, no change was more radical than the founding of the republic, and none seemed less appealing to the military mind. The loyalty crisis in the army implied a tense relationship with a rather unstable government that went through thirty different war ministers in just as many years. Suspected or actual disloyalty of generals led to what the military interpreted as harassment (Ritter 1970, 2: 34–37). In its power contest with the army, the civil government eventually forced the military leadership to "recognize the primacy of the law," but not before Marshal MacMahon could be removed from his position. The marshal was believed to protect and shield the generals, who supposedly were ready to make a coup d'etat in 1877.

It is not surprising that the officer corps enjoyed the support of the most nationalistic sector of French society, which advocated a war of revenge against Germany. The French were unable to get over the crushing defeat of 1870–71 and the loss of their eastern provinces of Alsace and Lorraine. The idea of revenge was popular indeed, and for a time no one proved more successful in capitalizing on it than General Georges Boulanger, the *Général de la Revanche*. At one point, he was expected to overturn the government and to assume dictatorial powers, but his political skills were not up to his own ambitions or to the expectations of his followers (Vagts 1959, 317–18).

In 1898 the Dreyfus affair exploded, doing immense damage to the moral authority of the officer corps, especially the General Staff, and to the right wing allies of the military establishment. The scandal following the conviction of an innocent officer by a military court aroused a storm of public controversy. "The attitudes and language of a great many officers, aware of the force of 'military power,' generated considerable inquietude" leading to a generalized revolt against the "military mind" (Monteilhet 1932, 243; Gorce 1963, 48). Hardly anything seems less consistent with the more pervasive forms of militarism than the military's loss of prestige, but this is exactly what happened in the wake of the Dreyfus affair. "Distaste for army life was not restricted to conservative bourgeois families, but extended to the levels of society that had looked on an officer's commission as a step up on the social ladder, almost as a claim to renown" (Gorce 1963, 50).

Following the Dreyfus affair, the republican government endeavored to purge the army of the "anti-republican, monarchist and clerical" officers who were regarded as a potential threat to the regime (Gorce 1963, 51–54).

Quite in contrast to the Prussian army, the French forces proved unable to build up a record of great military victories during the nineteenth century. Napoleon's attempt to conquer Europe resulted in disastrous defeat, and the professional army serving two kings, the First Republic, and the Second Empire failed to live up to the military traditions of France. Emulating the belligerent posture of his great-uncle, Napoleon III took part in the Crimean War, but he showed dissatisfaction with the mediocre performance of his troops. Although participation in the Italian War resulted in territorial gains (Nice and Savoy), the military achievements of the French army failed to meet the expectations of the emperor (Monteilhet 1932, 36). Napoleon's humiliating defeat in 1870–71 clearly demonstrated that the French professional army was no match for Prussian military might.

The indifferent performance of the French armed forces between the fall of Napoleon I and the dethronement of Napoleon III was due not only to political instability but also to technological and organizational obsolescence. The Infantry Maneuver Regulations of 1862, for example, reproduced those of 1831, and they were hardly more than a repetition of the regulations of 1791. The latter, however, copied the Prussian regulations of the mid-eighteenth century. Thus it happened that a young soldier of the Second Empire was trained to repeat the stiff gestures and movements of the recruits of Frederick the Great.

Napoleon III experienced the greatest difficulties in breaking down the opposition of his own High Command to the introduction of an early type of machine gun and the rifled cannon. And in 1870, a French cavalry general voiced his opinion that "maps, geography, and topography were a lot of foolishness that only served to fluster the mind of honest people" (Girardet 1953, 102, 109–10).

As much as obsolescence may be at variance with effective preparation for war, it does not seem to be inconsistent with militarism. When
confronted with major changes, the French officer corps did not behave
differently from those who were unprepared to cope with the novelty or
who regarded the change as a threat to their own position. In fact, the
attitudes of the German officer corps were hardly different from those of
the French officers, but the authoritarian structure of Germany proved
more effective in overcoming resistance to change than the parliamentary democracy of the Third Republic.

Although the prospect of rampant militarism never ceased to worry
French society, the military establishment found a safety valve for aggressive militarism in the conquest of a vast colonial empire. In sharpest
contrast to the instability of the domestic political scene, French colonialism never swerved from its chosen course of action during most of
the nineteenth century. Building on historical precedents traceable to
the sixteenth and seventeenth centuries, the French embarked on a long
series of conquests in Africa, Asia, and the Pacific. Algeria was brought
under French rule between 1830 and 1848. The conquest of Cochin
China was completed in 1862, and Cambodia fell to France in 1863.
Gabon and the Congo became French colonies in 1870, Tunisia in 1881,
and the conquest of French Indochina ended with the occupation of An-
nam and Tonkin. New Caledonia was taken in 1853, and Tahiti in 1842.

French military imperialism received vigorous support from large
landowners and winegrowers, a class that had no perceptible interest in
either Algeria or Indochina. These seemingly endless colonial campaigns were believed to stimulate the "military spirit" and to provide
desirable career opportunities for the officer corps. Still another consideration gained strength as the domestic birth rate continued to fall: The
colonies were perceived as reservoirs for military recruitment. Two voluntary associations reflected the imperialism and chauvinism of the
French officer corps: the *Ligue des patriotes* and the *Comité de l'Afrique
Française* (Vagts 1959, 384–85).

The image of French militarism remained rather indistinct up to the
time of the Franco-Prussian War (1870–71), but it moved into sharper
focus under the pressure of defeat and the desire to vindicate military
virtues and national honor. After almost a half-century, conscription was
reintroduced in 1872. The objective was the creation of a strong army,
strong in numbers and patriotism. Again, the "revolutionary" idea of the
armed nation gained currency, approaching, at least in rhetoric, one of
the basic aspects of militarism. The military spirit the army was expected
to instill in the French soldier, associated with the notion of the army's
becoming a "school for all," resembles the tenets of Prussian militarism.

In fact, France attempted to close the gap between French and German military development by systematically adopting German organizational and technological patterns, which were noticeable even in "the smallest details" (Monteilhet 1932, 127, 161, 166, 196). Clausewitz was rediscovered and heavily influenced French military teachings (Vagts 1959, 221).

The single act that greatly accelerated the armament race with Germany was the alliance with Russia in 1894. Intended to compensate for the numerical inferiority of available French armies, the alliance was gradually strengthened to make a two-front war more effective. The Franco-Russian pact hit the most sensitive spot in the defense system of the German General Staff, whose members feared nothing more than a two-front war. The alliance with Russia, later joined by Great Britain, also provided substance to the obsessive German preoccupation with "encirclement" (Einkreisung).

Russia's crushing defeat at the hands of the Japanese (1904–1905) temporarily dampened French expectations regarding the effectiveness of a second front in the East, but even though French society was still seething from the aftereffects of the Dreyfus affair, it found itself locked in a seemingly irreversible arms race with Germany. Military expenditures, which had increased no more than 42.0 percent between 1883 and 1908, jumped 86.3 percent between 1908 and 1913. Like Germany, France had developed its military-industrial complex. Schneider-Creusot, the French equivalent to Krupp, was vitally interested in speeding up the arms race, and like its German counterpart, it demonstrated its close connections with the military establishment by "employing" ex-admirals and ex-generals in leading positions (Vagts 1959, 309).

Fanned by an increasingly intransigent nationalism, the belief in the ineluctability of a major war grew stronger in both countries. Collective sentiments about France, the Erbfeind (hereditary enemy), were reflected in such favorite pieces of martial music as the Pariser Einzugsmarsch (Entrance March Into Paris) and Siegreich wollen wir Frankreich schlagen (Victoriously Shall We Beat France).

Like the German army, the French forces were hampered by an obsolete tradition. Gorce offers startling examples of the refusal to recognize the crucial significance of certain technological innovations. Asked about heavy German artillery, a member of the French General Staff declared (in 1910): "Thank God, we have none. French strength depends on the lightness of its cannon." In 1909, the officer in charge of acquisitions judged that the machine gun available at that time made "no difference at all," and an exhibition of military aircraft in 1910 prompted this comment from the commander of the Army School: "All this is just sport. For the army, the airplane equals zero" (Gorce 1963, 55). Like the Germans (and all other European peoples), the French cherished their cavalry to the point of having three times as many cavalrymen as could be used in the war (Vagts 1959, 230).

The outbreak of World War I was celebrated with the same indescribable enthusiasm as in Germany, and like the Germans, the French were convinced that "victory would be easy and rapid." As in the Wilhelmian empire, the French Socialists—traditionally antimilitaristic and averse to war—supported the conflict in the name of "right" and "freedom" (Gorce 1963, 100).

The French forces proved incapable of protecting the country against invasion by the hated *Boches*, who fought the whole war on French soil. Although France eventually won, the price of victory—five million soldiers killed, wounded, or captured—was high enough to instill permanent doubts about the desirability of militarism. In fact, recent French political history has been punctuated by occurrences that may be interpreted as a gradual decline of militaristic patterns. The extremely costly construction of the Maginot Line suggested an overwhelming desire for security from continuing threats of a warlike neighbor rather than the intention of meeting belligerency with an equally aggressive stance. France certainly failed to respond to the Nazi challenge with a commensurate military effort that might have prevented the country from being overrun by Hitler's armed forces.

If French colonialism was one of the most unequivocal manifestations of militarism in the past, the unsuccessful struggle for the preservation of the colonial empire may be considered a clear indication that militarism was losing momentum. The drawn-out war intended to restore French rule in Indochina came to an inglorious end with the crushing defeat of Dien Bien Phu (1954) and the subsequent withdrawal from Southeast Asia. More serious than the loss of Indochina was the rebellion of the Moslem population of Algeria against French rule. Algeria was considered an integral part of France, and its French population of nearly a million fiercely resisted any change that might have affected their own political and economic status. French-Algerian activists and high-ranking army officers joined forces in conspiracies intended to change the political structure of the Fourth Republic, whose decision-making capabilities were seriously impaired by its growing instability and internal divisiveness. Eventually, the prospect of a possible civil war induced the political leaders of the Fourth Republic to propose a return of General Charles de Gaulle to power. A change of the constitution provided the legal basis for a considerable concentration of power in the hands of the president. Yet for all his authoritarian bearing, the general inaugurated a regime that has been called "plebiscitary democracy," allowing him to approach the people directly without recourse to the intermediary role of the political parties (Hartley 1972, 300, 302). De Gaulle's rise to power continued the well-established pattern of "Bonapartism," defined as a "national feeling" that should be "incarnated in a leader/savior who would appear as the expression of the popular will" (Hartley 1972, 302).

The question here is whether de Gaulle's version of Bonapartism rekindled French militarism that had been on the wane. The general's lofty rhetoric abounded with utterances vaguely suggesting a revitalization of the military spirit: "Life is life—in other words a struggle, for a nation as for a man"; "France was made with the strokes of the sword"; and "the military body is the most complete expression of the spirit of the social system" (Hartley 1972, 2, 7, 8).

If de Gaulle's immense moral authority and his unlimited confidence in the historical mission of France helped restore the dignity and self-respect of the French people, there was no attempt to revive the kind of militarism that the term *Bonapartism* suggests. Militarism is almost implicitly associated with conquest, but de Gaulle repudiated conquest involving domination of societies with different cultures. The general thought that such peoples could not possibly be integrated with French society (Hartley 1972, 8). Of course, this point of view was incompatible with the traditional assimilation doctrine, one of the ideological mainstays of French colonialism according to which the inhabitants of all French possessions would eventually become assimilated to the French way of life and thus cease to be colonials.

Needless to say, the Asian and African peoples under French rule perceived the assimilation doctrine as a convenient disguise of "colonial exploitation." Acquiescing to insistent demands for political emancipation, the Fourth Republic proceeded to grant them increasing autonomy and, by 1960, complete independence, except for Algeria. But it was precisely Algeria that was prepared to go to any length to gain complete independence from France. It fell to President de Gaulle to find a way to end the war of liberation in a fashion that would satisfy the Moslems, the French colons, and the military. Thus, de Gaulle embarked on a long, troublesome process, full of ambiguities and groping attempts to find some compromise. Eventually, he decided for an independent Algeria against the intransigent opposition of Algeria's French population and the military, some of whom engaged in a *Putsch* against the Fifth Republic. Lack of solidarity among the generals and de Gaulle's iron will thwarted the *Putsch*, which almost certainly would have led to a civil war had a lesser man been in power.

It thus happened that a general who personified the most genuine and awesome form of military mentality became the final liquidator of a colonial empire that may be considered one of the most consistent manifestations of French militarism.

The single most persistent and fateful source of militarism in Europe undoubtedly was the "hereditary" enmity between France and Germany. Charles de Gaulle eradicated that source by bringing about a reconciliation with the German Federal Republic. It was the sharpest possible reversal of a trend that had dominated French military traditions up to the 1930s.

Charles de Gaulle frequently indulged in delusions of grandeur where the international role of France was concerned. No appeal to past glory and the proclaimed superiority of French culture could compensate for the profound changes in the international power structure that had affected the relative status of the great powers of yesterday and severely diminished their chances of prevailing in the international decision-making processes. To create at least a semblance of self-determination and military capability, de Gaulle withdrew the French forces from the integrated command structure of NATO and created the *force de frappe*, an atomic striking force intended to defend France against potential enemies. Yet whatever foes he had in mind, Germany was no longer one of them.

Great Britain

Of the several structural prerequisites for the rise of Prussian militarism, the most important was the emergence of the absolute monarchy. There was no way of establishing a permanent army without curtailing the power of the estates. It is a well-known fact that in Great Britain absolutism never gained the undisputed prevalence it enjoyed in Prussia and most of continental Europe. The English kings had to share power with Parliament. No matter how often and how far royal power encroached on Parliament, the two houses eventually recovered and legislation was enacted by "the King, Lords and Commons in Parliament assembled" (Wittke 1921, 18).

The power contest between the king and Parliament culminated in the English civil war in which Charles I lost to the parliamentary forces. The Levellers, the radical wing of the antiroyalist movement, put forward a reform program that demanded, among other things, the sole sovereignty and legislative monopoly of the House of Commons, a drastic reform of the legal system recognizing equal rights and liabilities for all regardless of birth and wealth, and a comprehensive tax reform. It was proposed that "all power originated in the people, who merely entrusted their elective representatives with as much of it as they chose" (Aylmer 1975, 13). Although the Restoration put an end to such radical demands, the English civil war reestablished the parliamentary tradition and retained the structural elements that would make it possible to resist the militarism that in Prussia and elsewhere throve under absolutism.

Nevertheless, the English civil war, like the French Revolution, created political conditions favorable to powerful bursts of militarism. In fact, not unlike Napoleon, albeit on a much more reduced scale, Oliver Cromwell created his own brand of militarism, which left a deep enough impression on the collective memory of England's ruling classes that any attempt to revive it during the two subsequent centuries, under whatever label and for whatever purpose, was doomed to failure. An unusually gifted soldier, Cromwell (1599–1658) fought against royal absolutism and Parliament, put down the Irish and the Scots, created a high sea fleet, and proceeded to wage war against the Dutch and the Spaniards. Eventually, he dissolved the House of Commons and assumed the title of "Lord Protector." Actually, his regime, supported by a strictly disciplined army, was at times indistinguishable from a military dictatorship.

The unresponsiveness of England's ruling classes to the lures of militarism has to be judged in the light of the country's insularity. None of the geopolitical determinants contributing to the conversion of Prussia into a warlike state were present in Great Britain. Without assuming too much of a risk, the country could afford to reject the idea of a standing army, which was felt to be a threat to liberty. Antimilitarism became a basic component of British libertarianism. British soldiers were held in greater contempt than those of France; nevertheless, most officers were noblemen, and commissions were for sale. There was no general staff, and civilian supremacy in military affairs was taken for granted (Ritter 1970, 2: 33–37).

Obviously, British antimilitarism hardly seems consistent with Britain's imperialism and the means it used to become a world power. The way England's ruling classes managed to reconcile domestic antimilitarism with the most blatant and persistent use of organized violence abroad has no parallel in European history. Apparently, the permanent existence of the largest and most powerful battle fleet in the world was not felt to be a threat to liberty and civilian dominance. The fleet had been entrusted with the historical mission "to keep the sea lanes open" and to protect British interests wherever they were believed to be in jeopardy. This proved to be an immense task, implying the delegation of extraordinary power to the commanders of fleets and individual ships.

The performance of such duties not only kept the fleet away from the home bases much of the time, but it also provided a way of deflecting possible militaristic designs from the political process in the homeland. As a matter of fact, British militarism found fertile ground in the colonies, particularly in India where it capitalized on its indigenous versions. The so-called martial races, seventeen altogether, provided most of the "warriors" British imperialism needed to maintain itself (Beaumont 1977, 6). Under the rule of the East India Company (1750–1858), English trade interests were protected by a relatively large army, which in 1857 included 40,000 British soldiers and 300,000 sepoys (Beaumont 1977, 106). Between 1749 and 1900, the Indian army engaged in 131 "principal actions." Britain's tenacious efforts to control an extremely unruly western "frontier" entailed almost continuous and mostly inconclusive fighting. (Incidentally, in 1847 a whole British-Indian army of 40,000 men perished in Afghanistan.)

Indian troops were afforded ample opportunity to fight and die for the British Empire. In World War I, the Indian army grew to 573,000 men, and 943,000 were sent to France, East Africa, the Persian Gulf, Egypt, Palestine, and Mesopotamia. By 1945, the Indian officer corps included 8,300 Indians and 34,500 Englishmen (Beaumont 1977, 125, 162, 174). The steady transfer of a large number of British officers to colonial duty may be considered another outlet for ambitious would-be militarists, who thus spared the homeland some of the political complications that affected the power contenders of continental Europe. Although conflict solution by negotiation was not totally rejected, Britain's imperial record has been called "truly militaristic." According to Otley, British forces were involved in no less than forty-nine major colonial campaigns between 1803 and 1901 (Otley 1968, 85).

For all its militaristic features, British colonial warfare, with its specific requirements in terms of strategy and weaponry, apparently delayed modernization of the metropolitan army. Military innovations were judged primarily for their serviceability on the "frontier." Often they were rejected for being useless in colonial warfare (Beaumont 1977, 128).

There were situations in which Great Britain's reluctance to muster a large home army had to yield to the threat of invasion from the Continent. The menace was particularly serious in view of Napoleon's determination to extend his domain to the British Isles. After 1804, Parliament approved a large increase of the armed forces, which in 1814 numbered a quarter of a million. In spite of its size, it was not felt to be a threat to the constitution because its officer corps—"the aristocratic element in Parliament and the countryside"—"was so much part and parcel of the governing order." But it was also an obsolete army and remained so for several decades (Finer 1975, 152–53).

In the context of growing international tension and an accelerating armament race, Great Britain's attitude toward militarism (as she understood it) could not continue indefinitely without hurting her credibility as a great power, especially as she allowed herself to get involved in conflicts that could not be classified as colonial wars in the usual sense of the word. The Crimean War, imposing "immense sacrifices in blood and money," demonstrated the obsolescence of British army organization. Even more ominous were the British defeats in the Boer War (1899). Abruptly, Britain changed the whole military system, and in the restructuring process, the German model was used extensively. A General Staff was created, army pay and benefits were greatly improved, and soldiers in general came to be more respected in British society. In fact, rearmament generated so much patriotic zeal that the Labor Party branded it a form of "Germanization" and "militarization" of the British nation. Reflections of "militarization" could be seen in the sudden emphasis placed on "military fitness" in a number of educational institutions (Ritter 1970, 2: 39–49).

Undoubtedly, Germany's increasingly blatant militarism on land and water was felt to imperil the political status quo. The most significant focus of military "reawakening" was, of course, the British navy. A supportive ideology called "navalism" declaimed the moral accomplishments of the fleet, which had served mankind "by destroying slave trade and piracy, by keeping order on every shore and protecting equally the traders of every nation" (Marder 1940, 15). With that kind of record, the British navy seemed entitled to world supremacy. Supporting England's response to the competing naval development programs of major power contenders, the "navalists" endorsed the view that war was not only inevitable but necessary, according to the teachings of social Darwinism. Like certain German ideologists, they asserted that nations achieved greatness through war, and if they proved unable or unwilling to wage war, deterioration and eventual loss of national identity would seal their fate. General Lord Wolseley, commander in chief of the British army, echoed the pronouncements of German militarists: "War with all its evils calls out and puts to the proof some of the highest and best qualities of man: Fearlessness, daring, endurance, contempt of death, self-sacrifice, readiness to die for country or some other sacred cause. . . . The training involved in all this preparation for war is an invigorating antidote against that luxury and effeminacy which destroys nations as well as individuals" (Marder 1940, 9).

In the 1890s, "war was universally regarded, in England at least, as fairly imminent, inevitable and not undesirable." Foreshadowing the events of a yet distant future, England as well as the continental powers expected sudden attack without declaration (Marder 1940, 20–21).

It is not surprising that a powerful "industrial-military complex" developed in the form of a vast, intricate network of relationships between manufacturers of war materiel and military officers. Many of the most eminent army and navy men had substantial holdings in, or were directors of, armament firms. Three generals and five admirals figured on Vickers' sharelist in 1904, and over three hundred officers owned shares. To popularize the naval construction program, the people were assured that "warship building means bread to the working man." Industrial and arsenal towns lent strong support to large construction programs. Thus, "commercialism and patriotism were neatly dovetailed" (Marder 1940, 27–38).

In contrast to the situation in Germany, British society did not have to be converted to the idea that a powerful fleet was essential to the survival of the empire. Only strong reminders were deemed necessary. Even so, a special associational device, the Navy League, was created to convey the message of navalism to the man in the street. The Navy League was founded in 1895. In 1900, some forty-four branches existed in England and the colonies, but its membership (15,000 in 1901) looks puny in comparison with the 600,000 Germans who joined the German Naval League. At any rate, the Navy League had a profound impact on certain sectors of the British educational system where paramilitary training began to be emphasized (Marder 1940, 53–55).

To reinforce the navalistic campaign and to shock the skeptics, a "starvation theory" was launched, according to which "national starvation, on a scale hitherto unknown, would be [Great Britain's] fate if she were unable to guard her ocean trade during any future naval war" (Marder 1940, 85).

Great Britain's military establishment was plagued by the same inconsistencies that delayed the modernization of certain branches of the German and French armies. For decades, the usefulness of the cavalry in a future war was a favorite subject of discussion. "The bloody and ineffectual cavalry charges of the Franco-Prussian and earlier wars were conveniently forgotten," and in spite of the increasing prevalence of automatic weaponry and field artillery, the most improbable arguments were advanced to oppose the abolition of the British cavalry. The controversy was shot through with irrational motivations, which made the lance appear as "a state of mind" and the charges as "a way of life" (Bond 1965, 100). As in Germany, horse and lance were symbols of a defunct life-style associated with the wealthy nobility, which provided a large proportion of the British officer corps. Their power was such that not only the cavalry survived but even the lance, which at one time had been replaced by the rifle as the principal weapon for dismounted action. Apparently, the "restoration of the lance" four years before World War I was, at least in part, determined by an uncritical adoption of the German model of the cavalryman whose dashing heroics on the maneuver field so fascinated the kaiser (Bond 1965, 104, 115).

Jingoism did not have the staying power to carry Britain into the First World War. By the turn of the nineteenth century, it was already a thing of the past, but naval expansion continued at full speed. When Britain entered the war, her navy was powerful enough to block any significant action of the German fleet, but at the Dardanelles it experienced a humiliating, unprecedented defeat at the hands of the "inferior" Turks. Victory proved unkind to the fleet, the most obvious symbol of British militarism. Costly beyond contemporary imagination, the war left the empire in economic straits serious enough to render a "navy beyond challenge" unaffordable. The treaty of 1922 marked the end of Britain's absolute control of the seas. A total of 657 ships had to be scrapped, and from that time the country had to reckon with the rising naval power of the United States and of Japan (Morris 1978, 217).

British imperialism did not survive the First World War unimpaired. No matter how glorious or lucrative the imperial tradition might have been, 700,000 dead British soldiers seemed an excessively high price to pay for the preservation of a precariously overextended political structure that was beginning to show the first ominous cracks. It was in Ireland, at a time when Britain was fully engaged in fighting Germany and its allies, "that the prototype of imperial revolution was launched— the precursor of all the coups, rebellions and civil wars which were to harass the British Empire from now until the end" (Morris 1978, 219).

Yet while the indications of revolt multiplied, Britain was still capable of assuming the suzerainty of Arabic lands that the Ottoman Empire had lost in the war: Egypt, Palestine, Transjordan, Iraq, sections of the western shores of the Persian Gulf, most of the southern coast of Arabia, and the port of Aden. "A new class of imperialists, the Anglo-Arabs, came into being to administer it, and some people hoped it would one day mature into a new brown Dominion, standing loyal, grateful and useful in oil between India and the Mediterranean" (Morris 1978, 248). It was a forlorn hope, of course. In the 1930s, the "new imperialism" was challenged by subversion and dissent, and in the decades following World War II, the "Anglo-Arabic empire" disintegrated into a number of sovereign states.

Pushed into World War II, for which she was woefully unprepared, Britain once more was able to rally the empire against the most powerful military alliance that had ever challenged its existence in virtually all parts of the world. It was, to repeat Morris's words, "a swan song of some splendor." Five million fighting troops were raised, and characteristically, India mobilized the "largest volunteer army in history which fought almost everywhere." Some defeats the British suffered at the hands of the Japanese and Germans clearly reflected the obsolescence of the military structure that had made the empire great, but perhaps no defeat was more indicative of its vulnerability than the fall of Singapore in 1942, which has been called "the most humiliating single disaster in British imperial history" (Morris 1978, 449).

The decades following Britain's Pyrrhic victory witnessed the gradual disintegration of the empire. As the former dominions and colonies gained independence, British militarism lost its *raison d'être*. The "martial races" of India were no longer needed or available to fight wherever British imperial interests were deemed in jeopardy. Deprived of its traditional function to provide liaison among the far-flung possessions, the fleet was reduced to a fraction of what it had been at the height of British sea power. While France fought desperately to keep its colonial empire intact, British resistance was neither massive nor protracted. De Gaulle's France bore at least a semblance of militarism, but Britain's political climate has been altogether unresponsive to a revival of militarism.

Russland/Soviet Union

Peter I, or Peter the Great (1682–1725), is considered the founder of modern Russia and its military might, but as in Prussia, the antecedents of its militarism can be traced to the Middle Ages. An event of basic significance was the conquest of European Russia, with the exception of Novgorod, by the Tartars during the first half of the thirteenth century. Two centuries of close contact between conquerors and native society generated complex processes of transfer. The Muskovite armies adopted Mongolian weapons, military formations, and tactics. The useful practice of registering the population for the purpose of military conscription and taxation was also borrowed from the Tartars (Duffy 1981, 2). Relevant in the present context is the convergence of two military traditions that permeated each other and eventually originated the kind of militarism that led to the formation of modern Russia.

The wars and conquests of the Muscovite rulers of the sixteenth century indicated a strongly pronounced imperialistic tendency. The conquest of the Tartar Empire of Kazan opened the way toward the east and south. Mongolian Astrakhan, and with it the lower course of the Volga, fell to the Russians. Victorious campaigns against Sweden contrasted with bloody defeats in Poland (Duffy 1981, 6). But the most impressive expansion of the Russian power domain occurred in Siberia, which performed for many generations the functions of a frontier. A long series of military expeditions, which began in 1483, continued throughout the sixteenth and seventeenth centuries. The native peoples were gradually brought under Russian rule, often after long and bloody wars in which the cossacks played a leading role (Lantzeff and Pierce 1973, *passim*). In 1581, most of Siberia was already under Russian control, and by 1700, Russian rule extended to the Amur River and the Pacific Ocean. Protected by units of cossacks and musketeers, Russian administrative centers were established, and Russian peasants began to settle in Siberia in the early seventeenth century (Bushkovitch 1980, 115).

An imperialistic tradition was thus established and subsequently pursued, with unswerving consistency, over a period of four centuries right up to the present time. Under Peter I, the czardom of Muscovy became the "Empire of all Russias" and a great European power. As in Prussia, a permanent army became a prime mover of political development. In 1699 began the formation of an army composed of volunteers and conscripted peasants. Initially, the permanent army was thirty-two thousand men strong, at least "on paper," but as soon as the czar became involved in a series of wars, it began to grow more rapidly.

As in Prussia, belligerency was determined largely by geographical factors. Lacking natural defenses, the huge Russian plains were invaded 133 times before 1462 and 136 times between 1500 and 1700. The rule of Peter the Great lasted thirty-five years, and Russia was at peace for just two years during his long reign (Klyuchevsky 1969, 58). Long before Peter's reign, the dividing line between defense and aggression had become blurred. After all, was there a more effective way of preventing further aggression than bringing the actual or potential invaders under permanent control of the czar?

In Europe, Russian expansionism was directed first against Sweden. After suffering a serious defeat at Narva (1700), the czar reorganized the Russian army, building it up to two hundred thousand men. The protracted campaigns against Sweden, ending with the conquest of the Baltic countries and Finland, were significant insofar as Sweden was then one of the great military powers of Europe. Livonia and Estonia became the Baltic provinces of Russia and thus began the "Germanization" of Russian culture, especially of the military. The upper class of the Baltic provinces was composed of Germans who had settled there centuries earlier, and many of them embarked on a military or diplomatic career in the service of the czar.

Peter's successors directed Russian expansionism primarily against Turkey, which in the course of several wars lost territories located north of the Black Sea and the Sea of Azov. More significant, however, was the first confrontation with Prussian militarism under Frederick the Great. The chancellor of Czarina Elizabeth Petrovna (1741–62) regarded Frederick's territorial expansionism as a threat to Russian interests in Kurland and Livonia. Russia entered the Seven Years' War as Austria's ally, but not without first reorganizing its army. In 1757, the Russian forces invaded Prussia and won their first victory in the battle of Gross-Jägersdorf (Duffy 1981, 80–81). In the following year, the Russians occupied East Prussia, which they intended to annex. The occupation of this Prussian province may be seen as a demonstration of Russian military superiority, which was further corroborated on the battlefields of Zorndorf, Paltzig, and Kunersdorf. In fact, the battle of Kunersdorf was celebrated as the "greatest Russian military feat of the eighteenth century." In 1760, a Russian unit, with Saxon and Austrian units, succeeded in occupying Berlin for a few days (Duffy 1981, 90, 95, 111, 114–15). Russia did not succeed in annexing East Prussia but did gain a large part of Poland, which in 1795 ceased to exist as an independent state.

In the nineteenth century, Russian rule in the Far East was consolidated with the acquisition of the Amur Territory (1858) and the founding of Vladivostok (1860). These were considered symbols of imperial power against the expanding influence of France and Great Britain (Geyer 1977, 72–73). Between 1864 and 1884, Russia conquered and annexed a huge area of central Asia extending to the borders of Afghanistan and China. The Caucasus had fallen under Russian control by 1856.

Colonial expansion of the Western nations served as both a model and a stimulant to the Russian power elites. Like the West, Russia claimed to carry out a "civilizing mission" among the "semi-savage peoples" of central Asia. Yet underlying such ideological trimmings was an anxious, almost obsessive search for "safe" border lines. As expansion proceeded, the border line receded in a kind of illusive game that the military skillfully played for its own purposes. The point is that the conquest of central Asia and other regions was not an outgrowth of "expansionist strategy of Russian commercial and industrial capital" but a ploy of the military, "whose self-determination again and again confronted Petersburg with *faits accomplis*. The military logic was such that always new actions were deemed inevitable" (Geyer 1977, 74–75). "The fight against militarily inferior tribes of Central Asia disguised the fact that the Russian army was not capable of conducting a major European war. The international attention these campaigns attracted always pleased the Russian military" (Geyer 1977, 78). Whatever economic interests were attached to conquest and annexation, they were afterthoughts formulated to justify allocation of scarce resources.

The incorporation of a vast array of heterogeneous peoples in central Asia proved a relatively safe way of competing with the great colonial powers of the West, whose military intervention in such remote areas seemed unlikely. Russia's most serious problems derived from the fact that its available economic resources failed to measure up to its political ambitions, geared as they were to territorial conquest or, at least, to a continuous expansion of the sphere of Russian political influence. Although exhausted from the war against Napoleon I, Russia fought Persia from 1826 to 1828 and Turkey from 1828 to 1829; it put down the Polish rebellion of 1830–31 and subjugated the Caucasian mountain peoples in the 1830s and 1840s. The expansionist thrust toward southeastern Europe and the Near East brought Russia into open conflict with Great Britain, France, Turkey, and Sardinia in the Crimean War (1854–56). Russia lost the war, but even so it made another attempt in 1877 to conquer the Bosporus and bring Turkey under Russian rule. International pressure and the presence of a British fleet in Constantinople induced the Russians eventually to accept a compromise without achieving their goal.

Pan-Slavism afforded a convenient ideological banner to liberate the Slavic peoples of the Balkans from the Turkish "yoke," yet a "deplorable financial situation" and military weakness prevented Russia from providing the assistance that would have been commensurate with its rhetoric about Pan-Slavism. At any rate, setbacks of the Serbian army in its war of liberation against Turkey caused such public excitement in Russia that military intervention became inevitable. Although Serbia and Montenegro achieved independence, the performance of the Russian troops did little to improve the military reputation of the country (Geyer 1977, 56, 60, 67). Even more frustrating was Russia's inability to assist the Slavic brethren in Bosnia and Herzegovina in their rebellion against Turkish rule (1875). Instead of incorporating the area into its own orbit, Russia had to compromise, recognizing Austria's "right" to occupy Bosnia-Herzegovina in exchange for Austrian neutrality in the impending war against Turkey.

It was, of course, the Hapsburg Empire that successfully competed with Russia for political dominance in the Balkans. Austria-Hungary was perceived as the enemy, and the hostility of the Russian power elites gradually developed into "savage hatred" of Austria (Ritter 1970, 2: 87). Prussia's rise to the status of a great military power led to the growing awareness of the Russian military that they would have to contend not only with the Hapsburg Empire but also with the "Central Powers." The "awakening" came with Austria's defeat at the hands of the Prussian army in 1866. The Franco-Prussian War of 1870–71 and the founding of the German Empire gradually convinced the Russians that violent confrontations with Austrian and German imperialism would be inevitable. In 1882, General Skobelev called for a Franco-Russian military alliance against the Central Powers, a suggestion that rapidly gained acceptance in Russian military circles (Ritter 1970, 2: 19, 80, 82). As noted before, the alliance, which increasingly stressed preparation for a two-front war against Germany, exacerbated the arms race and became a major factor leading to World War I.

While Russia attempted to gain political dominance in southeastern Europe, it concomitantly pursued imperialistic objectives in Siberia. The construction of the Trans-Siberian Railway was intended "to link 400 million Chinese and 35 million Japanese with Europe," enabling Russian commerce to win the economic struggle in the Pacific by deflecting trade from the existing routes. All this was supposed to happen by "peaceful penetration." Czar Nicolas II even dreamed of Korea, Tibet, and Persia under Russian rule (Geyer 1977, 145–46). It is not surprising that Russia's expansionism clashed with the political interests of Japan, a yet-untested power contender determined to use its growing military might to assert itself in the international concert of nations. Russia's humiliating and disastrous defeat in the war against Japan (1904) temporarily diminished its military effectiveness in a projected two-front war against Austria and Germany. It was not until 1910 that the czarist government was able to promote the idea that "Russia was returning to the number of great military powers" (Geyer 1977, 226). A ten-year plan of expansion and modernization of its armed forces was intended to bring Russia's military capabilities up to the level of those of the Central Powers. Russia's ten-year plan was actively supported by its military allies, particularly France, while Austria's extreme belligerency provided a convincing political justification for Russia's military preparations.

The Austrian General Staff had indeed developed into a center of intransigence and truculent militancy "that in the end overwhelmed all diplomatic efforts at compromise." Austria's chief of staff, Conrad von Hötzendorf, took the typically militaristic position "that the destinies of nations and dynasties are settled on the battlefield rather than at the conference table." Encouraged by Austria's military alliance with the German Empire, Von Hötzendorf advocated a preventive war against Italy, as well as the occupation of Serbia, Albania, and Montenegro. Strangely enough, he perceived war as a means of overcoming the ethnic discord that was undermining the political structure of the Austro-Hungarian Empire (Ritter 1970, 2: 227–31).

Serbia was, apart from Bulgaria, the only country in southeastern Europe that had remained within the Russian power domain. Its alliance with the czarist empire had assumed a symbolic meaning of such magnitude that Russia considered its own political future to be inexorably linked with that of Serbia. In fact, on the eve of World War I, the czar was convinced "that the Russian throne would be in peril if the Serbs were now abandoned to their fate" (Ritter 1970, 2: 89). When in 1914 Austrian forces invaded Serbia in retaliation for the assassination of the successor to the Hapsburg throne, and Germany did nothing to prevent further military sanctions against Serbia, the czar signed the declaration of war against the Central Powers. What contributed to this decision was the fact that Russian statesmen foresaw the collapse of the Turkish empire and the "need" for Russia to assume control of the Bosporus. Thus, Russia's entry into the war was determined by the conviction of the military elite that the imperial position of the country and the honor of the army demanded that Serbia be supported and that Constantinople should not fall into the hands of another power (Geyer 1977, 238). "The vision was of a reunited Poland attached to the Russian empire, Czecho-slovakia under a Russian prince, Serbia a Russian protectorate, Hungary and Romania falling into the Russian sphere, and part of east Prussia added to Russia" (Dallin 1951, 3).

Ritter argues that the Russian government's decision was not determined by "war-like ambitions, but political motives of prestige and self-assertion considered appropriate to great-power status" (Ritter 1970, 2: 89). The argument seems to imply the possibility of warlike ambitions existing in some sort of vacuum, apart from political and other motives. However, there appears to be no evidence that warlike ambitions *per se* actually cause war. Even the most warlike peoples always fight for something, be it retaliation, conversion, status, prestige, or economic resources of some kind, including territory. What actually characterizes a warlike or militaristic society is the preference of war to any other way of accommodating conflict. The fact that, over a period of four centuries, czarist Russia consistently chose war as a means of territorial expansion certainly puts it in the category of militaristic states. As in Prussia, an absolute monarchy, closely associated with a service nobility, provided the essential structural prerequisites for militaristic developments. As in Prussia, a disfranchised peasantry was available for recruitment purposes, but before the adoption of the Prussian system of universal conscription, there were no multinational mercenary armies in Russia.

It has been pointed out that, in contrast with most European armies of the eighteenth century, the Russian army constituted a homogeneous uninational body, integrated by the belief in a "national God." Furthermore, the ordinary soldier believed that all those killed on the battlefield would return, after three days, to a free and happy life in their native villages (Duffy 1981, 136). Many such beliefs faded away in the course of time, but many of them survived. Social and religious homogeneity and solidarity may have given the Russian infantry of the eighteenth century a relative superiority not to be found in other aspects of the Russian military system.

In comparing Russian with Prussian militarism, one cannot fail to discover, along with superficial similarities, profound structural differences that, at least in part, explain their diverse performance record.

It has already been made abundantly clear that the stability, continuity, and martial accomplishments of Prussian militarism were causally related to the extremely close ties between monarchy, nobility, and officer corps. To make such a cooperation fruitful, each of the three components must develop a high degree of internal consistency and the capability of concerted action. If the monarchy, nobility, and officer corps of czarist Russia are analyzed from this point of view, differences between it and Prussia become rather obvious. The major weakness of the Russian monarchy lay in the problem of succession that, more often than not, occurred in an atmosphere of political crisis accompanied by threats of violence or actual violence. Long before the actual investiture, some pretenders to the throne recruited private armies so that they could effectively carry through their claim. Peter I had to defend himself against the conspiracies of his sister Sophia. His accession to the crown became possible only after he had assured himself of the support of the nobility and the military. He killed his own son and further complicated the succession problem by abolishing primogeniture (Duffy 1981, 10). The death of Peter II led up to the plottings of the court nobility that eventually chose Anna, duchess of Kurland. Anna's demise was followed by the usual plots, in which the final decision was determined by the royal guard. Elizabeth Petrovna, daughter of Peter the Great, assumed the throne with the assistance of the military, and Peter III was deposed by his wife Catherine with the support of the guard and subsequently assassinated. Paul I (1796–1801) was murdered by his military retinue and officers of the royal guard. These and similar events indicate that the Russian monarchy was never entirely successful in its efforts to establish a tight relationship of loyalty with the nobility and the military leadership.

One of the most conspicuous characteristics of the Russian aristocracy was a heavily pronounced internal stratification. Immense latifundia worked by thousands of peasant serfs testified to the wealth and power of the highest aristocracy. At the beginning of the eighteenth century, the top stratum of Muscovite nobility constituted a tightly knit group of 137 families that owned a disproportionately large part of the existing 360,000 peasant households. Numerous members of those noble families played a leading role in the army and in the highest echelons of the bureaucracy (Duffy 1981, 136). In the sharpest possible contrast to those feudal lords stood the lower nobility, whose properties, reduced by repeated partitions, did not allow a way of life significantly different from that of free peasant landholders. In 1782, the male population of this stratum amounted to approximately 108,000. Most military officers, however, came from the middle nobility. The enormous social, political, and economic contrasts between these strata precluded the formation of a homogeneous class consciousness and a common political ideology. Internal differentiation was further accentuated by the policy of ennobling, indiscriminately, thousands who were willing to embark on a military officer's career. Peter the Great determined that *all* officers of bourgeois background were to be made members of the nobility and that all their descendants were also to be considered nobles. Needless to say, this policy entailed a considerable status depreciation among the nobility of ascent (Duffy 1981, 138). In sharp contrast to Russia, there was no heavy concentration of power in the higher ranks of the Prussian nobility, nor did ennoblement become a generic reward indiscriminately allotted to any individual upon joining the officer corps. Unlike the enormous estates of the Russian high nobility and their great wealth, the land-holdings of the Junkers were small, and their wealth, if it existed at all, tended to be on the modest side. Furthermore, living in a small country, the Prussian nobleman was never far from the royal court. This made control easy and breach of loyalty difficult.

The Russian officer corps was able to pursue power politics that often conflicted with the interests of the czar. Although intended to protect the monarch and the regime, the royal guard often played a leading role in overthrowing the government by means of violence (Duffy 1981, 140). The machinations and conspiracies involving many officers suggest a strongly pronounced political factionalism, which contrasts markedly with the political reliability and loyalty to the monarch characterizing the Prussian officer corps.

Another apparent difference was the inadequate professional training of the Russian officers. The members of the high aristocracy were particularly casual in the way they approached their military obligations. Although some military academies had existed since the early eighteenth century, only a small proportion of the officers received formal military training. A newly established cadet school educated so few officers that it fell woefully short of satisfying the army's demand for professional leadership (Duffy 1981, 143). Apparently, the officer's career proved so unattractive to native Russians that the ruler had to recruit foreign officers who, most notably under Peter I and Anna, represented one-third of the entire officer corps. In Prussia, the recruitment of Huguenot officers was a unique event, but the presence of numerous alien officers among the Russian military developed into a permanent institution that lasted far into the nineteenth century. More numerous than other alien groups, the German-Baltic officers ranked high among the protagonists of Russia's militaristic tradition.

Another trait that distinguished the Russian officer corps from Prussian and most other European officers was the lack of corporate pride and "knightly values" (Duffy 1981, 154). The structural weakness of the political trinity (monarchy-aristocracy-officer corps) reduced, from the very start, the chances of Russian militarism's success in the international power struggle of the nineteenth century. Since the social and political prestige of the Russian officer was "incomparably lower" than that of his Prussian peer, there was no incentive for other social classes to adopt martial modes of behavior in civilian pursuits. The rather unimpressive record of the Russian officer corps certainly stood in the way of social aspirations that, if fulfilled, might have placed the corps in a position similar to that of its Prussian counterpart (Ritter 1970, 2: 77).

One should not lose sight of the fact that the flowering of German militarism was based on the nearly unconditional support of a rapidly growing and increasingly prosperous bourgeoisie, whose rise was tied in with the industrial revolution of the Wilhelmian era. The Russian bourgeoisie was not only small but deeply divided. The bone of contention was not militarism but the autocratic regime itself, which was strongly resisted by various factions including Socialist groups far more inclined to radical revolutionary action than their German brethren.

Self-styled intellectuals and students demanded, among other things, abolition of servitude, and in the 1870s "students" attempted in vain to instigate the peasantry against the feudal landholders. Later, around the turn of the century, the growing industrial labor force of the cities became the target of revolutionary propaganda increasingly directed against the czarist regime. Among the revolutionaries, there were already groups of terrorists, and one of their victims was Czar Alexander II, assassinated in 1881. In 1905, when a crowd of workers demonstrated in front of the Winter Palace in Saint Petersburg, troops fired on the crowd and killed hundreds of demonstrators.

Shortly after 1874, the Russian government began to push military reforms stressing education and nationalistic indoctrination of the officer corps, but somehow the czar and his ministers proved unable to implant among the highest ranks the same degree of discipline that characterized the Prussian officer. Like all other armed forces, Russia's had a General Staff, but it was composed of "military bureaucrats unfamiliar with combat" and was quite unpopular among the armed forces (Ritter 1970, 2: 79–80).

The generals and the minister of foreign affairs who urged a reluctant czar to sign the mobilization order in July of 1914 apparently had no inkling of the implications of their action. Convinced that failure to assist Serbia would cause irreparable harm to Russia's regime and credibility as a great power, they entered the war grossly overrating their own strength and totally oblivious to the possibility that an unsuccessful war might threaten the very regime they were trying to preserve.

Russia's inability to wage a modern war became obvious almost immediately. Large Russian forces invaded eastern Germany, but in such an uncoordinated and utterly confused way that the initial success was rapidly transformed into a crushing defeat. The battle of Tannenberg (1914) sealed the fate of the invading forces, 150,000 of whom were captured by the Germans. From that time, the Russian military proved unable to prevent the war from being fought on Russian soil.

Final defeat on the battlefield created conditions leading to the destruction of the monarchy and its supporters. The Russian revolution of 1917 accomplished what the winners of the German revolution in 1918 failed to do, namely, a radical, violent transformation of the social structure. Instead of accommodating internal conflicts by compromise, as the Germans did, the Russian revolutionaries, once more preferring war to negotiated agreements, fought for years their internal enemies and their alien allies until they were able to consolidate the regime of their choice. They could not prevent the conversion of former Russian territories into independent states (Poland, Lithuania, Latvia, Estonia, and Finland), but they succeeded in establishing a totalitarian state whose ideological gospel and course of action were felt to be threats to the political stability of the Western nations.

A considerable proportion of the German officer corps survived the war and the revolution as a cohesive unit, assuming a leading position in the new army and preserving the militaristic tradition of the past, but no such continuity was even remotely possible in Soviet Russia. Years of civil war, following the revolution proper, acted as a selecting mechanism, forcing Russian armies to take sides for or against the Marxist regime. A substantial number of officers who decided to join the revolutionary armies found ample opportunity to demonstrate their loyalty to the Soviet state by fighting and possibly dying for it. Ex-czarist officers constituted the original cadres around which the Red Army could be organized.

There were early indications that Soviet Russia intended to develop a fighting machine far more militaristic than the czarist military establishment had ever been. The belief in the inevitability of war, so closely associated with German militarism, emerged within the context of Lenin's and Stalin's political doctrine: "The existence of the Soviet Republic, side by side with the imperialistic states, for a long time is unthinkable. One or the other must triumph in the end. And before that end supervenes a series of frightful collisions between the Soviet Republic and the bourgeois states will be inevitable. That means that if the ruling class, the proletariat, wants to hold sway, it must prove its capacity to do so by military organization also" (Lenin, as quoted in Tokaev 1956, 10). Since no lasting peace is conceivable while the Soviet state is threatened by capitalistic intervention, "the capitalistic encirclement must be destroyed." A war waged to liberate a country from "capitalistic domination" is *eo ipso* a "just" (and implicitly desirable) war (Tokaev 1956, 10).

Nevertheless, "the Soviet Union never initiates an aggressive war; it fights only in self-defense." Soviet propaganda has been absolutely consistent, although not always convincing, on this point. Even the conquest of the Ukraine and the independent Caucasian states in 1920–21 was carried out in the name of native self-determination. The Baltic states were absorbed "at their request." The Soviet war against Finland (1939–40) was "provoked by the Finns" (Dinerstein 1959, 209). And Soviet military intervention in Hungary, Czechoslovakia, and Afghanistan was carried out "at the request" of established governments allegedly threatened by forces hostile to socialism. Whatever ideological facade the Soviet powerholders wish to maintain, preparations for war have assumed such extraordinary proportions that a "pre-emptive strike" against any nation or alliance of nations must be considered a distinct possibility.

Whether offensive or defensive, modern war reaches the entire society; therefore, the civilian population must be trained for war in order to integrate it into the defense structure (Odom 1976, 34–35). In other words, one of the most relevant traits of militarism, namely, the permeation of a whole society with military modes of thinking and acting, was programmed and gradually put into practice by the powerholders of the Soviet state. Actually, the process was not limited to the transmission of military skills, values, and attitudes from the army to the civilian population. To understand the highly original nature of Soviet militarism, one has to be aware of the role the Communist Party has played in the process being examined.

Created by the Party, the Soviet army was used to seize power and to keep it. To preserve the dominant role of the Party, special structural devices had to be adopted to prevent the armed forces from gaining a measure of autonomy, which might conceivably lead to deviations from the established Party ideology. Much of what has been written about the relationships between the Party and the military seems to be based on the assumption that political and military interests do not mix, creating resentment, suspicion, and latent antagonisms between the two institutions. Actually, the Party-military relationship resembles a symbiosis rather than a coercive association shot through with veiled antagonisms. In fact, the controlling organ of the Party, the Main Political Administration, designed to prevent blatant disregard of Party directives by the army command, underwent intensive militarization insofar as its officers are an integral part of the military establishment "fully sharing its heroic traditions, privileges, prestige and responsibilities. The political officers assist line officers in maintaining discipline, high levels of professional competence and combat readiness, plus inculcation of the proper moral-political outlook" (Warner 1977, 74).

The linkage of Party and armed forces is achieved primarily by overlapping membership. The Communist Youth League *(Komsomol)* maintains cells in virtually all military units, and nearly 90 percent of all officers, warrant officers, and enlisted personnel are members of the Party or *Komsomol* (Scott 1979, 257). The integration of the Party and the army is institutionally sanctioned, at the highest level, in the form of a Council of Defense, a Party-military agency headed by Party Secretary and Marshal of the Soviet Union. At the Ministry of Defense level, there is a Main Military Council headed by the minister of defense, and similar councils supervise each of the five services (Scott 1979, 268–69).

Since integration does not mean loss of separate identity, the possibility of conflict between Party and military has to be admitted. It seems difficult to reconcile the accepted principle of "one-man leadership" with any given commander's dependence on Party "recommendations," which in reality tend to be orders rather than advice. To prevent such conflicts, military commanders are urged to assume leadership of Party units (Goldhamer 1975, 298).

The point here is that the Communist Party, in order to thoroughly politicize the armed forces, *underwent a process of militarization itself.* Incidentally, Stalin described the Party in military terms: "In our Party, if we have in mind its leading strata, there are about three to four thousand first rank leaders whom we would call our Party's General Staff. Then there are thirty to forty thousand middle rank leaders, who are our Party Corps of Officers. Then there are about a hundred to a hundred and fifty thousand of the lower rank Party Command Staff, who are so to speak our Party non-commissioned officers" (Mead 1951, 52).

Three interconnected facts point to a form of militarism especially adapted to the requirements of the Soviet state: (1) Within the Party cadres exists a highly specialized officer corps assigned to all army units to indoctrinate military personnel in the official political doctrine and to assure allegiance to the regime; (2) A very large proportion of the Party membership consists of military personnel; and (3) Many officers representing all levels of the military hierarchy occupy leading positions in the Communist Party.

A further hallmark of Soviet militarism is to be seen in the undisputed priority that the preparation for war has been given since the early 1930s. This aspect assumes particular relevance in view of the general state of underdevelopment of Russian society, aggravated by a lost war, years of civil strife, and the high cost of adapting a recalcitrant society to the exigencies of the officially approved Marxist-Leninist model. Only by ruthlessly imposing the most austere restraints upon the production of nonmilitary goods could the Soviet state hope to bridge the gap that separated its military technology from that of the Western nations. During the 1930s, the powers of a totalitarian regime were put to work to produce a vast arsenal of modern weaponry, the effectiveness of which, however, was diminished by Stalin's purges of the officer corps (Mackintosh 1965, 254; Zhilin 1969, 163).

World War II brought another invasion far more extensive and destructive than all previous ones combined. Only by relentlessly harnessing Russia's remaining human and material resources to the exigencies of total war were the Soviet powerholders able to defeat the German armies. In the final phase of the war, the rapidly advancing Russian armies found ample opportunity to revive the centuries-old tradition of territorial expansionism. Not only did they seize areas that had been under czarist control until World War I, but they also occupied whole countries that had never before been under Russian rule. In the East, Japan was forced to give up all continental possessions, as well as the Kuril Islands and southern Sakhalin, which were annexed by Russia. In the West, the three Baltic states and parts of East Prussia became Russian territory. The most significant accretions to the Soviet empire were undoubtedly the satellite states that indigenous Communist groups, protected and controlled by Soviet armies, were allowed to erect in Poland, East Germany, Czechoslovakia, Rumania, Bulgaria, Yugoslavia, Hungary, and Albania. Outright annexation of those countries would have imperiled the credibility of the Soviet regime that for decades had vociferously decried any form of colonialism and "imperialistic exploitation" of dependent peoples. Moreover, the Soviet Union was already saddled with the problems of a multiethnic society, and the dubious prospect of adding a number of other nations, each composed of diverse ethnic groups and set apart from each other by differing levels of socioeconomic development, probably contributed to the establishment of indirect rule. A formula had to be found that would reconcile the imperialistic tradition with ideological sanctions drawn from the Soviet version of Marxist doctrine. The fact that Yugoslavia had shaken off its satellite status as soon as the Soviet troops had left the country demonstrated that the presence of military force was essential to the maintenance of Soviet domination (Dallin 1951, 4). Rebellions in Poland, Hungary, and Czechoslovakia further indicated that the solidarity of the satellite Communist Party with the Russian Communist Party was not strong enough to override political particularism. No longer could it be assumed that the satellite parties were capable of retaining the power monopoly in their own countries, or that they would continue to respect the supreme authority of the Soviet state.

The Soviet Union had armed the satellite countries, but could their armies be trusted to remain docile instruments of the ruling party? The example of the Hungarian revolution suggested the opposite. The *ultima ratio* the Soviets resorted to was direct control of the least reliable satellite forces by Russian commanders. Furthermore, military occupation of most satellite nations was consolidated in the form of permanent garrisons, twenty-eight of which (in 1958) "are still needed to occupy Hungary while Hungarian soldiers, now commanded directly by Russian officers, can still not be trusted with weapons, and the situation is hardly much better elsewhere" (Arendt 1958, 42). The imposition of a Russian command structure on the Polish army was tried out in the 1950s, only to be abandoned at the insistence of the Polish government. Yet Russian garrisons became a permanent fixture in Poland, as they did in East Germany and Czechoslovakia (Staar 1958, 83).

Soviet dominance at the top level was established in 1955 by the Warsaw Pact. All satellite nations agreed on a joint military command under the supreme authority of a Soviet marshal (Staar 1958, 83).

If judged within the context of traditional Russian imperialism, the creation of the satellite states may be considered an outstanding achievement of centuries-old political aspirations. Like all earlier conquests, it was primarily a military achievement, and its permanence is predicated on military force rather than ideological control.

In addition to the revival of imperialism, the militarization of Russian society reflects and completes the portrait of a rather extreme form of militarism. Fifty percent of all men are inducted into the armed forces, usually at the age of eighteen. The other half receives some kind of military training beginning at the age of fifteen. Furthermore, a large proportion of the adult population is involved in mass defense activities, such as civil defense, patriotic assemblies, marches, rallies, physical training, and the like (Scott 1979, 69). Youth military training is centralized in the state-sponsored Volunteer Society for Cooperation with the Army, Aviation, and the Fleet (DOSAAF). Directed by a general of the army or air force, and staffed by numerous active duty officers and political officers, DOSAAF has 330,000 separate units, many of which are specialized in aviation, mechanics, and a large variety of sports, more or less closely associated with military interests. Boys and girls are recruited for such programs through the secondary schools. A total of 140 hours plus 40 hours in summer camps is devoted to military training activities (Scott 1979, 309–10, 316–17).

One can hardly explore the labyrinth of Soviet military training programs and structures without coming away with a sense of their pervasiveness and integration into all aspects of Soviet life. By the time a child is in the second grade, he receives his first formal instruction in survival in nuclear war. He learns not only that survival is possible but also how to go about saving himself personally. By his mid-teens, he confronts the "military supervisor" of his secondary school. About the same time, the local military commissariat is suggesting that he "volunteer" for one or more of the specialized military training courses offered by DOSAAF organizations. By age 18 or 19, he expects to be called to two years of active military service. If he matriculates at an institute of higher learning, he implicitly commits himself to becoming a reserve officer. If he wants to pursue any of a number of engineering specialties at the graduate level, he will learn that the best training in those areas—sometimes the only training—is found in military research facilities and in the graduate programs of military academies and schools. Even if he is a gifted musician and makes his way to the Moscow State Conservatory, he will not escape the militarization of Soviet education, for there he will find a military music department with generals as professors of directing and composition. If he becomes an economist and finds employment in GOSPLAN, discovering a General-Colonel in the post of a deputy chief would hardly surprise him (Odom 1976, 46).

Increasing efforts have been made "to surround military life with the rituals and appeals that associate the virtues of heroism, national service, and adventure with military life" (Goldhamer 1975, 23). To make the officer's career more attractive, pay and rank perquisites were adopted that put the professional army officer at a distinct advantage over civilians with comparable qualifications. "New salary scales increased divergence between officers and enlisted men and between senior and junior officers. Marshals, generals, field grade officers, and junior officers have their own messes and recreational facilities" (Goldhamer 1975, 25, 179). A colonel's pay of five hundred rubles a month was found to be equal to that of a factory manager, and the earnings of a marshal or admiral (two thousand rubles a month) are on the level of those of a cabinet minister. "More important than salary, however, is the officer's access to luxuries unavailable to most Soviet citizens. Officers enjoy free annual vacations at exclusive resorts, top-quality housing and privileges at shops that carry scarce imported foods" (*Time*, June 23, 1980, 31).

The officer corps obviously constitutes a privileged stratum of Russian society, but different arms and services apparently rank differently so far as levels of prestige are concerned. The navy ranks high, for example, and its relatively high position seems to be related to the emergence of a hereditary tradition in the officer corps (Goldhamer 1975, 24).

On the other hand, the Soviet military system has developed performance expectations that exceed even those of the Wilhelmian or National Socialist armed forces.

The demands made on personnel, both enlisted and commissioned, are relentless. Soviet military training is all the more onerous, all the more demanding, because it embraces not only the development of military skills in the conventional sense, but also a wide range of ideological, moral, and character traits and attitudes. Training so permeates the hour-to-hour and day-to-day activities of the Soviet forces that the distinction between operational and training activities becomes blurred (Goldhamer 1975, 321).

A comparison of the Soviet military system with that of Germany immediately yields one major difference: Soviet militarism is a creation of the state. All decisions relating to the preparation for war, the extent to which Russian society is to be militarized, and the ways and means of militarization emanate from the Supreme Soviet, which is virtually identical with the powerholders of the Communist Party. No other source of militarism is discernible in Soviet society. This means, of course, that all military decisions have to be implemented by different branches of the bureaucracy.

Without diminishing the determinant role the Prussian state performed in the creation of militarism, there is no doubt that, once it had taken hold, it developed dynamics of its own. Its extraordinary pervasiveness did not result from state-centered organizations and training programs, but from the fact that the meaning attached to an officer's commission, his paraphernalia, rank, attitudes, and deportment transcended the status prerogatives ascribed to professional groups in general. Militarism was implicitly and informally sanctioned by recognizing the officer corps as the top stratum of the social pyramid, and the officer's commission was widely used to move up to the top of the class structure. Furthermore, there was a profusion of voluntary associations with varying objectives and membership, but all shared a common denominator, namely, the cult of the military spirit. But what set German militarism even more apart from the Soviet version (and that of all other European nations) was *its tendency to encroach on all other professional sectors, causing their members to behave, in many situations, as if they were officers or enlisted men.* In other words, German militarism developed a social spontaneity that would be unthinkable in Soviet society. Soviet militarism tends to be pragmatic and goal oriented, while German militarism, at least in many of its ramifications, lost touch with military objectives only to become a kind of stylish game indulged in to validate status aspirations.

A comparison of Soviet militarism with its National Socialist version suggests parallels deriving from the totalitarian structure of both societies, but aside from the power monopoly vested in a single party and its leader, the structural differences between the two military systems are rather obvious. As indicated before, the Russian revolution of 1917 replaced the czarist forces with a new army created and controlled by the Communist Party. All competing armies were destroyed or forced to abandon Russian territory. However, Germany's aborted revolution of 1918 allowed the officer corps of the empire to assume command of the newly created army, which grew very powerful indeed. Far from becoming a docile instrument of the state, it stood for a political tradition opposed to republic, parliamentary democracy, and socialism. In contrast to the Soviet state, the Weimar Republic tolerated most of the private armies fighting for various causes, most of them incompatible with the regime. The strongest of those militias, the National Socialist storm troops, played a decisive role in the overthrow of the Weimar Republic.

Far from creating one monolithic military system, unambiguously and totally at the service of the regime, the victorious Hitler maintained his storm troops (SA) and praetorian guards (SS). True enough, the *Reichswehr* did nothing to prevent the Nazis from seizing power, nor was there any attempt to dissuade officers and enlisted men from joining the Party, but the German armed forces succeeded in keeping their separate identity. Hitler was known to harbor suspicions of the General Staff and his commanding generals, suspicions that at times bordered on the paranoid. He consistently retired generals who were known or suspected critics of the regime; nevertheless, the attempt to kill Hitler toward the end of World War II was carried out by conservative members of the officer corps.

The difference between the Nazi militias and the regular German army became quite apparent during the war. While Hitler's SA and SS transferred the pattern of domestic terrorism to the battlefields and occupied territories, the regular army by and large tended to abide by the norms of international conventions and a traditional honor code. The private army of the National Socialist Party was doubtlessly instrumental in securing Hitler's rise to power; it was equally effective in eliminating real and suspected enemies of the regime. Yet in purely military terms it was not only redundant and divisive but counterproductive insofar as its bestial style of warfare reinforced the determination of the Allies, particularly Russia, to erase Nazism from the face of the earth, regardless of the cost.

Before World War II, preparation for war and the militarization of the German people reached a pitch that surpassed military developments in Soviet Russia, but after 1945 the trend was reversed. The catastrophic defeat and political division of Germany caused militarism to subside, at least in the Federal Republic, but it has gained momentum in Russia, particularly since the 1960s. In fact, the militarization of Soviet Russia in recent years has dwarfed not only its own historical precedents but similar developments in contemporary Europe, including Wilhelmian and National Socialist Germany. Within the structural context of the Soviet empire, East Germany is merely an adjunct of Russian militarism. The organization, equipment, and indoctrination of its armed forces closely follow those of Soviet Russia, and to the extent that an East German militarism exists, it is tightly integrated with Soviet militarism. The East German soldier swears to fight side by side with the Soviet army and the armies of their Socialist allies to protect socialism, and his oath of allegiance forces him to obey unconditionally his military superiors (Forster 1968, 239).

The Fascist Interlude

All totalitarian regimes of the radical right are often subsumed under the generic concept of "fascism." The similarities between Italian fascism, National Socialism, and their different international offshoots allegedly justify the use of a generic term (Schieder 1976, 196; Payne 1980, 5). Chronologically, the Italian Fascist movement came first. It represented, as it were, the model for all other versions. Although there are obvious similarities, it should be pointed out that the roots of National Socialist militarism were quite different from those of Italian fascism. Hitler was able to connect directly with a tricentennial living tradition, but there was no such tradition in Italy. The ideologues of fascism tried to revive the symbols of Roman militarism, and the political elite took pride in the role of "heirs" to the Roman Empire. Mussolini called his militia *Fasci di Combattimento,* and the fasces of the Roman lictors were reinstated as symbols of authority and solidarity of the movement. What the doctrine of racial superiority meant for the National Socialists, Roman imperialism meant for the Italian Fascists (Smith 1976, 84). "Rome is our point of departure and our reference," wrote Mussolini. . . . "We dream of a Roman Italy, of an Italy wise and strong, disciplined and imperial. Much of the immortal spirit of Rome has been revived in Fascism. Roman are our lictor's rods, Roman is our fighting organization, Roman is our pride and our courage: *Civis romanus sum.* . . . The Romans were not only warriors but also formidable constructors who could defy and did defy time. In war and in victory Italy was Roman for the first time in fifteen centuries" (Florinsky 1936, 62–63).

These words contain a fateful misunderstanding. The culture of a country's past may be revived only to the extent that it consists of material elements such as buildings, tools, weapons, ornaments, images, or written documents. However, Roman militarism existed almost exclusively as an ensemble of values and patterns of behavior closely integrated with a particular social, political, and economic structure. As the Roman Empire declined and eventually ceased to exist, those patterns disappeared, that is, they were no longer handed down from one generation to the next, and the military tradition of ancient Rome came to a definitive end. A revival of this tradition was as impossible as a reconstruction of the political, economic, and social system of the Roman Empire. In contrast to the living tradition of German militarism, Roman militarism of Fascist Italy was no more than rhetoric and hyperbole. No military pageantry, mass meetings, parades, martial music, splendorous uniforms, and belligerent allocutions could change those facts. There were sallies into military conquest and colonization. Ethiopa fell to the Italian invaders, and the Fascist militias were given opportunity to test their military skills in the Spanish civil war. Italy seemed rapidly to become a thoroughly militarized nation, but Mussolini's decision to enter World War II on the side of Hitler soon exploded the myth of Italian militarism. No truly militaristic society rejects a major war as "unpopular," but the Italian people did. In doing so, they demonstrated that they had failed to assimilate the Fascist maxim of *"credere, obbedire, combattere"* (believe, obey, fight), which expresses the essence of militarism.

The people's unresponsiveness to Mussolini's idea that "the Italian character (had) to be formed through fighting" was compounded by the relative unpreparedness of the Italian army for the highly technified warfare that characterized World War II. Disastrous defeats in Greece, Crete, and North Africa laid to rest the naive presumption that militarism could be created by word of command and improvisation.

This brief comparison of Fascist with National Socialist militarism reveals fundamental differences that exclude the use of the term *fascism* as a generic concept. So far as attempts to transfer either form of radical political totalitarianism to other European countries, their failure can hardly be doubted. The diffusion of fascism or National Socialism (or a mixture of both) most often foundered on insurmountable cultural differences. In the present context, brief consideration will be given only to Great Britain and France.

British Fascisti parades were held as early as 1923, but at its peak, the movement, if one wishes to call it that, never counted more than a few thousand followers under the command of a brigadier general. Many of these "Fascisti" were absorbed by the founding of the British Union of Fascists in 1932, or the British Union of Fascists and National Socialists, as they began to call themselves in 1936. Their *duce* was Sir Oswald Mosley, and like their Italian brethren, they chose black as the color of their shirts. Ex-soldier and member of Parliament, Mosley shared with many of his followers a profound disillusionment with the social and economic effects of the Great War. He expected a major revolution in Britain, and his blackshirts wished to be ready to seize power when this Armageddon came about. In concord with the Fascist model, Mosley's blackshirts were organized along military lines. "Those who identified with the 'war generation' expected the values of war, the comradeship, the disciplined life, the responsibility, the danger and excitement, the freedom from the usual sexual inhibitions, to be carried over into civilian life" (Skidelsky 1975, 319). Thinking in terms of total war, General Fuller, Mosley's most outstanding military supporter, intended to "realize through fascism what the war had temporarily created—a social engine under unified political military direction" (Skidelsky 1975, 219). All the usual postures and symbols were transferred from the Italian and German models: the jackboots and the uniforms, the mass meetings and parades, as well as the violent confrontations with political adversaries.

In comparing British fascism with its Italian and German congeners, special attention should be given to one fact. Although the British Union, especially in its earlier period, was "organized as a military force, ready to seize power in a revolutionary situation," such a "revolutionary situation" *was not engendered by Mosley and his legion* but by the deterioration of Britain's economic and political conditions. The expected revolution failed to occur, and Mosley's fascism slowly moved into the limbo of redundancy. Unlike Mussolini and Hitler, Mosley never attempted to build his own revolution. This, of course, may be related to the lack of mass support in a society that, *on its home ground*, proved singularly unreceptive to dictatorial and militaristic enticements. Apparently, there were no more than 10,000 active and 30,000 nonactive members at the peak of the movement in 1934. Of these, hardly more than 1,000 black-shirts and 7,000 to 8,000 nonactive followers were left by 1940 (Skidelsky 1975, 331). The banning of uniforms by law in 1936 was a severe blow to the blackshirts, but it was Mosley's "opposition to the Second World War which ruined him with the British people" (Skidelsky 1975, 423).

The existence of a Fascist militia inevitably signifies an implicit or explicit challenge to the monopoly of organized violence held by the armed forces. Naturally, fascism exalts military values and generally be-stows status prerogatives upon the military profession. If a militarist tra-dition exists, the Fascist movement proceeds to cultivate and harness it for its own political ends. Yet the presumptive allegiance of the military establishment to the extant sociopolitical order puts it in opposition to the Fascist militias and their revolutionary objectives. Both Mussolini and Hitler distrusted the military, and both did the utmost to win them over to their cause, but they would probably have failed to gain power without deploying their private armies and conducting a demonstration of their own power capabilities.

Considering its modest size and the lack of revolutionary élan, Brit-ish fascism could not possibly be taken as a serious threat to the armed forces and their constitutional prerogatives.

Political instability and a history of militaristic adventurism seemed to make France a more promising ground for Fascist initiatives than Great Britain. Actually, there was no lack of initiatives that, regardless of self-classification and diversity of doctrine, bore at least some of the con-stitutive traits of fascism. But associated as it was with individualism, political instability proved to be an impediment rather than a stimulus to the formation of a sweeping Fascist movement. Individualism combined with instability implies, above all, a kind of pluralism that thrives on dissidence and deviation from established doctrine. Under those condi-tions, one might expect the availability of the Fascist model to generate not one but any number of competing movements attempting to implant conflicting versions of the same basic ideology. None is large or strong enough to become a serious threat to the established order, and none is capable of eliciting the blind devotion and martial discipline without which fascism has little chance of winning.

This is what happened in France, which initially provided an extraor-dinarily broad spectrum of political creeds, extending from the most archaic forms of conservatism to the most radical versions of socialism and nationalist revivalism. France had not been a monarchy since 1871, but several royalist groups survived until far into the present century.

The most influential of them undoubtedly was the *Ligue d'Action Fran-çaise*, which in spite of its early beginnings—it was launched in 1905—anticipated certain traits of fascism. *Action Française* advocated the restoration of the hereditary monarchy and was in principle opposed to "liberal-democratic capitalism." Determined to seize power by force, it organized two types of "shock troops," the *Camelots du Roi* and the *Étu-diants d'Action Française*. Only in a hyperbolic sense could these shock troops be classified as Fascist militias. Indeed, when fascism began to capture the attention of the more volatile French politicians, *Action Fran-çaise* indignantly denied that it was Fascist (Plumyène and Lasierra 1963, 23–27). If action rather than rhetoric is the benchmark of fascism, *Action Française* bore no more than a pallid resemblance to Mussolini's movement. This, however, did not prevent *Action Française* from becoming, however unwillingly, the matrix of several "Fascist" groups by the familiar process of apostasy and dissidence. *Le Faisceau* was one of these. Founded by George Valois, it has been called the first true French Fascist party. Like several other similar groups, it enjoyed the financial support of François Coty, the perfume manufacturer and indefatigable dabbler in politics. *L'Ami du Peuple*, Coty's newspaper, generated several political groups, two of which displayed Fascist traits, *La Solidarité Française* and *Francisme*. Wearing blue shirts and emphasizing strict discipline, the followers of *Solidarité Française* were hardly more than a praetorian guard of Jean Renaud, their commander. Devoid of any tangible political ideology, Renaud never counted more than fifteen hundred blueshirts (Plumyène and Lasierra 1963, 45).

Francisme, "of all French fascisms the most intransigent, the most systematic, the most fascist," never reached the proportions of a mass party. Its members, ten thousand at most, wore blue shirts and berets. Marcel Bucard, the leader of *Francisme*, exalted the "warrior spirit" and the "mystique of the fatherland." His movement enjoyed the support of the German occupation armies and lasted until the very end of Hitlerism (Plumyène and Lasierra 1963, 55).

The *Croix de Feu*, under the leadership of Colonel La Rocque, drew more attention than any other group of the radical right. Its membership was composed largely of veterans of World War I, and by 1934 it allegedly included ninety thousand men, organized into strictly disciplined and highly mobile shock troops. But La Rocque was no revolutionary preparing to seize power by force. On the contrary, his shock troops prepared to join the army and police to maintain the "law and order" that the colonel believed were threatened by the radical left. The "warrior spirit" of the *Croix de Feu* never crossed the threshold of conservative nationalism, and true to the prevailing pattern of individualism, La Rocque and his cohorts totally rejected any form of cooperation with similar groups (Plumyène and Lasierra 1963, 52–54).

At the opposite pole of the "Fascist" continuum lay the *Parti Populaire Français*, the "only authentic fascist party France produced." Jacque Doriot, its chief, had left the Communist Party to become anti-Communist and to organize a Fascist movement with a flag, a salute, and an anthem of its own. In 1937, Doriot's party allegedly commanded 130,000 followers, many of whom, including the chief, joined the legion of French volunteers to fight with the German troops on the Russian front (Plumyène and Lasierra 1963, 110, 125, 129, 138).

It was in France, during the politically tense 1920s, that leftist groups began to attach the label of fascism rather indiscriminately to any party or association they felt threatened by. Such intentional confusion distorted reality, but it also indicated a high degree of unresponsiveness to the Fascist gospel. In fact, Plumyène asserts that "ideological anti-fascism precedes organized fascism" (Plumyène and Lasierra 1963, 21). This would mean that a deliberately erected cultural barrier was already in place even before actual diffusion of Fascist elements began to take shape in the form of militant associations.

As attractive as fascism might have appeared to certain sectors of French society there was considerable reluctance to the uncritical transfer of an alien model without adaptive modifications designed to accommodate French nationalistic revivalism and pervasive factionalism. Thus, a hybrid breed of pseudofascism emerged that had some of the trappings but none of the constitutive traits of the model. The most remarkable example of this sort was probably the *Jeunesses Patriotes* led by Pierre Taittinger, who organized paramilitary commandos, but his program did not go beyond demanding a strengthening of the executive power and thus remained almost indistinguishable from that of any other rightist group (Plumyène and Lasierra 1963, 30).

Fragmentation, isolation, and ideological distortion rendered French "fascism" rather innocuous. To the extent that such Fascist groups can be called militaristic, they represented mere remnants or survivors of traditional French militarism. Instead of opposing or threatening the military monopoly of the French army, these so-called commandos or shock troops proposed to support it. Instead of preparing a revolution, these "Fascist" militias vowed to assist the army and the police in suppressing any revolution attempted by the radical left.

8

Changes in the International Power Structure
and their Impact on Military Policy
since World War II

The European nations that had suffered from the oppressive presence of
German occupation armies and the terror of Nazi storm troopers agreed
that only a "permanent and total deprivation of power" could prevent
the revival of German militarism. Never again should Germany have an
army. The country should even be divested of the economic prerequisites of rearmament. The Allies insisted upon a "reeducation" of the
German people, whose militaristic attitudes and values should be replaced by democratic and peaceful patterns of behavior (Wettig 1967,
647).

These intentions implied a controlled culture change of enormous
proportions, the difficulties of which were not clearly understood at the
end of the war. Although the elected representatives of the German people and German public opinion on the whole accepted the demilitariza-
tion plans of the Allies, the project was never really put to the test. Soon
it became obvious that the military policy of the Western powers was
based on totally erroneous assumptions. The crucial fact was the tremendous expansion of the Soviet power domain and the transformation of
formerly sovereign nations into satellites of the Soviet Union. Soon after
the end of the war, the desire of the United States to maintain the "alliance of the victorious powers" encountered the inflexible opposition of
the Soviet Union, and before long, relationships with Stalin's Russia assumed the characteristics of the "cold war." Without recapitulating well-
known facts, it must be emphasized that it took the Allies a long time to
react to the increasing pressure of Soviet expansionism and to decide on
inevitable changes in international military policy. The Western powers,
particularly the United States, were hardly aware that Soviet political

culture (following Marxist precepts) attached different meanings to conventional concepts. Thus, political negotiations between Soviet and Western diplomats were often vitiated by the West's unawareness that current terms meant one thing to Western representatives and something quite different to the Soviets. For example, in Western cultures, *peace* means "cessation of violent international conflict." Not so in Soviet terminology. All capitalistic societies are *eo ipso* imperialistic and aggressive. They are by nature bent on the annihilation of the "peace-loving," "progressive" Marxist-Leninist peoples. In other words, their enmity lasts forever, and to them *peace* means no more than "preparation for a new imperialistic war." Any war against the Soviet Union and its allies is necessarily an unjust war, while every struggle of the Soviet Union against aggression is believed to be thoroughly just. Since the Soviet Union cannot in any circumstances pursue objectives that are not "progressive" and "just," unjust wars are totally inconceivable (Wettig 1967, 490). All capitalist-imperialist nations are implicitly militaristic, while Marxist-Leninist societies cannot, under any conditions, be militaristic because they are totally averse to exploitative, imperialist wars. They struggle for a definitive, permanent peace that is contingent upon the abolition of the capitalist social order. All Socialist soldiers are therefore "peace fighters."

For the first time in history, the ideologues of Soviet imperialism justified territorial expansion with arguments that might sound convincing to Marxist-indoctrinated masses. The diplomats of czarist Russia shared their political logic with that of their Western colleagues so that international agreements carried identical meanings for both sides. However, it turned out to be extremely difficult, if not impossible, to reach such agreements with Soviet diplomats. Fundamental differences of this sort are rooted in genuine culture conflict that cannot be settled or "removed" by conferences. No adequate understanding of recent European military history can be reached without taking into account the irreconcilable nature of these differences.

Soviet ideology concerned with military matters and war may be interpreted as an attempt to camouflage the survival of Russian imperialism. Whether intended or not, the disguise has served its function not just for Soviet citizens but for the adherents of communism anywhere in the world.

Within the context of this ideology, Soviet disarmament would have been unthinkable after 1945. The alliance with the Western powers was no more than a pragmatic concession to a temporary calamity, and as soon as it ceased to exist, the alliance gave way to the cold war.

Nothing could more effectively elucidate the culture conflict between

East and West than the hasty demobilization of the Western powers, especially the United States. The concepts of *war* and *peace* had not changed their traditional meanings, which were naively believed to have universal validity. At the end of the war, 3.1 million American soldiers were posted in Europe. The following year, only 330,000 were left, and in 1948, the total had shrunk to two divisions. By 1946, the whole Canadian army was withdrawn from Europe, and of the 1.3 million British soldiers, no more than 450,000 were still in uniform. On the other hand, by the middle of 1946, the Soviet armed forces were four to five times larger than the American forces stationed in Europe (Wettig 1967, 130).

The demobilization of the Allies and the disarmament of Germany were carried out before the military threat from the East had been recognized. When it finally dawned on the Western nations that they were facing an implacable and intransigent adversary, they reacted in a way that contrasted sharply with the prevailing political orientation. On the one hand, the Western Allies, as well as West Germany, insisted on the continuation of the disarmament policy; on the other hand, there were those who demanded an immediate rearmament of occupied West Germany. Without Germany's participation, so they argued, Western Europe could not effectively be defended (Wettig 1967, 235). At this point, the West Germans attributed the responsibility for the defense of their country to the Allied forces, but before long, public opinion got caught in the inconsistencies that kept the military policy of the West in continuing disarray. The dread of a militaristic revival clashed with the fear of possible Soviet aggression. "Passionate controversies among scientists and theologians, but above all the negative attitudes of party leaders reinforced the widespread hostility against the creation of a new German army" (Geyer, Koch, and Auerbach 1976, 21). The Soviet blockade of Berlin and the invasion of South Korea by the armed forces of Communist North Korea were interpreted as Soviet operations that seemed to justify the fear of a far-flung Soviet policy of aggression (Wettig 1967, 306ff.).

The rearmament of the German Federal Republic, which at first had been discussed as possible or advisable, developed by 1950 into a "demand that the United States and its allies considered, for military reasons, as an absolute necessity" (Wettig 1967, 339). However, the negotiations, which had already dragged on for several years, proved extremely difficult. The nations of Western Europe, particularly France, seemed incapable of adapting to the radical changes in the international power structure. In the East, the situation was quite unambiguous. The formerly sovereign states, as well as the Soviet-occupied zone of Germany, were forced into a satellite relationship with the Soviet Union.

In the West, the existing political systems veiled, at least temporarily, the war-induced transformation of the international power structure. It could no longer be doubted that the economic recovery and the military defense of Western Europe depended, to a large degree, on the far-reaching participation of the United States. In other words, the great powers of Europe of yesteryear had been drawn into a dependency relationship implying a substantial limitation of their decision-making power. The outbreak and evolution of the cold war left little doubt that the rearmament of Germany was becoming a function of the growing antagonism between the United States and the Soviet Union, and that European opposition to the creation of a German army could not possibly be successful in the long run. The interminable conferences intended to establish a European defense organization were primarily concerned with surmounting France's tenacious opposition to an independent German army. The prevailing patterns of political behavior precluded authoritarian procedures by the United States. Only negotiations and "diplomatic pressure" were considered permissible means of conflict solution among the Western Allies. Even so, the European Defense Community turned out to be a failure when the French parliament refused to ratify the treaty. At any rate, the conferences, the endless discussions in the media and legislative bodies, and the varying position of the political parties served a function that should not be underestimated. Traditional attitudes, prejudices, and contrasting opinions were gradually changing, and in the end adaptation of international relationships to political reality could no longer be postponed. It was exactly the length of the process that made adaptation possible and that generated a new cultural model as new values and attitudes acquired stability. Agreement was finally reached in 1955, when West Germany was admitted to NATO and the sovereignty of the German Federal Republic was restored. Suddenly, this totally demilitarized country again became, almost against its own will, a major military power, an event that could not fail to affect its relative power position. The Western nations were compelled to make political concessions to appease the Germans opposing rearmament. The Federal Republic was able to demand, for example, full equality of its army with the military forces of the other NATO members. Another demand concerned the "rehabilitation of the German soldier" and therefore the question as to whether and to what extent the Prussian-German military tradition should be allowed to play a role in the organization of the new army. Members of the German government insisted on a revision of the "generalizing anathematization of German soldiership." How could a people be expected to perform "new military services" and at the same time accept the wholesale condemnation of its military tradition?

The inconsistency was quite obvious, and the problem has never ceased to cause controversy. At any rate, General Eisenhower, supreme commander of the NATO forces, complied with the request of the German government by correcting his own judgment and by publicly declaring "that there had been a real difference between the German soldiers and officers on the one hand and Hitler and his criminal cohorts on the other hand"; that the German soldier had "not lost his honor and that he had valiantly and honorably fought for his homeland" (Wettig 1967, 401).

The swift remilitarization of Soviet-occupied East Germany undoubtedly helped to weaken West German opposition to the creation of a new army. The outbreak of the Korean War alarmed West Germany, which felt threatened by the aggressive attitude of East Germany with its fighting force of seventy thousand men and its heavily armed "People's Police" (Wettig 1967, 310). The creation of a border police in 1950 and of a West German army *(Bundeswehr)* in 1955 marked the beginning of an armament race between East and West Germany, which developed within the high tension field of the NATO states and the nations of the Warsaw Pact, and which was to a large extent determined by the hostile posture of East Germany.

It should be observed here that this aspect of the East-West antagonism, as well as the entire armament race between the East Bloc countries and their Western rivals, was motivated by mutual fear, unverifiable accusations, and suspicions as much as by the statistics on the military buildup. Merely subjective judgments played as important a role as objective reasons, and the irrational components influenced the dynamics of the armament race as much as the rational ones.

The creation of the *Bundeswehr,* 462,000 strong in 1966, aroused little enthusiasm in West Germany. The catastrophe of 1945 "caused an understandable emotional withdrawal from everything related to security and defense." It is not surprising that the attitude of the people toward the *Bundeswehr* and NATO could be defined as "benevolent indifference" or "passive acceptance" (Geyer, Koch, and Auerbach 1976, 38). The realization that war could no longer solve international conflict had become a foregone conclusion, but the necessary redefinition of the function to be performed by the standing armies did not remain unopposed. West Germany accepted the assumption of the NATO allies that their own standing armies provided effective protection from aggression, which could come only from the members of the Warsaw Pact. The internal opponents of rearmament, however, were of the opinion that the danger of new conflicts lay exactly in the growing strength of the *Bundeswehr* and the NATO armies (Geyer, Koch, and Auerbach 1976, 48).

During the formative period of the new West German army, it became clear that a revival of traditional militarism was incompatible with the political structure of the Federal Republic. There was no party, social class, political group, or movement willing or powerful enough to foster effectively potential vestiges of militarism. In sharp contrast to the first republic, there was neither a "substitute emperor" nor nationalist myths that might have served as crystallization centers of a militaristic renaissance. The only such possibility lay in the development of the *Bundeswehr* into a relatively autonomous political power capable of prevailing against its opponents. However, unlike the Weimar Republic, the Federal Republic was not burdened with the problems an army of dubious loyalty might originate. Nor did the survival of the new regime, in obvious contrast to that of 1918, depend on the use of military forces. The new federal government felt unrestrained in the selection of officers whose loyalty to the regime was above suspicion.

Equally unopposed was the policy of the regime to integrate the new army into the existing political order in such a way that the military leadership remained subordinated to the constitutional government. This implied parliamentary control over the armed forces (de Maizière 1974, 24). Within the existing legal system, the supreme military command was not allowed to play an autonomous political role at all. Certain legal norms were enacted explicitly outlawing aggression and regulating the use of armed forces. Since the internal structure of the German armies had formerly contributed to the continuity of militarism, the traditional authoritarian organization was loosened to some degree. No longer was the soldier expected to obey commands that "violated his human dignity" or "demanded criminal actions." The soldier was promoted to the status of a "citizen in uniform," whose "political rights should be respected." The relationships between officers and rank and file were conceived in terms of a community built on reciprocal trust (Geyer, Koch, and Auerbach 1976, 51ff.). To carry out these changes, the "method" of "internal leadership" was invented with the intention of educating the soldier to share thoughts and responsibilities with his superiors (Von Bredow 1973, 53). *Internal leadership*, as defined by military authority, "is the task of all commanding officers to educate a soldier who is capable and willing to defend the freedom and the laws of the German people in hot and cold war against any aggressor. It (internal leadership) rests on political and social values of our democratic constitution, transfers proven soldierly virtues and experiences to our modern way of life and takes into account the consequences of the use and effects of modern technology" (as quoted in Von Bredow 1973, 98; Baudissin 1969, *passim*; and Ilsemann 1971, *passim*). The wishful image emerged of a reliable soldier who is loyal to the democratic state, who knows exactly what he fights for and against whom, who understands and spontaneously obeys the orders of his superiors, and who, in addition to everything else, is familiar with the technology of modern warfare. Different definitions and interpretations of internal leadership indicate the considerable flexibility of the concept. From the very beginning, the idea of internal leadership was caught in the crossfire of criticism. There was no consensus about the value or the significance of internal leadership, either within or outside the new army. Traditionalists opposed the reform, and before long, it became rather obvious that the implementation of the extremely demanding educational program of internal leadership failed to live up to the expectations of its originators and reformist legislators. The administrative offices in charge of the introduction and development of internal leadership had neither the necessary personnel nor the intention of actually carrying out the educational program. Even though well known, the concept was not considered legally or morally binding by many functionaries, who merely went through the motions of implementing something that should not, in their opinion, figure at all in the educational program (Genschel 1972, 226).

This undeniable difference between facade and reality was occasionally interpreted as an "internal and society-related partisan war in the realm of ideology" turned "against internal leadership and in favor of the traditional image of the soldier and his profession." It was directed "against public criticism refusing to accept the primacy of military thinking in politics" (Von Bredow 1973, 131).

The new army was, from the beginning, the focus of controversies that went much deeper than the problems of internal leadership and the control over forces that were, correctly or not, assumed to represent militaristic remnants. Actually, what was at issue was an internal inconsistency that brought into question the role of the military in general. Soldiers had always been expected to acquire fighting skills, to prepare for combat and, in militaristic societies, to desire war. Nowadays, however, each soldier learns "that he is no longer there to conduct war, but to prevent war. As soon as he was put in a position actually to use the weapons he had learned to employ, the purpose of his own existence would have been defeated because there is no defense against the new weapons. He can protect his fatherland only as long as he is not forced to engage in action" (Georg Picht as quoted in Von Bredow 1973, 61; also Thielen 1970, 31, 192). His only function is to "maintain the equilibrium of terror." This inherent inconsistency concerns all modern armies, at least to the extent that they are allied with either one of the two superpowers.

It is not our intent to reconstruct the details of this development. It is enough to note here that the rearmament of West Germany generated tensions and conflicts that went far beyond the question of whether or not the *Bundeswehr* could be integrated into the political order. Opposing rearmament on principle, some dissident groups have continuously advocated, since the very inception of the *Bundeswehr*, a more or less radical policy of disarmament.

Radical Socialist opponents to West German military policy believe the *Bundeswehr* is instrumental in the preservation of a capitalist society. In their opinion, the anti-Communist image of the enemy depicts no more than a "diabolization" of the adversary who, quite apart from his real behavior, is charged with "total militancy," an accusation intended to justify one's own aggressiveness (Thielen 1970, 36). On the other side are those who consider a constant readiness for war a basic prerequisite for the survival of the present social order or even of Western civilization in general. Between those two extremes is the amorphous mass of the indifferent and undecided. The picture is that of a disorganized society whose members adhere to mutually exclusive values and patterns of behavior, or drift bewildered and disoriented between alternatives of dubious validity.

Typical of the state of disorganization is the relative inability of a society to organize its internal network of relationships to reduce group tensions and conflicts as much as possible and, if they prove unavoidable, to provide solutions acceptable to the groups at variance with each other. A disorganized society therefore loses at least partial control over itself and thus the capability of making binding decisions. In order to assess concrete situations correctly, two kinds of conflicts ought to be distinguished. As in the case of the *Bundeswehr*, there may be differences about structural details, choice of armaments, or forms of political control that do not jeopardize its very existence. But there are also conflicts threatening the very survival of the military institution: Groups intent on the total abolition of the army intransigently confront those that are convinced of the absolute necessity of a defensive military force. Such conflicts concerning the existence or nonexistence of essential political institutions reflect a relatively high degree of disorganization, particularly if they are supported by large, militant groups. Furthermore, the development of such confrontations depends on the political climate of the society in which they occur. If they erupt in a democratic society, as in the German Federal Republic, the political proselytism of the contending groups is allowed to go almost unchecked.

To prevent misunderstandings, it should be emphasized that disorganizing processes very rarely affect *all* sectors of a society. If, as it happens in the German Federal Republic, disorganization involves problems of rearmament and military policy, the ability of the legislative and executive branches of the government to make binding decisions may be affected, especially since the existing tendency toward polarization may be aggravated by a growing fear of atomic aggression.

It hardly seems possible to overrate the impact these disorganizing processes may have on the future of militarism, whose existence is predicated on ideological and structural characteristics that have virtually disappeared from West German society. The primacy of military thinking and acting rested on the axiomatic assumption that war was an appropriate solution to international conflicts and therefore was capable of adaptive functions. This doctrine has now given way to the conviction that modern war, particularly atomic war, would bring the inevitable annihilation of society. Not actual battle but the frustration of warlike designs imputed to the enemy justifies, so it has been argued, the existence of a military force. The militarization of civil society, which played such an extraordinarily important role in the German past, has therefore become redundant and, if seriously attempted, would meet a virtually unanimous rejection by the postwar generation of West German society. In other words, militarism has lost its ideological foundations. Viewed from a structural standpoint, the evolution of militarism depends on societal consensus that supports, either spontaneously or under the pressure of sanctions and political indoctrination, the primacy of military ways of thinking and acting. Previous chapters emphasized the fundamental significance of societal consensus for the evolution of Prussian-German militarism. If there is no consensus or if there is, as in the German Federal Republic, a generalized, sharply pronounced disagreement about vital issues involving national survival, a renaissance of militarism seems utterly impossible. As a matter of fact, such a controversy transcends more or less amorphous, individual, and collective forms of disagreement about the importance and internal organization of the army; it is actually rooted in the political party system whose main components, the SPD (German Social Democratic Party) and CDU (Christian Democratic Union), represent points of view at variance with each other. The Social-Democratic government insisted on a "democratization" of the army. The defense minister of that period pursued the policy of definitively dissociating the army from the symbols, names, and traditions of Hitler's *Wehrmacht* on the grounds that a "regime of injustice" could not "build tradition" (*Der Spiegel*, No. 41, 1983, 20). If the position of the SPD was and still is antimilitaristic, the orientation of the CDU cannot, by any stretch of the imagination, be considered militaristic. It was rather the intention to "merge the valid heritage of the past with the army's appreciation for tradition." Deployment and leadership of the armed forces should take into account the experiences during the war. Soldierly virtues like "comradeship, loyalty and valor" should be revived, and military service should become again an "honorable service" (*Der Spiegel*, No. 41, 1983, 20–21).

The details of this party conflict are irrelevant in the present context, but it is important to remember that the military policies of the two parties differ from each other in most basic aspects. This means, of course, that a change of government implies a subsequent change of military policy. In other words, the political process lacks the continuity and stability considered to be prerequisites of a militaristic revival.

In view of this persistent disagreement and growing uncertainty, it hardly seems surprising that the *Bundeswehr* should be afflicted with a chronic "legitimacy" or "identity" crisis (*Der Spiegel*, No. 41, 1983, 21). It has often been emphasized that social disorganization, as understood here, constitutes an inevitable by-product or symptom of sociocultural change. In the case of the *Bundeswehr*, as of all other Western military forces, the prevailing change encompasses all these adaptive processes designed to reconcile social reality with the revolutionary transformations of military technology. Under the present conditions, it seems virtually impossible to predict the outcome of these adaptive attempts. However, there can be no doubt that in the Western democracies the extraordinary magnitude of military preparations is inversely proportional to the actual willingness of these peoples to get involved in wars. The considerable growth of the peace movement and the rapidly increasing number of "conscientious objectors" suggest a clear departure from the traditional forms of militarism.

Rearmament of the Soviet-occupied zone of Germany was quite different. Immediately after the cessation of the war in 1945, leading German Communists, exiled in Russia, were returned to Berlin and other urban centers under Soviet control and charged with the organization of a centralized administration in accordance with Soviet models. Furthermore, as in all other East European countries, a governmental system was set up that proved willing to follow political guidelines dictated by Moscow. In 1945, rearmament in the Soviet zone began with the establishment of the so-called People's Police, followed in the same year by the Border Police, which in 1946 reached an effective force of 18,000. In 1948, the first military cadre units were set up, and in 1950, the German Democratic Republic had an army of 70,000. In 1953, it had grown to 100,000 and shortly thereafter to 204,000 (Jungermann 1973, 70–75; Nawrocki 1979, 11; Geyer, Koch, and Auerbach 1976, 9).

Since rearmament of East Germany was carried out by the Soviet

Union, under Soviet control and exclusively with Soviet military equipment, it was almost a foregone conclusion that it should become a scaled-down copy of Soviet military organization. However, the Soviet version of militarism accompanying the massive transfer of modern weaponry proved adaptable to the specific political conditions of the German Democratic Republic (DDR). The militarization of East Germany was a function of the power monopoly of the Socialist Unitary Party of Germany (SED), which was charged with the task of streamlining political thinking and acting among the people. Any attempt to identify the specific characteristics of East German militarism ought to consider at least the following facts:

1. The preamble to the military service law of 1956 reads that "the revival of aggressive militarism in West Germany and the establishment of a West German army . . . imply a constant menace to the German and all other peoples of Europe" (Geyer, Koch, and Auerbach 1976, 15). Defined as a "capitalistic" country, West Germany is implicitly aggressive, imperialistic, and militaristic, according to Marxist-Leninist doctrine. Sooner or later, so goes the argument, the machinations of the "revanchist, fascist German Federal Republic" will lead to a violent confrontation with the peace-loving German Democratic Republic. In the end, war is assumed to be inevitable, and the DDR should be well prepared.

In contrast to the armies of other satellite states, the National People's Army had a "double-gauged fighting task," namely, the defense of socialism on all fronts *and* the liberation of West Germany from the shackles of monopolistic capitalism. From the very beginning, it was the objective of the army and of the other East German military organizations to create "an uninhibited feeling of hatred, the will to annihilate the West German soldier" (Jungermann 1973, 229). The *Bundeswehr* has been represented as a "thoroughly reactionary and imperialistic army," which, under the command of a "fascist leadership clique," was "essentially undistinguishable from Hitler's army" and had therefore a "criminal character, hostile to the people" (Jungermann 1973, 238).

Since the predicted West German aggression failed to materialize, an abstruse aggression doctrine was launched that imputed to the "militarists" and "fascists" of West Germany the intention of promoting "indirect," "economic," and "ideological" aggression. Furthermore, the idea of "covert war" somewhere in East Germany, but not necessarily near the border, has played a significant role in the military doctrine of Communist Germany (Jungermann 1973, 232). As with so many other terms, the concept of aggressor has been given a different meaning in East Germany. The initiator of military operations is usually considered the aggressor, but the defense minister of Communist Germany does not think that the characteristics of war are necessarily determined by the party that actually started it (Henrich 1978, 45). The ambiguity of this and similar statements created almost unlimited possibilities to justify the "liberating mission" of the National People's Army against the German Federal Republic whenever the situation seemed ripe for military action. Nevertheless, in the official Party terminology, the soldier is designated *peace fighter*. The use of the term agrees with the Marxist-Leninist dictionary, which defines *peace* as a "condition the existence of which is contingent upon the annihilation of class society." The struggle for peace is therefore the revolution that brings about the global destruction of the prevailing social structure (Eisenfeld 1978, 25).

Thus, orthodox Marxist-Leninist doctrine postulates that the resolution of conflict between East and West, between communism and capitalism, cannot be achieved without war. Such a war is not only inevitable but also just and desirable. Following Soviet lines of thought, the military ideologues of East Germany justified the morality of military violence on the grounds that the "socialist human community" had a "moral obligation" to support the "liberation struggle of the communist movement" (Jungermann 1973, 201).

2. In accordance with the Soviet model, the East German military did not consider a strong, well-equipped army to be sufficient to ensure the final victory of communism. The entire society had to be militarized; "military education ought to begin in Kindergarden and constitute a unified system" (Marks 1970, 7). In 1952, the Society for Sport and Technology (GST) was established to prepare East German youth for military service (Nawrocki 1979, 125), and to familiarize them with the use of firearms and technical specialties of military significance. Membership in the GST is voluntary, but military education has been an integral part of the curriculum of all schools and universities (Marks 1970, 32). Within the framework of militarization, the so-called Fighter Groups of the Working Class play a particularly important role. They are composed of heavily armed units under direct control of the Party. In 1962, they were 350,000 strong, of whom about 150,000 were combat ready (Kabel 1966, 51). The predecessors of these Fighter Groups were the Worker's Militia in Large-Scale Socialist Factories. Their beginnings were probably related to the popular revolt of 1953 (Nawrocki 1979, 148).

3. The command structure of the National People's Army has, in contrast with the *Bundeswehr*, an absolute character. The official designation "Democratic Centralism" means that decisions made by "each superior

organ are absolutely binding for all subordinate organs" (Marks 1970, 32). The soldier has no right to question the moral quality of orders. The highest and unappealable authority is vested in the Socialist Unitary Party, which demands total subordination from the soldier. The Party constitutes, so to speak, the brain, the soldier no more than the executing arm (Geyer, Koch, and Auerbach 1976, 82; Kreusel 1971, 264; Jungermann 1973, 203).

4. In a previous chapter, considerable emphasis was placed on the decisive role the social rise of the military profession played during the formative period of Prussian militarism. Once the traditional image of the soldier had faded, a revalorization process of the military career was deemed opportune by the East German leadership. Soldiers and officers again were taught that "it was an honor and a patriotic duty to serve in the National People's Army" (Kreusel 1971, 269). Political expediency brought about an unexpected revival of Prussianism. In contrast to the *Bundeswehr*, the East German army took up in many details "the traditions of the German *Wehrmacht* and the Prussian army. Cultivation of those patterns obviously meant to convey to the soldiers of the National People's Army a historical identity, to give them the feeling that they are fostering and protecting the most valuable traditions of the German people. The uniforms . . . resemble in almost every detail those of the old *Wehrmacht*. Only the egg-shaped steelhelmet looks different, and part of the winter uniform is a fur hat after the Russian model. But the mug, the goosestep, the parade of the guard, the beating of the tattoo including the York March and even some of the orders and decorations relate to Prussian traditions" (Nawrocki 1979, 59–60).

History is taught with an emphasis on events that can be interpreted as armed conflicts designed to liberate the lower classes. The Peasant War (1524–25) and the revolutions of 1848 and 1918 are stressed, but so, unexpectedly, are the Wars of Liberation (1813–14), although they were not related to the social class system at all. Military leaders, such as Blücher and Gneisenau, are included in the pantheon of East German freedom fighters (Geyer, Koch, and Auerbach 1976, 36), and one of the films on "socialist military education" deals with Scharnhorst, who is presented as "creator of the people's army" and "co-fighter in the liberation wars against Napoleon's alien rule" (Henrich 1978, 133). Obviously, all these efforts are intended to mold the army into a central, integrating factor of a new nation, which is quite different from what has occurred in West Germany. The development of a separate "socialist national consciousness" and the image of an implacable enemy may be necessary to maintain the internal solidarity of the German Democratic Republic (Geyer, Koch, and Auerbach 1976, 72). The militarization of East German society would therefore perform a function that has very little to do with the alleged threats of "fascist revanchists" of the West.

The fact that the militarization of East Germany seems to have met little resistance may be attributed to structural conditions of the country, which formed part of the core area of Prussian militarism where the traditional pattern of subordination to power and authority had been particularly strong (Geyer, Koch, and Auerbach 1976, 71). It should not be overlooked either that the Communist regime was established almost immediately after the invasion of the Soviet army. In contrast to West Germany, there was no time lapse between the fall of National Socialist totalitarianism and the rise of Soviet totalitarianism, between disarmament and rearmament, between the dissolution of Hitler's *Wehrmacht* and the creation of a new army. In other words, there really was not enough time to develop new models and modes of behavior that might have delayed or deflected remilitarization. In general, the discipline and combat capabilities of the East German army are believed to be equal or superior to those of all other satellite armies. However, there are differences of opinion about the discipline of the Soviet elite divisions stationed in East Germany. Apparently, there are problems that are said to play no role at all in the National People's Army (Geyer, Koch, and Auerbach 1976, 9; Nawrocki 1979, 191).

The relative success of East Germany's remilitarization is based largely on conditions nonexistent in the *Bundesrepublik*, namely, the concentration of political power in a single party and its dependent government. Furthermore, a combination of negative (or punitive) and positive (or rewarding) sanctions and relentless indoctrination have generated a degree of consensus that would be unthinkable in the *Bundesrepublik* or any other democracy. This does not imply absence of political opposition in East Germany. The uprising of 1953, the flight of innumerable citizens to West Germany, and the desertion of thousands of military personnel can only be interpreted as unmistakable signs of discontent. About ten years ago, the number of military deserters was estimated to be nearly 25,000 (Jungermann 1973, 235).

In contrast to West Germany, there are, publicly at least, no doubts about the army's task. Its mission is combat rather than prevention of armed conflict. There is no doubt about the imminent aggression of the capitalist-imperialistic powers, but neither is there any uncertainty concerning the definitive victory of the united Socialist armies. The entire military doctrine of East Germany rests on the belief that a modern war, even an atomic war, could be won. However, the credibility of this doctrine seems questionable to some of its citizens, because even in East Germany the almost universal peace movement has been gaining ground. Apparently, this movement has found asylum, at least for the time being, in the churches of East Germany. Since "bourgeois" pacifism is, according to Communist doctrine, a contemptible and counterrevolutionary attitude, repressive reactions are to be expected.

The militarization of a society implies, as pointed out repeatedly, the danger of increasing political importance of the military. Without structural restraints, the officer corps may become a state within the state, or even a breeding ground of political subversion. In the German Democratic Republic, considerable effort has been made to prevent this possibility through the use of such devices as the selection of officer candidates from the "proletariat" and the structural interlocking of the officer corps with the Socialist Unitary Party. From the very beginning, the proportion of officers of working class origin has been high, amounting to 83 percent in 1974 (Studiengruppe Militärpolitik 1976, 140). Although the precision of the working class concept leaves much to be desired, the social homogeneity of the officer corps appears to be beyond doubt. An officer of "proletarian" background can hardly fail to interpret his career as social ascent. He is most probably aware that the state of "workers and peasants" made his ascent possible. This linkage of a personal career with the social structure may contribute, quite apart from all political indoctrination, to the development of intense loyalty (Geyer, Koch, and Auerbach 1976, 70). As in the Soviet Union, the formation of an independent power center in the army should be prevented by enlisting the largest possible number of officers in the Socialist Unitary Party. By 1974, 99 percent of all officers had allegedly become members of the Party. This interlocking membership suggests a growing influence of the military on the political leadership (Studiengruppe Militärpolitik 1976, 41). Although complete identity of military and political interests is supposed to exist, or is at least intended, the possibility of a power dislocation within the Party structure in favor of the military should not be rejected out of hand. Antagonisms between military and political leadership are extraordinarily difficult to avoid, particularly when financial support for a steadily growing military buildup is at stake. Under such conditions, an ideologically disguised military regime may develop, in which the Party becomes the vehicle of a de facto ruling officer clique.

Another hallmark of East German militarism is the way it deals with conscientious objectors to military service. Refusal to bear arms cannot be reconciled, as indicated before, with the basic principle of militarism. Nevertheless, the East German government has made certain concessions to the churches that try to protect conscientious objectors. Yet the compromise itself bears signs of militarism. The conscientious objectors are not forced to bear arms, but they have to serve in working details charged with the construction of military facilities. Their organization is thoroughly military, they wear uniforms, and even though unarmed, they have to undergo military training. They are also forced to swear an oath of allegiance that differs little from that of the armed forces in general. Those who totally refuse to join the army run the risk of prison sentences. Since the political and professional prospects of conscientious objectors are not promising, relatively few young men are willing to take the risks involved in such an option (Eisenfeld 1978, 73).

East German militarism may be said to move on two different but interrelated levels. In the first place, it is undoubtedly an offshoot of Soviet militarism, not only in ideology but in organization and technology as well. At the same time, East German militarism has been specifically directed against West Germany, and in a way that is probably unique in contemporary history. The pronounced aggressiveness of the German Democratic Republic rests on the conviction that West Germany's army is a reactionary force at the service of imperialism and ready for imminent assault. The whole process of militarizing East German society appears to rest on that assumption, which is astonishingly out of touch with international political reality. More than three decades have elapsed since the rearmament of East Germany, but the expected attack of West German imperialism and its "Fascist" generals has failed to materialize and is not going to take place in the foreseeable future. Ideologies based on unfulfilled predictions do not have an unlimited life span. One wonders how long it will take until the East German military buildup can no longer be justified by an ideology of aggression whose credibility is wearing thin.

9

The Evolutionary Dynamics of Prussian-German Militarism: A Summary

The structural groundwork of Prussian militarism was laid in the Middle Ages by the Teutonic Knights, conquerors and rulers of Prussia for two centuries, and by the warlike, expansionist principality of Brandenburg. A merger of those two states and their military traditions led to a new polity whose rulers strove to convert it into an absolute monarchy. Whatever military developments subsequently occurred, they have to be understood in the light of the military revolution, which radically transformed medieval forms of warcraft. For at least a century, Prussia remained at the receiving end of technical and organizational innovations borrowed from neighboring societies.

After many years of conflict with the estates, the Great Elector succeeded in imposing two major changes representing the first steps toward a militaristic state: absolute fiscal control and the establishment of a standing army. It was the beginning of a long series of evolutionary changes determined by the absolute power of the Prussian rulers.

Induced to accept the role of military leadership, the land-holding nobility began to provide the manpower for the officer corps, a service that gradually developed into a coveted privilege. In contrast to the old officer corps of uncouth, socially low-ranking mercenaries of questionable loyalty was the group the Prussian ruler now commanded: socially high-ranking, respected officers bound to him by close ties of personal allegiance and controlled by a self-imposed honor code.

The next major changes came with tighter military discipline, standardized equipment, and new training methods intended to provide a maneuverability never before attained in any European army. The introduction of the cantonal system, based on a Dutch model, constituted the first step toward conscription and attempted to correct some of the shortcomings of the mercenary army. As the army grew, its role in nonmilitary sectors of Prussian society expanded. In fact, military norms and modes of behavior served as models for the organization of the new bureaucracy.

During the late seventeenth century, the alliance between crown, nobility, and army took definite shape, forming the foundation for further militaristic developments. The victorious wars of the eighteenth century established Prussia as one of Europe's great military powers.

Toward the end of the eighteenth century, three of the five constituent attributes of Prussian militarism were firmly in place: (1) Discretionary appropriation of resources to maintain and develop a permanent army had long since become an undisputed prerogative of the king. (2) Because of the close association of the officer corps with the king and the Junker nobility, its political power had been firmly established. And the tendency to use war as a means of conflict solution had taken shape under Frederick the Great. (3) The militarization of Prussian society had affected the peasantry, the bureaucracy, the judiciary, and the educational system, but the urban bourgeoisie had not yet been touched by military concerns. In fact, it was the king's intention that "the peaceful burghers should not even notice when the king fought his battles."

Far from weakening the military tradition of the Prussian state, the lost war of 1806 had a powerfully invigorating influence on its further development. Prussian nationalism was born, and one of its first fruits was the successful role the reorganized Prussian armies played in the final defeat of Napoleon. With the introduction of universal conscription, the status of soldier was elevated to that of an honorable, admired profession.

The social and military reforms following the defeat of 1806 provide an illuminating example of the interplay between evolutionary change and tradition. The protagonists of Prussianism correctly perceived change as a means of salvaging the militaristic legacy of the past, but political opposition was still strong enough to prevent the most radical of the intended changes from being sanctioned by the monarch.

Militant nationalism began to prevail in the area of ideological confrontations. Increasingly, family, community, and school proceeded to inculcate in the young the military virtues of discipline and unconditional respect for authority. While peasantry and nobility had been militarized in the eighteenth century, the urban bourgeoisie now began to be confronted with the ideological attractions of a militant nationalism. However, the bourgeoisie was divided and refused to yield to the enticement of a militaristic state without considerable resistance that eventually led to the democratic revolution of 1848. A democratization of the political structure of Prussia and the other German states might have curtailed the power of the monarchs and the military, but the revolution was beaten down by the army. From that time, the liberal bourgeoisie and the decimated democratic movement entered upon separate courses. The political unification of all German lands and the founding of a strong national state prevailed over democratization.

Among the most significant changes characterizing the development of the military establishment, the General Staff ranks as high as the most effective technological innovations of the century. Pulling together all available knowledge about the conduct of war and transforming it into a science, the General Staff operated on a corporate, superindividual level, free from political interference and accountable only to the monarch.

Industrialization and economic prosperity reinforced the position of the militaristic state. A mutually dependent relationship between the army and the armament industry provided continuity and furthered technological innovations. Churches and educational institutions lent ideological support to the political designs of the state. As never before, war was glorified and interpreted as a source of national vigor. The educational system, from the grammar school to the university, lent its support to the task of perpetuating and strengthening the military tradition, and so did a variety of voluntary associations. The institution of the reserve officer became an important channel for diffusing militaristic values and attitudes throughout the middle and upper classes, while the ubiquitous figure of the retired noncommissioned officer instilled military modes of behavior in the lower levels of the social structure.

As militarism turned into imperialism, a large battle fleet was built, primarily to challenge the maritime hegemony of Great Britain. Yet far from serving as an effective tool of victory in World War I, the German fleet became a distinct liability to the warlords. It was obviously a bad investment, diverting scarce resources from other sectors of the war economy where they were sorely needed; and it was among the mutinous crews of the battleships that the collapse of the German armed forces began. In addition to the battle fleet, other branches of the German armed forces proved to be liabilities in that they prevented the nation from maximizing the development of military resources.

Germany's defeat in World War I failed to eradicate militarism. Lack of support, threats, and actual attempts at subversion from the radical left and right induced the republican regime to compromise with political forces that succeeded in salvaging the militaristic tradition. A regime that could have destroyed militarism thus paved the way to the most fateful change ever to befall Germany: the rise of National Socialism.

The disintegration of the powerful, highly differentiated military complex in the wake of the defeat of 1918 turned into a sort of military pluralism unheard of in Prussian-German history. The situation is perhaps best defined in terms of a civil war in which the so-called Free Corps fought against each other, against the republican regime, and against Polish insurgents. The loss of all former support structures and the strictures imposed by the peace treaty deprived the new army of the means to reinstate the rule of the law, again a situation without precedent in three centuries of militarism. The violent power contest of those postwar years engendered the novel pattern of militarized political parties. With Hitler's victory in 1933, the Party militia became a permanent institution. Thereafter, there were two military complexes, each adhering to different standards of behavior and each performing different functions. Since, for the first time in history, the political regime was clearly dictatorial, the opposition, real or imaginary, could be eliminated by the use of organized violence.

The revival of German militarism under Hitler again reveals the interplay between change and tradition. In spite of the lost war, the military tradition was still widely supported, not only by the officer corps of the *Reichswehr* but also by conservative political parties, militant associations of ex-combatants, and large sectors of the German bourgeoisie. Determined to shake off the "yoke of Versailles" and to reestablish Germany as a great power, these groups perceived Hitler and his rapidly growing party as saviors of a tradition "which had made Germany great."

To gain the support of the armed forces and to legitimize his regime, Hitler and the Nazi elite proclaimed themselves protagonists of Prussianism and its military tradition. The ploy succeeded insofar as it enabled Hitler to gain wide support for changes he intended to carry out.

A direct link between the military tradition and the changes proposed by the Nazi regime was provided by the twice-elected president of the republic, General Field Marshal Paul von Hindenburg, Junker and revered war hero who represented the rallying symbol of the nationalistic awakening of the 1920s. The crucial step was President Von Hindenburg's decision to invite Hitler to assume the chancellorship of the Reich. Once installed in the second highest office of the republic, Hitler usurped the position of the dying president and forthwith merged the presidency with his own office. The Nazis' assumption of power was tantamount to preparation for war on a scale never seen before. Unencumbered by an arsenal of obsolete weaponry, the Nazis were able to build a modern war machine that was technologically ahead of that of any other nation, at least temporarily.

Initially, the demonstration of power capabilities, short of actual war, proved eminently successful insofar as territorial expansion was concerned, but the invasion of Poland marked the beginning of actual war in which the conjunction of traditional militarism with the massing of technological resources secured a long series of victorious invasions with few parallels in European history.

Total war, initiated by the Germans, met total defeat. The conclusion that modern warfare was highly nonadaptive after all seemed inescapable. Unparalleled devastation, enormous casualties, total occupation by enemy forces, political division into two separate, mutually incompatible states, and the annexation of the eastern territories by Poland and Russia destroyed the conditions under which militarism had thrived in the past. However, total defeat also meant a reversal of attitudes about militarism. In taking a strong stand against it, German society came full circle, beginning with the implanting of militarism in the seventeenth century, against the interests of the estates, and its development as a means of self-assertion and territorial expansion. The essence of Prussian militarism emerged as military modes of thinking and acting gradually pervaded all sectors and strata of the society to the point of creating "a structure common to army and nation," to use Herbert Spencer's words. The outcome of World War I strongly suggested the obsolescence of traditional militarism, but once again it survived to launch into a convulsive struggle of unprecedented furor. Total defeat was followed by determined rejection of the militaristic tradition. The circle was completed.

The historical facts do not suggest the inevitability of militarism, which, after all, was no more than one component among many of political evolution. It began as the deliberate creation of a ruler struggling, as so many others did, to establish absolutism. Its consolidation succeeded only after decades of internal strife. Once consolidated, it became a self-perpetuating system propelled by built-in rewards flowing to the dynasty, to the nobility, and later to an upwardly mobile bourgeoisie.

Self-perpetuation also derived from the continuous interaction—antagonistic, competitive, or cooperative—with other militaristic nation-states. As an evolutionary process, militarism implied both continuity and changes, the latter being determined, to a large extent, by exogenous models. Whatever their origin, changes were dictated by the need to preserve the viability of the system, and by the will to push it to its limit in terms of conquerable and exploitable human and natural resources.

These evolutionary changes implied not only almost continuous expansion and internal differentiation of the military complex proper, but also a gradual diffusion of military modes of behavior to all sectors of the society until, during the period of efflorescence, militarism came to be a major integrator of German society.

The militarization of German society proceeded on the assumption that, in the long run, war was inevitable and that, in spite of its high costs in human lives and economic resources, it would eventually result in tangible benefits to the nation. This doctrine was, *mutatis mutandis,* shared by most nations, particularly during the era of European imperialism, but in Germany it was allowed to outlast its usefulness. In fact, under the Nazi regime it reached utopian proportions, totally out of step with reality. Perhaps it was not so much war in and of itself as the Nazi version of total war that caused enough collective resistance to destroy the regime, its warlords, and the foundations of German militarism.

The facts presented in previous chapters confirmed our initial assumption that the definitions of militarism proposed by different analysts at different times fully apply to its Prussian-German version. The preferential use of organized violence to resolve conflict, both international and national, clearly prevailed from the military suppression of the revolution of 1848 to World War II. The parallel development of a war ideology encompassed the belief in the inevitability of violent confrontations as well as the dogma of the regenerative effects of war.

The German officer corps retained its privileged status as a self-recruiting body, disdainful of the burgeoning political party system, and derived its power from close association with the monarch and the ultra-conservative nobility. The fact that both emperors (William I and William II) perceived their role primarily as supreme military commander reinforced the privileged position of the military. Under Hitler, the status of the professional officer corps lost much of its traditional superiority to the military elite of the National Socialist Party.

In spite of all attempts to bring the military budget under parliamentary control, the emperor and his ministers, supported by public opinion and most parties, obtained approval of all long-range armament projects. Discretionary appropriation of human and economic resources for military purposes reached its climax during the two world wars.

Rigid discipline in the sense of "blind" obedience to orders issued by superior authority proved feasible only after the mercenary armies had been replaced by a homogeneous national army in the early nineteenth century.

The gradual revaluation of the military profession was followed by increasing respect and reverence for military status symbols, but this trend should be understood in the context of the general militarization of civilian society and the glorification of war and warrior. The diffusion of military ways of conduct was not just the result of a deliberate plan to transform recruits into "soldiers for life," but the spontaneous desire of an upwardly mobile bourgeoisie to be socially and politically acceptable to the ruling classes.

The uniqueness of Prussian-German militarism becomes obvious if it is compared with that of its major power contenders, namely, Great Britain, France, and Russia: In none of the three nations—with the possible exception of present-day Russia—did militarism become as pervasive as it did during the German Empire and the National Socialist regime. The militarization of German society went far enough to virtually obliterate the civilian-military dichotomy. In Great Britain, not only had civilian authority remained undisputed since Oliver Cromwell, but anti-militarism became a distinct trait of British society. Yet the conquest and retention of a world empire would have been unthinkable without a colonial militarism based largely on the harnessing of warlike traditions of indigenous peoples to the political designs of the homeland. Except in periods of acute danger, antimilitarism seemed affordable because of England's insularity. It would be difficult to imagine a more striking contrast than that between the geopolitical realities at the roots of Prussian militarism and those of the British Isles, where a similar orientation would have been clearly dysfunctional.

Nor did French militarism develop under the pressure of compelling geographical determinants. Unlike Prussia, France enjoyed territorial contiguity, and natural barriers protected most of its borders from invasion. Nevertheless, the French Revolution prepared the ground for Napoleon's brand of imperialism, which initiated a new era of warfare far more formidable than anything Europe had known before. Perhaps the most significant innovation was that war and preparation for war involved the nation as a whole and thus laid the groundwork for the idea of total war. Instead of gathering new strength from lost battles, as Prussia did after 1806, France reacted to Napoleon's defeat with a persistent, deep distrust of things military. Political instability and repeated changes of regime prevented the French army from developing lasting loyalty to any political system. In contrast to their Prussian counterparts, the French military never succeeded in gaining the public support that comes from significant victories on the battlefield. The disastrous defeat at the hands of the Prussian army in 1870–71 generated a desire for revenge, yet the rapidly improving credibility of the French armed forces suffered a setback from the moral impact of the Dreyfus affair. In contrast to the continuity of the Prussian-German militaristic tradition, French militarism was handicapped by intermittence and ambivalence. However, like Great Britain, France consistently pursued a vast program of colonial conquest, absorbing military ambitions that found no outlet in the homeland.

Again in sharp contrast to Germany, the extremely costly victory in World War I put a damper on British and French militarism. Both countries were affected by the Fascist tide, but neither one proved responsive enough to change the direction of political process that slowly drifted away from the military tradition of the past. While Nazi Germany prepared for war on a scale unprecedented in history, France and Britain did little to meet the impending onslaught. World War II wrought radical changes in the international power structure, which not only brought to an end three centuries of German militarism but also forced Great Britain and France to relinquish their colonial empires, the most enduring symbols of the militaristic tradition.

In a superficial way, the military history of Russia resembled that of Prussia and Germany. The wide, open Russian plains repeatedly served as invasion routes and contributed to an almost obsessive concern about secure borders. Much earlier than Prussia, Russia chose war as the preferred means of territorial expansion. In the sixteenth century, the foundations of a militaristic tradition were laid that proved as consistent and continuous as its Prussian counterpart. Russian warfare was successful against tribal or semitribal societies, but it failed against the military might of the Western powers and Japan. The structural prerequisites that generated Prussian militarism were almost totally absent in Russia, whose political aspirations consistently exceeded the social, economic, and technological realities of the country. While German society reached a rare degree of consensus about the military designs of its ruling classes, the social structure of Russian society was breaking up under the strain of class conflict. The Russian revolution of 1917 marked the beginning of a radically different military organization, while the German revolution of 1918 failed to reorganize the armed forces and thus created the conditions for a revival of the militaristic tradition.

Germany tolerated hostile private armies that emerged in the wake of the lost war, but Russia stamped out all internal enemy forces fighting on its soil. The 1930s saw the beginning of an enormous rearmament program, rendered relatively ineffectual, however, because of a purge of the officer corps by Stalin's henchmen. In World War II, Russia again fell victim to the German invader, but in the final phase of the war, the advancing Russian armies resumed the imperialistic tradition of conquest and territorial expansion.

The Russian experiences of World War II undoubtedly contributed to the greatest military buildup of all history. But militarism is to be seen not so much in the accumulation of weaponry of all kinds as in the far-reaching militarization of Russian society. The most remarkable step in this direction was the attempted integration of the Communist Party and the armed forces into a single structure that would eradicate the much-feared civilian-military dichotomy as a possible source of internal strife. The emergence of this structural innovation was accompanied by a comprehensive program of paramilitary training. Military initiatives of any kind have been monopolized by the state, while German militarism, though originated and forcefully promoted by the state, developed a spontaneity of its own, manifest above all in numerous voluntary associations and later in the proliferation of private armies. The seizure of power by the National Socialist Party resulted in the preservation of Hitler's private army and eventually in the development of a military dualism totally abhorrent to Soviet Russia.

The rearmament of the two Germanys was unrelated to the evolutionary cycle of German militarism ending on the battlefields of World War II. The decision to raise a modern army in West Germany did not originate with that country but with the United States and its allies. In fact, the decision was strongly resisted at first, and when it was eventually and very reluctantly approved by the West German government, it failed to gain popular support. There was a lack of consensus then, and now, more than a quarter of a century later, opinions are still sharply divided about the alleged need for a large military force. Nor is there general agreement about the kind of ideological orientation that should be instilled in the soldier. The facts previously presented clearly show that none of the constituent attributes of militarism applies to the military institutions of West Germany. If anything at all, the current doctrine of deterrence contradicts the basic principle of militarism: The West German soldier is taught that his task is no longer to fight but to prevent fighting merely by demonstrating "power capabilities."

The rearmament of East Germany was imposed by the Soviet Union and by the Communist regime installed under the protection of the Soviet occupation armies. It happened almost immediately after the end of World War II, and proceeding rapidly, it was unambiguously directed against West Germany. In fact, it was one of the major determinants of West Germany's willingness to rearm.

Since the rearmament of East Germany was carried out under Soviet control, with Soviet military equipment, and under the exclusive influence of the orthodox Marxist-Leninist doctrine, it is not surprising that the East German army should have become a replica of the Soviet military establishment, slightly overlaid with elements symbolizing Prussia's military tradition and skillfully adapted to the prevailing ideological context. Soviet militarism in East Germany is manifest in the fusion of army leadership with the Communist Party, through which the generals are allowed to exercise powers. Military discipline closely resembles the Prussian model: Obedience to orders issued by superior authority is unconditional. A Marxist-Leninist version of the inevitability of war is maintained, and the East German soldier is trained to fight rather than to prevent fighting. A thorough militarization of East German society closely resembles the Soviet model, and as in Soviet Russia, war, even an atomic war, is officially believed to be winnable.

The political antagonism between East and West Germany appears to be a function of the far more comprehensive and seemingly inextricable conflict between the NATO powers and the East Bloc. The most striking difference between prewar Germany and its successors is that neither country has been able to preserve its political capability to decide freely on the use of its military potential in international conflicts. Such decisions are monopolized by the two superpowers. Russian divisions stationed in the German Democratic Republic and American divisions garrisoned in the German Federal Republic would certainly prevent any attempt of the East or West German ally to stray from the prescribed course of political action.

Bibliography

Albertini, Luigi. *The Origins of the War of 1914*. Vol. 3. London: Oxford University Press, 1957.

Anderson, Charles W. "Toward a Theory of Latin American Politics." Graduate Center for Latin American Studies, Vanderbilt University, Nashville. Occasional Papers No. 2, 1964.

Arendt, Hannah. "Totalitarian Imperialism: Reflections of the Hungarian Revolution." In *The Soviet Satellite Nations: A Study of the New Imperialism*, edited by John H. Hallowell. Gainesville: Kallmann Publishing Co., 1958.

Ashkenasi, Abraham. *Modern German Nationalism*. New York: John Wiley & Sons, 1976.

Aubin, Hermann. "The Lands East of the Elbe and German Colonization Eastwards." In *The Cambridge Economic History of Europe*, edited by J. H. Clapham and Eileen Power, vol. 1. Cambridge: Cambridge University Press, 1941.

Augstein, Rudolf. *Preussens Friedrich und die Deutschen*. Berlin: S. Fischer Verlag, 1968.

Aylmer, G. E., ed. *The Levellers in the English Revolution*. Ithaca: Cornell University Press, 1975.

Baudissin, W. Graf von. *Soldat für den Frieden. Entwürfe für eine zeitgemässe Bundeswehr*. Munich: P. von Schubert, 1969.

Baumgart, Peter. "Epochen der preussischen Monarchie im 18. Jahrhundert." In *Das Preussenbild in der Geschichte*, edited by Otto Büsch. Berlin: Walter de Gruyter, 1981.

Beaumont, Roger. *Sword of the Raj: The British Army in India (1747–1947)*. Indianapolis: Bobbs-Merrill Co., 1977.

Berghahn, Volker R. *Militarismus: The History of an International Debate*. New York: St. Martin's Press, 1982.

Bernhardi, Friedrich von. *Deutschland und der nächste Krieg*. Stuttgart and Berlin: J. G. Cotta'sche Buchhandlung, 1913.

Bond, Brian James. "Doctrine and Training in the British Cavalry, 1870–1914." In *The Theory and Practice of War*, edited by Michael Howard. New York: Praeger, 1965.

Bracher, Karl Dietrich. *Die Auflösung der Weimarer Republik*. 3d ed. Villingen: Ring-Verlag, 1960.

Brandt, Peter, Thomas Hofmann, and Reiner Zilkenat. Preussen: *Zur Sozialgeschichte eines Stattes*. Reinbeck bei Hamburg: Rowohlt Taschenbuchverlag, 1981.

Bredow, Wilfried von. *Die unbewältigte Bundeswehr*. Frankfurt: Fischer Taschenbuch Verlag, 1973.

Briefs, Goetz. "Betriebssoziologie." In *Handwörterbuch der Soziologie*, edited by Alfred Vierkandt. Stuttgart: Enke Verlag, 1931.

Bruck, W. F. *Social and Economic History of Germany from William II to Hitler*. London: Oxford University Press, 1938.

Büsch, Otto. Militärsystem und Sozialleben im alten Preussen, 1713–1807. Berlin: Walter de Gruyter & Co., 1962.

———. "Die Militarisierung von Staat und Gesellschaft im alten Preussen." In *Preussen: Beiträge zu einer politischen Kultur*, edited by Manfred Schlenke. Reinbeck bei Hamburg: Rowohlt Taschenbuch Verlag, 1981.

Bushkovitch, Paul. *The Merchants of Moscow, 1580–1650*. Cambridge: Cambridge University Press, 1980.

Carroll, Berence A. *Design for Total War: Arms and Economics in the Third Reich*. The Hague: Mouton, 1968.

Carsten, Francis L. *The Origins of Prussia*. London: Oxford University Press, 1954.

———. *The Reichswehr in Politics, 1918 to 1919*. Oxford: Clarendon Press, 1966.

———. *Revolution in Central Europe, 1918 to 1919*. Berkeley and Los Angeles: University of California Press, 1972.

Clark, George. *War and Society in the Seventeenth Century*. Cambridge: Cambridge University Press, 1958.

Clausewitz, Carl von. *Vom Kriege*. Hamburg: Rowohlt, 1963.

Constitution of the Kingdom of Prussia. Philadelphia: American Academy of Political and Social Science, 1894.

Craig, Gordon A. *The Politics of the Prussian Army, 1640–1945*. New York: Oxford University Press, 1955.

Dallin, David J. *The New Soviet Empire*. New Haven: Yale University Press, 1951.

Dehio, L. *Deutschland und die Weltpolitik im 20. Jahrhundert*. Munich: Kopernikus Verlag, 1955.

Demeter, Karl. *The German Officer Corps in Society and State, 1650–1945*. New York: Praeger, 1965.

Der Spiegel. Das Deutsche Nachrichten Magazin. No. 41, October 10, 1983.

Deuerlein, Ernst. *Der Aufstieg der NSOAP in Augenzeugenberichten*. Munich: Deutscher Taschenbuch Verlag, 1968.

Dinerstein, H. S. *War and the Soviet Union*. New York: Praeger, 1959.

Domarus, Max. *Hitler. Reden und Proklamationen, 1932–1945*. Vol. 1. Munich: Süddeutscher Verlag, 1965.

Dorwart, Reinhold August. *The Administrative Reforms of Frederick William I of Prussia*. Cambridge: Harvard University Press, 1953.

Duffy, Christopher. *Russia's Military Way to the West: Origins and Nature of Russian Military Power, 1700–1800*. London: Routledge & Kegan Paul, 1981.

Eisenfeld, Bernd. *Kriegsdienstverweigerung in der DDR-ein Friedensdienst?* Frankfurt: Haag und Herchen Verlag, 1978.

Endres, Franz Carl. "Militarismus als Geistesverfassung des Nichtmilitärs." In *Militarismus*, edited by Volker R. Berghahn. Cologne: Kiepenheuer und Witsch, 1975.

Erbe, Helmut. *Die Hugenotten in Deutschland*. Essen: Essener Verlagsanstalt, 1937.

Ergang, Robert. *The Potsdam Führer*. New York: Columbia University Press, 1941.

Fichte, Johann Gottlieb. *Addresses to the German Nation*. Chicago and London: Open Court Publishing Co., 1922.

Fick, Heinz-Erich. *Der deutsche Militarismus der Vorkriegszeit*. Rostock: Spezial-Druckerei für Dissertationen, 1930.

Finer, Samuel E. "State- and Nation-Building in Europe: The Role of the Military." In *The Formation of National States in Europe*, edited by Charles Tilly. Princeton: Princeton University Press, 1975.

Fischer, Fritz. *Der Griff nach der Weltmacht*. Düsseldorf: Droste Verlag, 1962.

Flitner, Andreas. *Die politische Erziehung in Deutschland*. Tübingen: Max Niemeyer Verlag, 1957.

Florinsky, Michael T. *Fascism and National Socialism*. New York: Macmillan, 1936.

Forster, Thomas M. *The East German Army*. New York: A. S. Barnes & Co., 1968.

Fried, Hans Ernest. *The Guilt of the German Army*. New York: Macmillan, 1942.

Genschel, Dietrich. *Wehrreform und Reaktion. Die Vorbereitung der inneren Führung 1951–1965*. Hamburg: R. V. Decker's Verlag G. Schenk, 1972.

Geyer, Dietrich. *Der russische Imperialismus*. Göttingen: Naderhoek & Rupprecht, 1977.

Geyer, Rolf, Heinrich Otto Koch, and Ludwig Auerbach. *Streitkräfte im geteilten Deutschland*. Munich: Kopernikus Verlag, 1976.

Girardet, Raoul. *La Société militaire dans la France contemporaine, 1815–1939*. Paris: Librairie Plon, 1953.

Goedecke, Paul. "Der Reichsgedanke im Schrifttum von 1919–1935." Ph.D. diss., Marburg University, 1951.

Goldhamer, Herbert. *The Soviet Soldier*. New York: Crane, Russak & Co., 1975.

Gorce, Paul-Marie de la. *The French Army: A Military-Political History*. New York: George Braziller, 1963.

Görlitz, Walter. *Der deutsche Generalstab*. Frankfurt: Verlag der Frankfurter Hefte, 1950.

Grinnell, George Bird. *The Fighting Cheyennes*. Norman: University of Oklahoma Press, 1956.

Groh, Dieter. *Negative Integrierung und revolutionärer Attentismus: Die deutsche Sozialdemokratische Partei am Vorabend des ersten Weltkrieges*. Frankfurt and Berlin: Verlag Ullstein, 1973.

Gruner, Wolf D. *Das Bayerische Heer, 1825 bis 1864*. Boppard am Rhein: Harold Boldt Verlag, 1972.

Hartley, Anthony. *Gaullism: The Rise and Fall of a Political Movement*. London: Routledge & Kegan Paul, 1972.

Henning, E. W. *Die Industrialisierung in Deutschland, 1800–1914*. Paderborn: Verlag Ferdinand Schöningh, 1973.

Henrich, Wolfgang. *Wehrkunde in der DDR: Die neue Regelung ab 1. September 1978*. Bonn: Hohwacht Verlag, 1978.

Herwig, Holger H. "The First German Congress of Workers' and Soldiers' Councils and the Problem of Military Reform." *Central European History*, 1 (June 1968).

———. *The German Naval Officer Corps*. Oxford: Clarendon Press, 1973.

Hillgruber, Andreas. *Grossmachtpolitik und Militarismus im 20. Jahrhundert*. Düsseldorf: Droste Verlag, 1974.

Hintze, Otto. *Die Hohenzollern und ihr Werk*. Berlin: Verlag von Paul Parey, 1915.

———. "Staatsverfassung und Heeresverfassung." In *Militarismus*, edited by Volker R. Berghahn. Cologne: Kiepenheuer und Witsch, 1975.

Höhn, Reinhard. *Die Armee als Erziehungsschule der Nation*. Bad Harzburg: Verlag für Wissenschaft, Wirtschaft und Technik, 1963.

Höhne, Heinz. *Der Orden unter dem Totenkopf*. Gütersloh: Sigbert Mohn Verlag, 1967.

Holborn, Hajo. *A History of Modern Germany, 1648–1840*. New York: Knopf, 1964.

Huber, Ernst Rudolf. *Deutsche Verfassungsgeschichte seit 1789*. Vol. 3. Stuttgart: W. Kohlhammer, 1963.

Huntington, Samuel P. *The Soldier and the State*. Cambridge: Harvard University Press, 1957.

Ilsemann, Carl-Gero von. *Die Bundeswehr in der Demokratie: Zeit der inneren Führung*. Hamburg: R. V. Decker's Verlag G. Schenk, 1971.

Jähns, Max. *Heeresverfassungen und Völkerleben*. Berlin: Allgemeiner Verein für deutsche Literatur, 1885.

———. *Geschichte der Kriegswissenschaft*. Vol. 1. Munich and Leipzig: R. Oldenburg, 1889.

Janowitz, Morris. "Armed Forces and Society: A World Perspective." In *Armed Forces and Society*, edited by Jacques van Doorn. The Hague: Mouton, 1968.

———. *Military Conflict: Essays in the Institutional Analysis of War and Peace*. Beverly Hills and London: Sage Publications, 1975.

Jany, Curt. *Geschichte der preussischen Armee vom 15. Jahrhundert bis 1914*. 4 vols. Osnabrück: Biblio Verlag, 1967.

———. "Die Kantonverfassung des altpreussischen Heeres." In *Moderne preussische Geschichte, 1648–1947*, edited by Otto Büsch and Wolfgang Neugebauer, vol. 2. Berlin: Walter de Gruyter, 1981.

Johnson, John J. *The Military and Society in Latin America*. Stanford: Stanford University Press, 1964.

Jünger, Ernst. *Sämtliche Werke*. Vol. 7. Stuttgart: Klott-Cotta, 1980.

Jungermann, Peter. *Die Wehrideologie der SED und das Leitbild der Nationalen Volksarmee vom sozialistischen deutschen Soldaten*. Stuttgart: Seewald Verlag, 1973.

Kabel, Rudolf. *Die Militarisierung der Sowjetischen Besatzungszone Deutschlands.* Bonn and Berlin: Deutscher Bundesverlag, 1966.

Kehr, Eckart. "Zur Genesis des Königlich-preussischen Reserveoffiziers." In *Moderne preussische Geschichte, 1648–1947,* edited by Otto Büsch and Wolfgang Neugebauer, vol. 2. Berlin: Walter de Gruyter, 1981.

Kitchen, Martin. *The German Officer Corps, 1890–1914.* Oxford: Clarendon Press, 1968.

———. *The Silent Dictatorship: The Politics of the German High Command under Hindenburg and Ludendorff, 1916–1918.* New York: Holmes & Meier, 1976.

Klöne, Arno. *Hitlerjugend: Die Jugend und ihre Organisation im Dritten Reich.* Hannover and Frankfurt: Norddeutsche Verlagsanstalt O. Goedel, 1960.

Klyuchevsky, Vasili. *Peter the Great.* New York: St. Martin's Press, 1969.

Kreusel, Dietmar. *Nation und Vaterland in der Militärpresse der DDR.* Stuttgart: Seewald Verlag, 1971.

Lamprecht, Karl. *Deutsche Geschichte.* Vol. 3. Berlin: Weidmannsche Buchhandlung, 1913.

Lantzeff, George V., and Richard A. Pierce. *Eastward to Empire: Exploration and Conquest on the Russian Open Frontier to 1750.* Montreal: McGill-Queens University Press, 1973.

Liebknecht, Karl. *Militarismus und Antimilitarismus.* Berlin: A. Hoffmann's Verlag, 1907.

Lieuwen, Edwin. *Arms and Politics in Latin America.* New York: Praeger, 1960.

Lowie, Robert H. *The German People: A Social Portrait to 1914.* New York: Rinehart & Co., 1945.

Ludovici, Jacob Friederich. *Einleitung zum Kriegs-Prozess.* Halle: Verlegung des Waysenhauses, 1749.

Mackintosh, Malcolm. "The Development of Soviet Military Doctrine since 1918." In *The Theory and Practice of War,* edited by Michael Howard. New York: Praeger, 1965.

Maizière, Ulrich de. *Führen—im Frieden.* Munich: Bernhard und Graefe Verlag, 1974.

Marder, Arthur J. *The Anatomy of British Sea Power.* New York: Knopf, 1940.

Marks, Heinz. *GST—Vormilitärische Ausbildung in der DDR.* Cologne: Markus Verlag, 1970.

Mead, Margaret. *Soviet Attitudes Toward Authority.* New York: McGraw-Hill, 1951.

Messerschmidt, Manfred. *Die Wehrmacht im NS-Staat: Zeit der Indoktrination.* Hamburg: R. V. Decker's Verlag G. Schenck, 1969.

Meyer, Folkert. "Das konservative Schulregiment in Preussen während der 80er Jahre." In *Preussen in der deutschen Geschichte,* edited by Dirk Blasius. Königstein: Verlag Anton Hein Meisenheim, 1980.

Militärgeschichtliches Forschungsamt. *Offiziere im Bild von Dokumenten aus drei Jahrhunderten.* Stuttgart: Deutsche Verlagsanstalt, 1964.

Moeller van den Bruck. *Das dritte Reich.* Hamburg: Hanseatische Verlagsanstalt, 1931.

Monteilhet, J. *Les Institutions Militaires de la France, 1814–1932.* Paris: Librairie Félix Alcan, 1932.

Morris, James. *Farewell the Trumpets: An Imperial Retreat.* New York: Harcourt Brace Jovanovich, 1978.

Muncy, Lysbeth Walker. *The Junker in the Prussian Administration under William II, 1888–1914.* Providence: Brown University Press, 1944.

Nawrocki, Joachim. *Bewaffnete Organe in der DDR.* Berlin: Verlag Gebr. Holzapfel, 1979.

Nusser, Von Houst G. W. *Konservative Wehrverbände in Bayern, Preussen und Oesterreich, 1918–1933.* Munich: Nusser Verlag, 1973.

Obermann, Emil. *Soldaten, Bürger, Militaristen.* Stuttgart: J. G. Cotta'sche Buchhandlung, 1958.

Odom, William E. "The Militarization of Soviet Society." *Problems of Communism* (Sept.–Oct. 1976).

Oman, C. W. C. *The Art of War in the Middle Ages, A.D. 378–1515.* Ithaca: Cornell University Press, 1953.

Otley, C. B. "Militarism and the Social Affiliations of the British Army Elite." In *Armed Forces and Society,* edited by Jacques van Doorn. The Hague: Mouton, 1968.

Paulsen, Friedrich. *The German Universities and University Study.* New York: Charles Scribner's Sons, 1906.

Payne, Stanley G. *Fascism, Comparison and Definition.* Madison: University of Wisconsin Press, 1980.

Plumyène, J., and R. Lasierra. *Les Fascismes Français, 1923–1963.* Paris: Editions du Seuil, 1963.

Ranke, Winfried. "Preussen—ein Kunststück." In *Preussen: Versuch einer Bilanz,* edited by Gottfried Korff, Hrsg. Hamburg: Rowohlt Taschenbuch Verlag, 1981.

Ritter, Gerhard. "Das Problem des Militarismus in Deutschland." In *Historische Zeitschrift.* Munich: Verlag von K. Oldenbourg, 1954.

———. *Frederick the Great, A Historical Profile.* Berkeley and Los Angeles: University of California Press, 1968.

———. *The Sword and the Scepter.* Vol. 1, *The Prussian Tradition, 1740–1890.* Miami: University of Miami Press, 1969.

———. *The Sword and the Scepter.* Vol. 2, *The European Powers and the Wilhelmian Empire, 1890–1914.* Miami: University of Miami Press, 1970.

———. *The Sword and the Scepter.* Vol. 3, *The Tragedy of Statesmanship: Bethmann-Hollweg as War Chancellor, 1914–1917.* Miami: University of Miami Press, 1973.

———. *The Sword and the Scepter.* Vol. 4, *The Reign of German Militarism and the Disaster of 1918.* Miami: University of Miami Press, 1973.

Roberts, Michael. *Essays in Swedish History.* London: Weidenfeld and Nicolson, 1967.

Roghmann, Klaus, and Rolf Ziegler. "Militärsoziologie." In *Handbuch der empirischen Sozialforschung,* edited by René König, vol. 9. *Organisation. Militär.* Stuttgart: Enke Verlag, 1977.

Rohe, Karl. "Militarismus, soldatische Haltung und Führerideologie." In *Militarismus,* edited by Volker R. Berghahn. Cologne: Kiepenheuer und Witsch, 1975.

Rosenberg, Hans. *Bureaucracy, Aristocracy and Autocracy: The Prussian Experience, 1660–1815.* Boston: Beacon Press, 1958.

――――. "Die Ausprägung der Junkerherrschaft in Brandenberg-Preussen: 1410–1618." In *Preussen in der deutschen Geschichte,* edited by Dirk Blasius. Königstein: Verlag Anton Hein Meisenheim, 1980.

Ruge, Friederich. *Politik, Militär, Bündnis.* Stuttgart: Deutsche Verlagsanstalt, 1963.

Rumschöttel, Herman. *Das Bayerische Offizierskorps, 1806–1914.* Berlin: Duncker & Humblot, 1973.

Schäfer, Wolfgang. *NSDAP Entwicklung und Struktur der Staatspartei des Dritten Reiches.* Hannover and Frankfurt: Norddeutsche Verlagsanstalt O. Goedel, 1957.

Schermer, David. *Blackshirts: Fascism in Britain.* New York: Ballantine Books, 1971.

Schieder, Wolfgang. *Faschismus als soziale Bewegung: Deutschland und Italien im Vergleich.* Hamburg: Hoffmann und Campe, 1976.

Schleier, Hans. *Sybel und Treitschke: Antidemokratismus und Militarismus im historisch-politischen Denken grossbourgeoiser Geschichtsideolologien.* Berlin: Akademie Verlag, 1965.

Schlenke, Manfred. "Nationalsozialismus und Preussentum." In *Das Preussenbild in der Geschichte,* edited by Otto Büsch. Berlin: Walter de Gruyter, 1981.

Schmoller, Gustav. *The Mercantile System and Its Historical Significance.* New York: Peter Smith, 1931.

――――. "Die Entstehung des preussischen Heeres von 1640 bis 1740." In *Moderne preussische Geschichte, 1648–1947,* edited by Otto Büsch and Wolfgang Neugebauer, vol. 2. Berlin: Walter de Gruyter, 1981.

Schwabe, Klaus. *Wissenschaft und Kriegsmoral.* Göttingen: Musterschmidt Verlag, 1969.

Schwieger, Klaus. "Militär und Bürgertum: Zur gesellschaftlichen Prägkraft des preussischen Militärsystems im 18. Jahrhundert." In *Preussen in der deutschen Geschichte,* edited by Dirk Blasius. Königstein: Verlag Anton Hein Meisenheim, 1980.

Schweigler, Gebhard Ludwig. *National Consciousness in Divided Germany.* London and Beverly Hills: Sage Publications, 1975.

Schwierskott, Hans-Joachim. *Arthur Moeller van den Bruck und der revolutionäre Nationalismus in der Weimarer Republik.* Göttingen: Musterschmidt Verlag, 1962.

Scott, Harriet Fast, and William F. Scott. *The Armed Forces of the USSR.* Boulder, Colo.: Westview Press, 1979.

Seignobos, Charles. *Histoire Sincère de la Nation Française.* Paris: Presses Universitaires de France, 1969.

Senghaas, Dieter. "Ueberlegungen zur gegenwärtigen Militarismus Problematik." In *Militarismus,* edited by Volker R. Berghahn. Cologne: Kiepenheuer und Witsch, 1975.

Service, Elman R. "War and Our Contemporary Ancestors." In *War: The An-*

thropology of Armed Conflict and Aggression. Morton H. Fried et al., eds. New York: Natural History Press, 1967.

Shanahan, William O. *Prussian Military Reforms, 1786–1812*. New York: Columbia University Press, 1945.

Simon, Walter M. *The Failure of the Prussian Reform Movement, 1807–1819*. Ithaca: Cornell University Press, 1955.

Skidelsky, Robert. *Oswald Mosley*. New York: Holt, Rinehart & Winston, 1975.

Smith, Dennis Mack. *Mussolini's Roman Empire*. New York: Viking Press, 1976.

Snell, John L. *The Democratic Movement in Germany, 1789–1914*. Chapel Hill: University of North Carolina Press, 1976.

Sombart, Werner. *Deutscher Sozialismus*. Charlottenburg: Mittler, 1934.

Speier, Hans. *Social Order and the Risks of War*. New York: George W. Stewart, 1952.

Spengler, Oswald. *The Hour of Decision*. New York: Knopf, 1934.

Staar, Richard F. "The New Course in Poland." In *The Soviet Satellite Nations: A Study of the New Imperialism*, edited by John H. Hallowell. Gainesville: Kallmann Publishing Co., 1958.

Studiengruppe Militärpolitik. *Die nationake Volksarmee: Ein Anti-Weissbuch zum Militär in der DDR*. Reinbek bei Hamburg: Rohwolt Taschenbuch Verlag, 1976.

Tazerout. "La Pensée Politique de Moeller van den Bruck." *Revue Internationale de Sociologie* 44 (1936).

Thayer, William Roscoe. *Out of Their Mouths*. New York: D. Appleton & Co., 1917.

Thielen, Hans Helmut. *Der Verfall der inneren Führung: Politische Bewusstseinsbildung in der Bundeswehr*. Frankfurt: Europäische Verlagsanstalt, 1970.

Time, June 23, 1980.

Tokaev. G. A. *Soviet Imperialism*. New York: Philosophical Library, 1956.

Toynbee, Arnold J. *War and Civilization*. New York: Oxford University Press, 1950.

Treitschke, Heinrich von. *The Origins of Prussianism (The Teutonic Knights)*. Translated by Eden and Cedar Paul. London: Allen & Unwin, 1942.

———. *Politik*. Vol. 2. Leipzig: S. Hinzel, 1898.

Vagts, Alfred. *A History of Militarism*. London: Meridian Books, 1959.

Veblen, Thorstein. *Imperial Germany and the Industrial Revolution*. New York: Viking Press, 1939.

Viénot, John. *Histoire de la Réforme Française de l'Édit de Nantes à sa Revocation*. Paris: Librairie Fischbacher, 1934.

von Archenholz, J. W. "Gemälde der preussischen Armee vor und in dem Siebenjährigen Kriege." In *Preussisches Soldatenleben in der Fridericianischen Zeit*, edited by Raimund Steinert. Leipzig: R. Voigtlanders Verlag, n/d.

Wallace, Ernest, and E. Adamson Hoebel. *The Comanches: Lords of the South Plains*. Norman: University of Oklahoma Press, 1952.

Warner, Edward L. III. *The Military in Contemporary Politics*. New York: Praeger, 1977.

Webster, David L. "On Theocracies." *American Anthropologist* 78, no. 4 (1976).

Weingartner, James J. *Hitler's Guard*. Carbondale: Southern Illinois University Press, 1968.

Wettig, Gerhard. *Entmilitarisierung und Wiederbewaffnung in Deutschland, 1943–1955*. Munich: R. Oldenbourg Verlag, 1967.

Williams, Warren E. "Versuch einer Definition Paramilitärischer Organisationen." In *Militarismus*, edited by Volker R. Berghahn. Cologne: Kiepenheuer und Witsch, 1975.

Willoweit, Dietmar. "Das Modell des preussischen Staates: Grundlagen-Auflösung-Nachwirkungen." In *Das Preussenbild in der Geschichte*, edited by Otto Büsch. Berlin: Walter de Gruyter, 1981.

Wippermann, Wolfgang. "Ordensstaat, Hohenzollernmonarchie und Drittes Reich." In *Preussen: Beiträge zu einer politischen Kultur*, edited by Manfred Schlenke. Hamburg: Rowohlt Taschenbuch Verlag, 1981.

Wittke, Carl. *The History of English Parliamentary Privilege*. Columbus: Ohio State University Press, 1921.

Wright, Quincy. *A Study of War*. Chicago: University of Chicago Press, 1965.

Zhilin, P. "The Armed Forces of the Soviet State." In *Military Profession and Military Regimes*, edited by Jacques van Doorn. The Hague: Mouton, 1969.

Index

221